AN INTRODUCTION TO APPLIED ECONOMETRIC ANALYSIS

— AN INTRODUCTION TO APPLIED ECONOMETRIC ANALYSIS —

R. F. WYNN AND K. HOLDEN

A HALSTED PRESS BOOK

JOHN WILEY & SONS
New York

330.018
W 988

First published in the United Kingdom in 1974 by
The Macmillan Press Ltd

Published in the U.S.A.
by Halsted Press, a Division
of John Wiley & Sons, Inc.,
New York

ISBN 0 470-96898-2
Library of Congress Catalog Card Number 74-3665

Printed in Great Britain

To A. and J.

Contents

Preface

Our principal aim in writing this book has been to help meet the growing need for an introduction to applied econometrics at the advanced undergraduate level. In particular, we believe that undergraduates derive more benefit from a course in econometric methods if it is supported by discussion of how these methods relate to applied work and thereby to other fields of economic science. Furthermore, an early introduction to applied econometrics has the additional advantages, through encouraging the use of computer and library facilities, of fostering research interests and skills and of bringing the student closer to the current literature in at least some areas of economics. It is also hoped that our efforts may help postgraduates and others who are not intending to specialise in econometrics but who nevertheless need to make use of econometric methods in their research.

Given these objectives we have in no way attempted to give a comprehensive account of any particular aspect of applied econometric analysis, nor have we attempted a review of the literature in any particular field of applied econometric research. Rather we have concentrated on presenting an account of what is involved in expressing economic theory in the form of an econometric model, in testing models against observation and in preparing and analysing forecasts. Only four areas of applied econometrics have been referred to in order to illustrate these matters. This has meant that many special points of interest relating to other topics have been omitted, but we believe these four areas are sufficiently distinctive to provide a basis for an introduction to the subject. The problems and limitations of dealing with data and of assessing empirical results are discussed, and the student is encouraged to consult the literature for himself through a guide to further reading at the end of each chapter.

We assume a knowledge of at least elementary economic theory, statistics, algebra and calculus, and that the reader has taken, or is taking, an introductory course in econometric methods. A knowledge of the basic matrix operations (addition, multiplication and inversion) and of determinants is desirable for certain topics. Despite these prerequisites, however, we believe that there is some value in reviewing in an introductory chapter those econometric methods that are almost universally used in applied work. In Chapter 1 we have therefore summarised the way in which regression and econometric results are used in hypothesis testing and prediction, and also the usual tests of the assumptions of the classical linear regression model. Problems that arise in the use of certain kinds of data or models are pointed out where necessary in the chapters that follow.

The chapters dealing with investment, the production function and wage-price models share a common approach. In each case theory relating to the specification of alternative models is reviewed together with ways in which these models might be tested. This is followed by examples of published empirical results. The final two chapters consider macro-economic models. In dealing with the specification of such models, selected references to seven published studies are used to illustrate the way in which the structure and scope of these models have been adapted to serve different purposes, and, in particular, the need for a more comprehensive treatment of macro-economic systems. The second of the chapters on macro-economic models is a review of matters relating to the preparation of forecasts from an econometric model, the theoretical and practical attractions of different ways of evaluating forecasts and the preparation and analysis of multipliers. Again a limited selection of published work is reviewed.

Although all six chapters have been much improved as a result of the suggestions and reactions of both co-authors, R. F. Wynn was responsible for the preparation of Chapters 1, 5 and 6 and K. Holden for Chapters 2, 3 and 4. The final draft of the book remains our responsibility alone of course and yet we must express our gratitude to all those who have given us the benefit of their advice in the various stages of preparation, especially R. W. Latham, D. A. Peel, P. J. M. Stoney and A. E. Woodfield. We should also like to thank those whose skill and patience has turned our handwritten material into typescript, particularly Mrs A. Burgess and Mrs D. Lewis. Finally the permission of the following publishers to reprint the tables specified is gratefully acknowledged: Centro de Economia e Finanças, Lisbon (Tables 6.1 and 6.5); the editors of the *American Economic Review* (Table 6.2); the Economics Research Unit, Wharton School of Finance and Commerce, University of Pennsylvania (Table 6.4); the editors of the *Review of Economic Studies* (Tables 6.6 and 6.7); and the Brookings Institution (Table 6.8).

April 1974   R. F. WYNN
                                                                      K. HOLDEN

1. Introduction

1.1 THE OBJECTIVES AND METHODS OF APPLIED ECONOMETRICS

Broadly speaking econometric analysis can be said to be concerned with developing means by which hypotheses about economic systems can be tested with reference to observation. One of the first objectives of this kind of study must therefore be the specification of a *model* which it is believed adequately represents the relationship between a given set of variables. Given the quantitative nature of information about these variables, the model may conveniently be expressed as a mathematical function, the simplest example of which can be found in the familiar regression model

$$Y_i = \alpha + \beta X_i + u_i \qquad (1.1)$$

in which the dependent variable Y is shown to be a linear function of a single independent variable (or explanatory variable or regressor) X and a random or stochastic variable u. The subscript i refers to a particular observation on X and Y.

The simplicity of (1.1) rests on three features: its linearity, the appearance of only two variables in the exact or non-stochastic part of the function and the use of only one relationship relating Y and X. These are restrictions which can, however, be relaxed to some extent to cope with some of the demands of a more complex reality and yet retain the convenience of the linear character of (1.1). Thus the addition of further independent variables on the right hand side requires only a generalisation of regression methods applicable to (1.1) while the linearity assumption itself can be modified somewhat by allowing variables like X to represent other variables such as Z^n, $1/Z^m$, Z_1^n/Z_2^m or $\ln Z$ so that the model is no longer linear in variables, providing it remains linear in parameters and providing the way in which the disturbance term is incorporated in the model also conforms to this principle, which means, for example, that the disturbance in

$$Y = \alpha X^\beta u \qquad (1.2)$$

has to be multiplicative for it to be additive in the linear equivalent of (1.2)

$$\ln Y = \ln \alpha + \beta \ln X + \ln u \qquad (1.3)$$

In addition, a model may consist of more than one equation which is linear in parameters, even if these equations relate a set of mutually determined variables, without creating serious problems in the adaptation of the kind of econometric analysis which is applicable to a single equation model.

The need for a disturbance term in the specification of a regression model is a reflection of the kind of information which is available on economic variables in practice. Thus while it may be postulated that the observed behaviour of Y is closely associated with that of X, this behaviour is not something which can be studied under controlled experimental conditions in economic science and other factors which have a bearing on the behaviour of Y may also be subject to change from one observation to the next. The shifts in Y associated with these other factors may be conveniently accounted for by the single, composite variable u. The use of this device means that observations on the dependent variable inevitably constitute a sample. In the case of *time-series data*, which relate to the same economic unit over a number of intervals of time, this is so for other reasons since the population, or complete array of all possible observations, or outcomes, is infinite but even if *cross-section data*, which relate to a number of economic units at a point in time, are available on *all* the units involved, this information must be regarded as a sample since the Y's are observed for only a selection of values of the factors accounted for by the disturbance term u. Thus econometrics is essentially concerned with *statistical inference*, or the use of sample information to obtain some idea of the characteristics of a population.

Both theoretical and applied interests may be identified in demarcating more precisely the scope of econometric analysis. The first is concerned with establishing the kind of conclusions that can be drawn from sample data using certain analytical procedures and subject to certain assumptions about the model used including, in particular, the properties of the disturbance term employed. The method or formulae used to estimate population parameters, like α and β in (1.1), is central to this discussion. These formulae are referred to as *estimators* in order to distinguish them from the *estimates*, or numerical results, obtained from their application to a given series of data. One such method of estimation, based on the 'least squares' principle, is of special interest in view of certain well-known attractive properties if the assumptions of the 'classical normal linear regression model' are valid. According to the least squares criterion estimates of population parameters such as α and β in (1.1) are sought so as to minimise the sum of the squares of *residuals*

$$\hat{u}_i = Y_i - \hat{Y}_i \tag{1.4}$$

which separate observed values of Y from values predicted by the estimated model

$$\hat{Y}_i = \hat{\alpha} + \hat{\beta} X_i \tag{1.5}$$

The resulting formulae are referred to as *least squares estimators* for α and β.

A study of what happens to the properties of these estimators if the assumptions of the classical model are relaxed constitutes a starting point of what may be regarded as econometrics proper. Broadly speaking, interest centres on dealing with three problems for each assumption in turn: what happens to the properties of the least squares estimator if the assumption is relaxed, how can the validity of the assumption be tested in practice and what can be done to retrieve any useful properties that would otherwise obtain if the assumption is in fact found untenable?

Some of the essential tasks of applied econometrics follow from the application of methods suggested by theory for dealing with the second and third of these issues in practice. Others, concerning the specification of a model, the organisation of data, comparisons of empirical evidence with what might be expected on *a priori* grounds and tests on the practical value of an econometric model in, say, forecasting, need to be added. Although it is difficult to generalise about what is involved in applied econometric analysis in view of the different uses that may be made of econometric statistics and of the conclusions of economic and econometric theory in building, testing and applying econometric models in different branches of economic science, the sequence of steps normally undertaken can be summarised, broadly speaking, as follows.

To begin with the objectives of a study should be stated clearly together with a review of the relevant theory and of any knowledge of the way the variables concerned are believed to be related in reality. So far as the last of these matters is concerned, if, for example, the behaviour of a variable is determined, whether wholly or only partially, by forces such as government regulations then it is obviously important to know this. However, to the extent that it may not be possible for the analyst to be entirely certain about some institutional arrangements, such as private agreements, or about the motivations which dictate the behaviour of certain economic units, he may well be reduced to advancing nothing more than a suspicion which is related neither to formal logic nor to well-found information. It is therefore often pointed out that the formulation of hypotheses is as much an art as a science and in view of these qualifications it is not surprising that the result is usually far from unambiguous.

Secondly, using as many functional forms as may be considered relevant, the conclusions reached this far must be used to specify hypotheses in the form of mathematical functions relating those variables which it is reasoned are principally involved and assigning all other influences to disturbance terms which are incorporated in these functions in appropriate ways. Logic and a knowledge of how things work in practice will at best provide only an incomplete view of the characteristics of the mathematical functions to be used and of any lag between the timing of observations on a dependent and an independent variable. It is to be expected, therefore, that doubts will often remain concerning the variables to be explicitly taken account of in expressing a hypothesis, the precise form of the mathematical relationship to be employed and the number of relationships involved.

Thirdly, it is necessary to seek out relevant published information, to reorganise what data there are in published form to suit the objectives of a study and to undertake *ad hoc* inquiries if necessary to augment what information is already available. The way in which information should be collected is a subject in itself, while in practice this is a task which usually has to be left to others or to a separate study in view of the time and cost involved.

Fourthly, it must be asked before proceeding further whether the specification of the model adopted infringes the assumptions of the classical regression model. Evidence to this effect may already be available on *a priori* grounds but it is also something which must be the subject of various tests on the data used. Since most of these tests are performed on the residuals of a fitted model, estimation of the model takes a high priority in the computational work involved in econometric analysis but it should be emphasised that, at this stage, estimation is directed mainly at getting some idea of the behaviour of residuals.

Fifthly, if it is suspected that certain assumptions on which the analysis relies are not tenable then re-specifications of the model or different estimation procedures may be in order so that the analysis may proceed further.

Sixthly, having reached this far it should be possible to assess the extent to which the hypotheses used are supported by the available empirical evidence. The answer depends on how closely an estimated model fits the data, on whether the signs and orders of magnitude of estimated parameters are the same as those expected from theoretical, and other, considerations, and on how well the estimated model predicts.

Next, reformulations of the hypotheses originally advanced may seem in order for various reasons in the light of the empirical evidence available to this point so that, lastly, but perhaps repeatedly, the analysis from step three may be undertaken again for new hypotheses.

Ideally, the results which emerge have three characteristics. In the first place, one theoretically explicable hypothesis would clearly prove to be more consistent with the available data than any other rival hypothesis. Secondly, all the estimated parameters of this model would be highly significant so that they could be safely assumed to be accurate estimates of population parameters. Thirdly, the ability to produce accurate forecasts is often regarded as an important property of an estimated model so that it would be helpful if it were to perform well on this count also. Anyone who has had practical experience of applied econometric analysis will know just how elusive a result this is. However, econometric studies succeed or fail according to the way in which results which fall short of this ideal are interpreted and are used as the basis of further, perhaps more illuminating, inquiry. It is hoped that what follows may provide some introductory guide-lines in this respect as well as the other issues of applied econometric analysis set out above.

1.2. THE PRESENTATION AND INTERPRETATION OF BASIC REGRESSION RESULTS

For the generalised multiple regression model

$$Y_i = \beta_1 + \beta_2 X_{2i} + \beta_3 X_{3i} + \ldots + \beta_K X_{Ki} + u_i \qquad (1.6)$$

sample statistics obtained from regression analysis are usually presented using the following format

$$\hat{Y}_i = \hat{\beta}_1 + \hat{\beta}_2 X_{2i} + \hat{\beta}_3 X_{3i} + \ldots + \hat{\beta}_K X_{Ki} \qquad \bar{R}^2 \qquad (1.7)$$
$$(\text{s.e. } \hat{\beta}_1) \ (\text{s.e. } \hat{\beta}_2) \ (\text{s.e. } \hat{\beta}_3) \qquad (\text{s.e. } \hat{\beta}_K) \qquad F$$

The formulae concerned in arriving at these results are not given here and indeed are not often referred to in practice since the weight of computational work usually encountered is such that a computer, and therefore a suitably comprehensive computer program, is used. Those not familiar with these formulae may consult the standard texts, to which a guide is given in Section 1.4, although some explanation of the interpretation of (1.7) is perhaps in order in view of the frequent references to regression results over the chapters that follow.

The quantity in parentheses below each parameter estimate, for example $\hat{\beta}_k$, is the estimated standard error of the sampling distribution of this estimate which is required in testing hypotheses concerning the size of the corresponding population parameter, β_k. Where interest is confined to testing whether each $\hat{\beta}_k$ is different from zero simply as a result of having to use sample information to obtain *estimates*, these standard errors can be conveniently replaced by the ratio $\hat{\beta}_k/(\text{s.e. } \hat{\beta}_k)$ which, subject to the usual assumptions, is a statistic which has a t distribution and which can therefore be compared with tabulated values of the t distribution, $t_{\varepsilon/2, (N-K)}$, for different levels of significance, ε, and the number of degrees of freedom involved, in this case $(N - K)$ if N is the sample size. If $\hat{\beta}_k/(\text{s.e. } \hat{\beta}_k) > t_{\varepsilon/2, (N-K)}$, the null hypothesis

$$H_0 : \beta_k = 0$$

is rejected at the level of significance chosen and on the basis of the available evidence represented by the sample used while it is not rejected, subject to the same qualifications, otherwise.[1] Stated in these terms the hypothesis tested can be seen to be equivalent to the null hypothesis that the true or population mean value of Y_i is not linearly dependent on X_{ki} which is often simply referred to as the hypothesis that Y is not linearly dependent on X_k. If it is concluded that this hypothesis cannot be rejected on the basis of the available evidence it is then sometimes said that the estimate of β_k is 'not significant' and *vice versa*.

Alternatively, the null hypothesis may be that the population parameter is β_k rather than zero in which case the appropriate test statistic becomes $(\hat{\beta}_k - \beta_k)/(\text{s.e. } \hat{\beta}_k)$ while a hypothesis that the parameters of a model conform to a linear restriction, such as, in general terms,

$$H_0 : a_2 \beta_2 + a_3 \beta_3 + \ldots + a_K \beta_K = b,$$

[1] The reader should be aware that if it is clear on theoretical grounds that β_k must be positive, or, alternatively, that it must be negative, then a one-tailed test applies rather than the two-tailed test above and the level of significance is $\varepsilon/2$.

where $a_2, a_3, \ldots, a_K$ and b are constants, can also be tested with reference to the t distribution. The appropriate formula and an illustration of its use is given by Johnston (1972) pp. 155–6.

A second statistic, F, can be used to extend the kind of statistical inference that is made possible by the test statistic t for an individual regressor to all the regressors of a multiple regression model. Indeed in the case of the simplest regression model (1.1) $t^2 = F$ while F and $\bar{R}^2$ are related by (1.11) and (1.12) given below. The statistic $\bar{R}^2$ is the familiar coefficient of determination, R^2, corrected for degrees of freedom. The uncorrected statistic R^2 is an estimate of that proportion of the variation of Y which is associated with variation of the explanatory variables of a model. Using lower-case letters to denote deviations from sample means, e.g. $y_i = Y_i - \bar{Y}$,

$$R^2 = \sum_{i=1}^{N} \hat{y}_i^2 \bigg/ \sum_{i=1}^{N} y_i^2 \tag{1.8}$$

This may be compared with the test statistic F since it can be shown, first, that subject to certain assumptions the ratio between the variance of $\hat{Y}$ and that of the residuals

$$F = \frac{\sum_{i=1}^{N} \hat{y}_i^2}{(K-1)} \bigg/ \frac{\sum_{i=1}^{N} \hat{u}^2}{(N-K)} \tag{1.9}$$

has the F distribution with $(K-1)$ and $(N-K)$ degrees of freedom and, secondly, that

$$\sum_{i=1}^{N} y_i^2 = \sum_{i=1}^{N} \hat{y}^2 + \sum_{i=1}^{N} \hat{u}^2 \tag{1.10}$$

so that it follows

$$F = \frac{R^2(N-K)}{(1-R^2)(K-1)} \tag{1.11}$$

Because F is a ratio between variances it has the advantage over R^2 of being correct for the degrees of freedom involved in the computation of the quantities in its numerator and denominator. The effect of this shortcoming in R^2 is that it remains at least constant on adding an irrelevant regressor, for which the true value of the corresponding parameter β_k is zero, to a model, but more often some increase is recorded owing to sampling. This snag is avoided if R^2 is also corrected for degrees of freedom by computing

$$\bar{R}^2 = 1 - \frac{N-1}{N-K}(1-R^2) \tag{1.12}$$

Although the coefficient of determination and the test statistic F are related each serves a different purpose, the first as a convenient expression of how well an estimated model fits a given series of data and the second as a means of testing the hypothesis that none of the explanatory variables of a model is linearly associated with the true mean of Y_t. The latter requires a test of whether an estimate of F is significantly different from one, which is effected by comparing it with a tabulated value of a point on the F distribution for the degrees of freedom found in the numerator $(K - 1)$ and denominator $(N - K)$ and the required level of significance.[1] The same test can be extended to a sub-group of the regressors on replacing the numerator in (1.9) by the difference between an estimate of the variation of Y that is associated with the variation of K regressors and that which is associated with the variation of, say, L regressors, divided by, in this case, $(K - L)$. The denominator remains equal to the variance of the residuals that are obtained on regressing Y against all K regressors.[2]

Lastly among these points concerning the interpretation of regression results brief reference is made to the use of statistical inference in testing the forecast performance of a fitted model. In particular, it is often of interest to know whether the value of Y forecast by an estimate of a model like (1.1) for a particular value, X_0, of the independent variable,

$$\hat{Y}_0 = \hat{\alpha} + \hat{\beta} X_0 \tag{1.14}$$

is sufficiently different from what is observed, Y_0, to suggest that the forecast error $(\hat{Y}_0 - Y_0)$ is not zero not simply because of sampling. Again subject to the usual assumptions, the ratio of the statistic $(\hat{Y}_0 - Y_0)$ to an estimate of its standard error has a t distribution with, in this case, $(N - 2)$ degrees of freedom, so that this measure can be used to test a null hypothesis concerning the size of $(\hat{Y}_0 - Y_0)$ in the same way as for hypotheses concerning the true values of regression coefficients.[3] Furthermore, just as the hypothesis that the

---

[1] It may be that measures of the test statistic t for the $\hat{\beta}_k$ of a multiple regression model suggest that a null hypothesis that *all* the corresponding true parameters are equal to zero cannot be rejected while an estimate of F is greater than a tabulated value of F using the same level of significance. This can happen if there is a strong linear association between two or more explanatory variables so that *as a group* they account for sufficient of the observed variation of Y to suggest that the null hypothesis tested with reference to the F statistic be rejected.

[2] Sometimes the variance of the residuals,

$$\hat{\sigma}_u^2 = \sum_{i=1}^{N} \hat{u}_i^2 / (N - K) \tag{1.13}$$

often referred to as the *variance of the regression*, is quoted as another or an alternative measure of the fit a model to a set of observations. Like $\bar{R}^2$ this too is a statistic corrected for degrees of freedom but it is less useful and is superfluous where $\bar{R}^2$ is quoted. (The notation s^2 is often adopted rather than $\hat{\sigma}^2$.)

[3] Just as before, a one- or a two-tailed test may be adopted depending on whether there are firm grounds for believing that positive or negative forecast errors alone are to be expected or not.

true values of a set of parameters are all equal to zero can be tested with reference to the F statistic, so also can the true values of a set of forecast errors relating to a series of predictions. The appropriate formula is discussed by C. F. Christ (1966) pp. 557–61.

1.3 THE INTERPRETATION AND USE OF THE RESULTS OF ELEMENTARY ECONOMETRIC ANALYSIS

As noted in Section 1.1, it remains necessary to ask what needs to be done in an applied study to test the assumptions on which the interpretation of the results of regression analysis discussed in the previous section rests. In addition, where these tests indicate that it seems unreasonable to assume that these assumptions hold it will be necessary to go on to consider what can be done in order to be able to use sample information to test theory and to forecast. Four topics which are of more or less general concern in applied work, are briefly referred to here. These are autocorrelated and heteroscedastic disturbances, multicollinearity and specification errors. Other problems which are also commonly encountered include some which inevitably follow from the use of certain kinds of model and which are not therefore, generally speaking, the subject of tests to see whether they apply to a given set of observations. In particular, special problems are often incurred *a priori* in the context of binary variables, lagged dependent variables and simultaneous equations, examples of which are referred to in the chapters that follow.[1] Errors in variables represent a fourth, in this case more generally applicable, area of interest, the relevance of which does not need to be established with reference to some specially designed test. Rather this is a possibility which should be examined in the light of knowledge about the collection, processing and presentation of the data used in a study. Thus it may be that the available data do not quite relate to the variable required in theory, or observations may themselves be sample statistics, or they may have been condensed in their published form to the point that frequencies alone are known for given ranges of values of a variable so that the average for each interval of observations has to be estimated by, say, the midpoint of the interval. This is a problem which is briefly discussed in Chapter 3, Section 3.5.

Autocorrelated disturbances

Violation of the assumption that the disturbances of a regression model are not autocorrelated is essentially the result of two things: one of the variables assigned to the disturbance term is highly correlated with the dependent variable and observations on this variable are correlated with other observations on the same variable. The same conclusions may apply equally well to an autocorrelated group of variables which in concert exhibit a pre-eminent linear

[1] See, respectively, Chapter 3, Section 3.5, Chapter 2, Section 2.4, Chapter 4, Section 4.4, and Chapter 5, Section 5.3.

association with a dependent variable. This being so it can be expected that the phenomenon of autocorrelated, or serially correlated, disturbances will be encountered only rarely in dealing with cross-section data since there can be few instances where the value recorded for a particular variable for a particular sample unit of a cross section of sample units (e.g., firms, industries, countries, etc.) will be correlated with the value recorded for another unit of the sample. In contrast, the cyclical movements displayed by many economic variables means that examples of autocorrelated disturbances are encountered only too often when using time-series data. (In recognition of the special need to test for autocorrelated disturbances in dealing with time-series data, the subscript 't' is used rather than 'i' in this sub-section in referring to a particular observation while T is used in place of N in referring to the sample size.)

The consequences of autocorrelated disturbances are, broadly speaking, twofold. In the first place ordinary least squares (OLS) estimators no longer have the property of having a sampling distribution which has the smallest variance among the class of linear unbiased estimators. This property passes to the generalised least squares (GLS) estimator which is referred to again later. Secondly, the two formulae used to estimate the standard error of an OLS estimator of a parameter are biased, usually so as to tend to produce an underestimate of the true figure, while quite apart from this problem the test statistics referred to in Section 1.2 no longer apply.

These are serious consequences of course and they apply, albeit with varying degrees of seriousness, whatever the form or scheme that the autocorrelation takes. It is general practice, however, to test the null hypothesis that the disturbances of a model are not autocorrelated only with reference to the first-order scheme

$$u_t = \rho u_{t-1} + \varepsilon_t, \tag{1.15}$$

where ε_t is also a stochastic variable, unless there are firm *a priori* grounds for suspecting a higher order scheme. This being so it is necessary to test the hypothesis

$$H_0 : \rho = 0$$

against the alternative hypothesis of first-order autocorrelation. Such a test is conveniently available in the form of the *Durbin–Watson test* in which the test statistic

$$d = \sum_{t=2}^{T} (\hat{u}_t - \hat{u}_{t-1})^2 / \sum_{t=1}^{T} \hat{u}_t^2 \tag{1.16}$$

is required. Unfortunately, the sampling distribution of this statistic depends on the observed values of the independent variables but subject to this qualification population values for d can be expected to range between zero, where the population parameter ρ is 1, through 2, where $\rho = 0$, to 4, where $\rho = -1$. Because of the qualification published values of d also indicate a range for which the test is inconclusive, which is demarcated by upper and lower limits d_U and d_L for different sample sizes, numbers of independent variables and probabilities. Thus, for example, for a sample size of 20 and a model which has three independent variables (excluding the constant term) the tabulated values of d_U and d_L required for testing at the 1 and 5 per cent levels of significance are as follows

	d_U	d_L
1 per cent	1·41	0·77
5 per cent	1·68	1·00

These limits demarcate, for positive autocorrelation,[1] five intervals for which the conclusions to be drawn for a given estimate of d are as follows:

$0 \leq d < 0\cdot77$ Null hypothesis (H_0) rejected at both the 1 and 5 per cent levels of significance.

$0\cdot77 < d < 1\cdot00$ H_0 rejected at 5 per cent level; test inconclusive at 1 per cent level.

$1\cdot00 < d < 1\cdot41$ Test inconclusive at both levels.

$1\cdot41 < d < 1\cdot68$ H_0 not rejected at 1 per cent level; test inconclusive at 5 per cent level.

$1\cdot68 < d \leq 2\cdot00$ H_0 not rejected at both levels.

Christ (1966), pp. 527–8, and Johnston (1972) pp. 252 and 258, review evidence which suggests that the upper limit d_U is to be regarded as being closer to the correct acceptance limit of this test. Hence where there is doubt d_U alone may be used; this will mean that the test errs on the side of indicating first-order serial correlation when this may not be so, but as Johnston notes, p. 258, 'since the consequences of incorrectly accepting the null hypothesis . . . are so much more serious than those of incorrectly rejecting it, one might have a preference for rejecting the null hypothesis in cases of doubt'.

Where a model includes regressors which are lagged terms in the dependent variable the Durbin–Watson statistic is seriously biased against the discovery of serial correlation. However, Durbin (1970) has developed a test for auto-correlated disturbances which is applicable to this kind of model where a large sample (T) is available. The relevant test statistic is

$$h = \hat{\rho}\sqrt{\frac{T}{1 - T\hat{V}(\hat{\beta}_1)}} \qquad (1.17)$$

where $\hat{\rho}$ is an estimate of the parameter ρ of the first-order scheme (1.15) that can be obtained from

$$\hat{\rho} = \sum_{t=2}^{T} \hat{u}_t \hat{u}_{t-1} / \sum_{t=2}^{T} \hat{u}_{t-1}^2 \qquad (1.18)$$

using OLS residuals and $\hat{V}(\hat{\beta}_1)$ is an estimate of the sampling variance of $\hat{\beta}_1$,

---

[1] Where the estimated value of d exceeds 2, the null hypothesis can be tested against the alternative hypothesis of negative first-order autocorrelation by subtracting it from 4 and using the same tabulated values of d.

the OLS estimate of the coefficient of Y_{t-1}, which alone is required without regard to any other lagged terms in the dependent variable. The test statistic h can be compared with tabulated values (one tail) of the normal distribution for different levels of significance to test the null hypothesis

$$H_0 : \rho = 0$$

in the usual way. Unfortunately, the test clearly breaks down if $T\hat{V}(\hat{\beta}_1) \geq 1$.

Two approaches to removing autocorrelated disturbances may be adopted. The first is suggested by the point made at the start of this sub-section that the underlying cause of autocorrelated disturbances can be traced to a specification error of the kind where an important and autocorrelated variable, or group of variables, has been assigned to the collective disturbance term, u_i. Hence the appropriate, and in this sense the most satisfactory, solution to the problem is to correct this fault in the specification of the model used by adding a variable which is both closely correlated with the dependent variable and which is auto-correlated in the same way as the disturbances of the original model. A test would be to regress candidate variables (Z_t) on u_t or simply include Z_t in the original model and test again for autocorrelation.

Only in the event of failure to resolve the underlying specification problem should resort be made to an alternative approach based on a transformation of the available data. This alternative follows from the substitution of the disturbance variable, u in, for example,

$$Y_t = \alpha + \beta X_t + u_t \tag{1.19}$$

by the disturbance ε in the first-order scheme (1.15) on subtracting ρ times (1.19) lagged back one interval from (1.19). The result is

$$Y_t - \rho Y_{t-1} = \alpha(1 - \rho) + \beta(X_t - \rho X_{t-1}) + (u_t - \rho u_{t-1}) \tag{1.20}$$

so that if ε has the same properties that are otherwise normally assumed to apply to u the assumptions of the classical linear regression model are restored on adopting (1.20).[1] If the first values of the transformed variables take the form

$$\sqrt{1 - \rho^2}\, Y_1, \qquad \sqrt{1 - \rho^2}\, X_1$$

while the remaining values, $t = 2, 3, \ldots, T$, take the form indicated by (1.20), then the OLS estimator of the parameters α and β in (1.20) is equivalent to the GLS estimator of these parameters. The problem is that ρ is unknown but if it is substituted by a suitable estimate at least approximate GLS estimates can be

---

[1] Thus it is that the use of data in the form of first differences, e.g. $(Y_t - Y_{t-1})$, will help to reduce the strength of a first-order scheme of autocorrelated disturbances (i.e., in the transformed model) if ρ is close to 1. However, where the value of ρ is close to zero then the reverse applies. It is also interesting to note that if $\rho = 1$ the transformed model has no intercept, unless there is a linear time trend in the original model, while the use of first differencing produces negative autocorrelation if the disturbances of the original model are positively autocorrelated.

computed. One convenient way of estimating ρ, proposed by Durbin, which has as much to commend it as any other, is to obtain an OLS estimate of the parameter of Y_{t-1} in a rearrangement of a model like (1.20)

$$Y_t = \alpha(1 - \rho) + \rho Y_{t-1} + \beta X_t - \beta \rho X_{t-1} + u_t, \qquad t = 2, \ldots, T. \quad (1.21)$$

In principle higher order autocorrelation schemes may be dealt with along the same lines. For example, the second-order autoregressive model

$$u_t = \rho_1 u_{t-1} + \rho_2 u_{t-2} + \varepsilon_t \quad (1.22)$$

requires that the variables of (1.19) be transformed so that

$$Y_t - \rho_1 Y_{t-1} - \rho_2 Y_{t-2} = \alpha(1 - \rho_1 - \rho_2) + \beta(X_t - \rho_1 X_{t-1} \\ -\rho_2 X_{t-2}) + (u_t - \rho_1 u_{t-1} - \rho_2 u_{t-2}). \quad (1.23)$$

In the case of the above two-stage estimation procedure, the first stage would consist of finding OLS estimates of the parameters ρ_1 and ρ_2 of (1.23) on transferring $\rho_1 Y_{t-1}$ and $\rho_2 Y_{t-2}$ to the right-hand side while the second stage would involve OLS estimation of (1.23) after having replaced ρ_1 and ρ_2 with the OLS first-stage estimates of these parameters. (Should the Durbin–Watson test statistic still indicate autocorrelated disturbances after having allowed for first-order autocorrelated disturbances using an estimate of ρ, then the hypothesis that the disturbances follow a second-order scheme cannot be rejected.)

Lastly, it should be mentioned that when autocorrelated disturbances have been detected and once a transformed model such as (1.20) has been estimated, then that transformed model should be used for the purposes of prediction

$$\hat{Y}_{t+1} = \hat{\alpha}(1 - \hat{\rho}) + \hat{\beta}(X_{t+1} - \hat{\rho} X_t) + \hat{\rho} Y_t \quad (1.24a)$$
$$= \hat{\alpha} + \hat{\beta} X_{t+1} + \hat{\rho}[Y_t - (\hat{\alpha} + \hat{\beta} X_t)] \quad (1.24b)$$

since it can be seen from (1.24b) that in this case not only will an estimate of the parameter of an autoregressive disturbance model be used in computing the estimates $\hat{\alpha}, \hat{\beta}$ but it will also be used to make an allowance for the influence of the disturbance of the previous time interval on Y_{t+1}.

Heteroscedastic disturbances

Violation of the assumption that the disturbances share a common variance is usually referred to as the problem of heteroscedastic disturbances, or even simply heteroscedasticity. The effects of this phenomenon on the properties of the OLS estimators are essentially the same as those noted above for auto-correlated disturbances. However, in contrast to the latter it might be expected that heteroscedastic disturbances are more likely to be encountered in dealing with cross-section data than in the use of time-series data. This is because it seems reasonable to postulate that the variance of the disturbance u_i corresponding to a particular observation on, say, a single independent variable X_i is more likely to be different from the variance of the disturbance u_k if the observations X_i, X_j on the independent variable X relate to members of a heterogeneous population, such as firms of widely different scales of operation, households of widely different income levels, etc. Such sources of heterogeneity may be contrasted with the constancy inherent in observing a particular economic unit through time, even though it should be added that large changes in the observed values of a variable through time may well be associated with changes in variance.

In order to test the null hypothesis that the disturbances associated with given sample information share a common variance what is wanted ideally is repeated observations on the dependent variable for each set of values of the independent variables. This is too much to expect so far as observations on economic variables are concerned but given a large sample observations can be grouped, the variance of the residuals for each group computed and the standard test applied as given in Mood (1950) pp. 269–70. Alternatively, it might be reasonable to advance a plausible scheme for the heteroscedasticity so that this scheme can be tested against observation rather than a general hypothesis. A simple example would be to write the variance as being proportional to a power of some variable Z,

$$\sigma_i^2 = kZ_i^n. \tag{1.25}$$

A particular scheme of heteroscedasticity might then substitute an explanatory variable for Z,

$$\sigma_i^2 = kX_i^n. \tag{1.26}$$

This would be a useful form in dealing with a demand analysis problem where it is suspected that the variation displayed in *per capita* expenditure (Y_i) on a given commodity may increase as income levels *per capita* (X_i) increase. A test of the significance of an estimate of n can be used to test the null hypothesis of homoscedastic disturbances, at least, that is, with reference to the particular scheme (1.26). A maximum likelihood estimator for n is discussed in Kmenta (1971) pp. 263–4, using a trial and error approach to maximise the appropriate likelihood function. A large sample estimate of the variance of this estimator is also given.

A small sample test of (1.26) for the hypothesis

$$H_0 : n = 2$$

as opposed to the alternative hypothesis

$$H_A : n \neq 2$$

which uses the F-statistic has been developed by Goldfeld and Quandt (1965) while Glejser (1969) has proposed a procedure which can be used to test, separately, different hypotheses concerning the value of n.

Where a particular hypothesis about n appears to be supported by the available data, GLS estimates can be obtained as in the case of autocorrelated disturbances by an appropriate data transformation followed by OLS estimation using these transformed data. If $n = 2$ in (1.26) then for the model

$$Y_i = \alpha + \beta X_i + u_i$$

the transformed observations required are Y_i/X_i and $1/X_i$ so that the model becomes

$$\frac{Y_i}{X_i} = \frac{\alpha}{X_i} + \beta + \frac{u_i}{X_i}$$

the disturbances of which share the common variance k.

Multicollinearity

The term multicollinearity is used to refer to a linear dependence or (sample) correlation between two or more of the explanatory variables of a regression model, the consequences of which depend on how strong this correlation is. In the extreme situation where it is perfect, so that movements in a particular explanatory variable are exactly paralleled by movements in another explanatory variable, or a linear combination of other explanatory variables, it is quite impossible to distinguish between the way in which the values of a dependent variable are related to the first explanatory variable and the second explanatory variable(s) and the least squares estimator breaks down completely. However, where the correlation is less, and yet is still considerable, then there is usually an increase in the variances of estimated regression coefficients which means that the test procedures looked at in Section 1.2 are more likely to err on the side of the conclusion that a particular estimate does not appear to be significantly different from zero. However, where the purpose of estimating a model is to predict rather than to obtain reliable estimates of the parameters of a model, multicollinearity may present no serious problem if much the same interrelationships between regressors obtain also in the forecast situation.

Since multicollinearity need not be confined to a pair of regressors, inspection of a (symmetric) *matrix of zero-order correlation coefficients*, which displays the zero-order, or simple, correlation coefficients between each pair of explanatory variables, excluding the 'variable' which effectively forms the intercept but including the correlation coefficients $r_{X_k X_k}$ so that the diagonal elements are all unity,

$$\mathbf{r} = \begin{bmatrix} r_{X_2 X_2} \, r_{X_2 X_3} \cdots r_{X_2 X_K} \\ r_{X_2 X_3} \, r_{X_3 X_3} \qquad r_{X_3 X_K} \\ \cdot \qquad \cdot \qquad \cdot \qquad \cdot \\ \cdot \qquad \cdot \qquad \cdot \qquad \cdot \\ \cdot \qquad \cdot \qquad \cdot \qquad \cdot \\ r_{X_2 X_K} \, r_{X_3 X_K} \cdots r_{X_K X_K} \end{bmatrix} \tag{1.28}$$

provides only a limited check on multicollinearity except, of course, where there are only two regressors. A more general check is available in the determinant expansion of **r**, referred to as the *correlation determinant* (c.d.), $|\mathbf{r}|$, which has the boundaries 0 and 1, demarcating the range between perfect multicollinearity and a total absence of any linear independence between regressors. The first occurs, for example, if X_2 is perfectly correlated with X_3 so that X_2 has the same zero-order correlation coefficient with X_4, X_5, . . . as has X_3. The elements of the first two rows and columns in **r** then exactly correspond in which case its determinant expansion is zero. The second occurs in, for example, the simplest multiple regression model if the statistic $r_{X_2 X_3}$ is zero so that

$$|\mathbf{r}| = \begin{vmatrix} 1 & 0 \\ 0 & 1 \end{vmatrix} = 1.$$

Although the value of $|\mathbf{r}|$ is affected by the dispersion of the observed values of regressors it is perhaps the best available single measure of the degree of multicollinearity.

Other consequences of multicollinearity may be used to detect its presence. Thus multicollinearity is indicated where the test statistics $\hat{\beta}_k/(\text{s.e. } \hat{\beta}_k)$ for a multiple regression model are low and yet a high estimated value for $\bar{R}^2$ is recorded and the test statistic F for the explanatory variables as a group is significantly different from zero. In this case it may be that one or more of the regressors *is* significantly associated with the dependent variable but that a close association between the regressors has masked this. Secondly, possible interrelationships between regressors can be investigated with reference to estimates of $\bar{R}^2$ for regressions of each regressor in turn on all others. Thirdly, multicollinearity may be suspected if the estimated parameters of the other explanatory variables of a model are sensitive to whether a particular variable appears in the specification of a model or not.

These various tests share a common drawback in that none of them produces a sharp, unambiguous distinction between what is 'serious' multicollinearity and what is only the usual and 'acceptable' multicollinearity to be expected when using sample data. However, together they give the applied econometrician, and those who reads his results, a fairly clear idea of whether these results have been seriously affected by multicollinearity. As a rough guide as to what to do in practice, the results of some or all of the above tests should be presented if multicollinearity is suspected as being a problem from an estimate of $|\mathbf{r}|$ and estimates of the sampling variances of regression coefficients.

Since multicollinearity is essentially a shortcoming in the available data there is very little that can be done about overcoming the problems it raises other than a search for new data or the imposition of restrictions on the parameters to be estimated from what data there are available so that its deficiencies are less serious in relation to more limited information required from it. The opportunity to extend a sample or to use other compatible information to provide an alternative means of estimating the parameter of a troublesome explanatory variable, so that it can be removed to the left-hand side of a regression model and its values incorporated with those of the dependent variable, is something which is rarely encountered in practice. However, the second alternative may more readily offer means by which the separate appearance of a regressor which is strongly correlated with other regressors may be avoided.[1] In this case *a priori* information may suggest, for example, that the sum or the ratio of two variables may be taken to be a constant. Thus if the production function

$$Y_i = \beta_1 X_{2i}^{\beta_2} X_{3i}^{\beta_3} u_i \qquad (1.29)$$

cannot be reliably estimated for given observations on Y, X_2 and X_3 then the number of references can be reduced by one on setting the sum of β_2 and β_3 equal to one, i.e. assuming constant returns to scale, when (1.29) becomes

$$Y_i = \beta_1 (X_{2i} X_{3i}^{-1})^{\beta_2} X_{3i} u_i$$

or
$$Y_i / X_{3i} = \beta_1 (X_{2i} / X_{3i})^{\beta_2} u_i. \qquad (1.30)$$

Specification errors

The form of the mathematical function used to express a regression model and the assumptions made concerning its explanatory variables and disturbances may be collectively referred to as the specification of the model. Hence if this mathematical function or any of the other assumptions made about the model are inappropriate it could be said that a specification error had been made. The term *specification error* is, however, usually used in a narrower sense, and reference is made here in particular to three kinds of fault relating to assumptions made about the exact part of a regression model: the omission of a relevant regressor, the inclusion of an irrelevant regressor, and the use of an incorrect mathematical form.

The first of these errors results in biased estimates, the seriousness of which increases the stronger the correlations between included and excluded variables and the direction of which depends on the signs of the parameters of the excluded variables and of the correlations between included and excluded variables. Estimates of the variances of estimated parameters are also biased, upward in this case, with the result that the tests reviewed in Section 1.2 may lead to incorrect inferences concerning the magnitudes of population parameters.

It is somewhat difficult to generalise in reviewing tests of this source of

---

[1] It should be noted that the valid use of other sample information to reduce the sampling variances of regression coefficients should be encouraged, quite apart from any need to do this because of serious multicollinearity and that use should be made of plausible *a priori* restrictions on the parameters wherever possible with the same objective. This advice extends to both slope and intercept parameters. Thus if there are strong *a priori* grounds for believing that a regression model passes through the origin then there is no need to estimate the intercept of the model and observations on the variables may be taken as being already in the form of deviations from the sample mean (which will be different from the true mean only as a result of sampling).

specification error since the omitted variable(s) may be one of a variety of alternatives and its absence may only be conjectured from perhaps no more than the surprising size, sign or significance of a variable included in a model where these characteristics are supported by firm *a priori* reasoning. A more systematic test of the absence of an important variable is suggested, however, by the effect that this omission may have on the properties of the disturbance variable of the incorrectly specified model. One effect is that the expected values, or population mean values, of disturbances may no longer be zero. An example may be found in an examination of the association between two variables across firms in different industries. It may be that there are other, perhaps unknown or unquantifiable, variables which are also relevant and which take on different values for different industries. The expected value of the disturbance for firms in different industries is then different too, with the result that the distribution of the residuals of the fitted regression will tend to be clustered above or below the fitted line for different industries. A pattern is therefore found in the residuals in just the same way as a pattern is found when the disturbances are autocorrelated. Although in this case the sequence in the clustering above and below the fitted regression is arbitrary since the ordering of the industries is arbitrary, as also is the ordering of the residuals within each industry, the Durbin–Watson statistic may be used to provide an objective test of the significance of this clustering. Inspection of the observed residuals may then indicate whether the clustering corresponds to industries and hence whether other variables are required in the model, for example binary variables corresponding to the different industries.

If, in contrast to the first of these three specification errors, an irrelevant variable is included in a model then the least squares estimators of the parameters of other explanatory variables remain unbiased while unbiased estimates of the true variances of estimates of these parameters are also obtained from the usual formulae. These conclusions do not mean, however, that a regression model may be littered with regressors, selected simply on a 'try and see' basis, without penalty. In the first place there is the possibility that as a result of sampling, a variable that does not belong to the model is nevertheless shown to be significantly associated with the dependent variable. This may be an acceptable risk for one or two variables and, indeed, the procedure constitutes a test of this particular source of specification error. However, the risk of the test producing an incorrect result is increased the larger the number of variables that appear as regressors. Secondly, from what has been noted earlier on the subject of multicollinearity, it will be appreciated that the variance of the least squares estimator of the parameter an explanatory variable which is, say, appropriately included in the model, will be increased if another, perhaps irrelevant, regressor is also included unless the sample correlation between the two variables is zero. This result may be regarded as the opposite to the gain in the reliability of estimates when restrictions on the parameters of a regression model are used to reduce the number of parameters to be estimated (see footnote, p. 16). Thus if an additional variable is indeed irrelevant there will almost certainly be an unnecessary fall in the accuracy of inferences based on estimates of regression coefficients.

Turning to the last of the specification errors discussed in this section it is noted first that where it is assumed that a dependent variable is a linear function of some variable when a quadratic, cubic or some higher order polynomial would have been more appropriate, the consequences are the same as when any other relevant variable has been overlooked. To the extent that Taylor's theorem can be used to represent many functions in the form of a power series, providing, at least in most cases, the series converges, this conclusion has more general application. Thus it is often possible to expand a function of some regressor X as a power series in X about a constant, the sample mean $\bar{X}$ or zero are obvious choices,

$$f(X) = f(\bar{X}) + \frac{f'(\bar{X})}{1!}(X - \bar{X}) + \frac{f''(\bar{X})}{2!}(X - \bar{X})^2 + \dots \quad (1.31)$$

so that the simple model (1.1) may be regarded as a drastic simplification of a more general representation of a relationship between two variables and an additive disturbance,

$$Y_i = f(X_i) + u_i. \quad (1.32)$$

Although there may be some appeal in the simplicity of the linear function, if there are no strong *a priori* reasons for adopting models like (1.1) it may be useful to test the linearity assumption against observation. Where there is nothing to suggest that some trial non-linear function should exhibit more than one, if any, finite maximum or minimum then the statistical significance of the estimate γ in the fitted quadratic

$$Y_i = \alpha + \beta X_i + \gamma X_i^2 \quad (1.33)$$

may be used as a rough guide as to whether the true relationship between Y and X is linear or not.[1] The use of a quadratic for this purpose not only serves

---

[1] Another kind of non-linearity which can be tested in this way is found in the use of special transformations of variables where the marginal relationship between two variables is believed to be a function of a third variable rather than a constant. The usual example quoted is the influence of family size (Z) on the income (X) marginal propensity to consume certain commodities such as food. Thus if expenditure on food is represented by Y, the model

$$Y_i = \alpha + \beta X_i + \gamma X_i Z_i + u_i, \quad (1.34)$$

when

$$\partial E(Y_i)\partial X_i = \beta + \gamma Z_i, \quad (1.35)$$

may be preferred to

$$Y_i = \alpha + \beta X_i + \gamma Z_i + u_i. \quad (1.36)$$

(The notational form $E(Y_i)$ is used to refer to the population mean value, or expected value, of Y_i.) Whether Y can be regarded, on the basis of the available sample information, to be a linear function of X then requires a test of the hypothesis

$$H_0: \beta = \gamma = 0$$

while a test of the hypothesis

$$H_0: \gamma = 0$$

can be used to check on the validity of (1.35).

to allow the fitted line to curve but may also be regarded as a closer approximation to the Taylor's expansion (1.31), expanded about $X = 0$ if the model is fitted to actual observations on X or about $X = \bar{X}$ if deviations from sample means are used. Alternatively, a logarithmic transformation of the data might be used as in (1.3), particularly if there is good reason to believe that the trial function should have no finite maximum or minimum; in this case the comparison should be based on a test of the closeness of the fits of the two alternative regression results to the data.

A second approach to a test of the appropriateness of the functional form used is indicated by the conclusion that if a linear model is used incorrectly in the place of some non-linear model, or *vice versa*, then the residuals of the fitted regression will not only estimate the disturbances of the correct model but will also reflect divergences between this result and the underlying correct model. If these divergences relate to, say, the variable X then they will give rise to a pattern in the residuals in the X–Y plane as the correct relationship passes above and below the fitted relationship. Such a pattern will have a similar appearance to the pattern found in the time-Y plane in the case of auto-correlated disturbances which suggests yet another instance in which the Durbin–Watson statistic may be used to test the non-randomness of residuals, i.e. when they are ordered according to the ranking of a particular regressor, X. It will be evident that one snag in this arises when time-series data are used and the ranking of X roughly corresponds to the time ordering of observations on X. In this case a test of first-order autocorrelated disturbances is confused with that of the appropriateness of the functional form adopted with respect to X.

1.4 FURTHER READING

This chapter has done no more than review the scope of applied econometrics and look at some of the results of statistical theory relating to hypothesis testing and of econometric theory relating to tests of the assumptions of the classical regression model. It cannot be emphasised too strongly that intelligent and sensitive use of these procedures requires a sound understanding of the theory to which they relate and those who have found themselves unfamiliar with the concepts, assumptions, methods of analysis and formulae discussed or simply mentioned so far must remedy this before venturing further. In addition it is necessary to build up a knowledge of those other areas of econometric theory, the conclusions of which are variously called on in dealing with different problems encountered in applied work.

There are a number of excellent texts now available which may be used to provide these theoretical foundations. Six texts in particular are referred to here as being sufficiently comprehensive without entirely overstepping the introductory nature of the discussion pursued over the chapters that follow. Roughly in order of increasing difficulty of treatment these include texts by Koutsoyiannis (1973), Kmenta (1971), Wonnacott and Wonnacott (1970),

Johnston (1972), Goldberger (1964) and Theil (1971). References have also been given earlier with respect to some tests which are not dealt with by all of these texts.

Both Koutsoyiannis and Kmenta provide a relatively gradual introduction to the subject. In particular each includes a review of those elements of statistical theory which are necessary for an understanding of the principles of estimation and of hypothesis testing while both authors have chosen to explain and discuss using the simplest possible mathematical tools, especially avoiding matrix algebra wherever possible. In addition theoretical results are illustrated with reference to numerical examples throughout. However, despite these aids to the beginner, the size of the texts means that they remain essentially comprehensive. Indeed both give detailed attention to several topics which are of special interest in applied work: this applies in particular to Koutsoyiannis's treatment of distributed lag models and Kmenta's treatment of estimation when some observations are missing, specification errors, non-linear models, models with restricted coefficients and the pooling of cross-section and time-series data.

The Wonnacotts' text is divided into two parts so as to cover roughly the same ground at two different levels. Part One provides an introduction to important statistical concepts used in econometrics and to the main problems which are encountered on weakening the assumptions of the classical regression model; Part Two is a generalisation of Part One and relies heavily on matrix algebra. Vector geometry is used extensively to interpret regression and correlation theory and the use of instrumental variables in tackling the related problems of estimating when using regressors which are subject to errors of measurement and of estimating simultaneous equation models.

Johnston's thorough development and explanation of econometric methods has been a standard text at both the undergraduate and graduate levels for many years, while a recent second edition has kept it abreast of the advance of the subject. A knowledge of basic mathematical statistics is assumed but the essentials of matrix algebra are provided in an early chapter and this method of exposition is used throughout the rest of the book. Topics covered in the second edition of Johnston's book which are either not dealt with at all, or which are dealt with in much less detail, by the three texts referred to so far, include seasonal adjustment, covariance analysis and other multivariate methods including principal components, canonical correlations and discriminant analysis.

The last two texts referred to here are aimed essentially at the graduate level. Goldberger's text remains extremely valuable in this respect as a concise and advanced treatment of the subject despite developments since its publication. Theil's book has the advantage of being organised so as to provide a choice of courses of instruction at different levels including a special topics course centred around consumer demand theory. Other differences include an introduction to aggregation theory, a review of the frontiers of econometrics and an extensive bibliography.

1.5 REFERENCES

Christ, C. F. (1966), *Econometric Models and Methods* (New York: John Wiley).

Durbin, J. (1970), 'Testing for Serial Correlation in Least-Squares Regression when Some of the Regressors are Lagged Dependent Variables', *Econometrica*, vol. 38, 410–21.

Glejser, H. (1969), 'A New Test for Heteroscedasticity', *Journal of the American Statistical Association*, vol. 64, 316–23.

Goldberger, A. S. (1964), *Econometric Theory* (New York: John Wiley).

Goldfeld, S. M. and Quandt, R. E. (1965), 'Some Tests for Heteroscedasticity', *Journal of the American Statistical Association*, vol. 60, 538–47.

Johnston, J. (1972), *Econometric Methods*, 2nd ed. (New York: McGraw-Hill).

Koutsoyiannis, A. (1973), *Theory of Econometrics* (London: Macmillan).

Kmenta, J. (1971), *Elements of Econometrics* (New York: Macmillan).

Mood, A. M. (1950), *Introduction to the Theory of Statistics* (New York: McGraw-Hill).

Theil, H. (1971), *Principles of Econometrics* (New York: John Wiley).

Wonnacott, R. J. and Wonnacott, T. H. (1970) *Econometrics* (New York: John Wiley).

2. Investment

2.1 INTRODUCTION

In the study of economic behaviour one of the variables which is important at all levels of economic activity is investment: that is, the value of goods bought by the producing sector which will provide services in the future. This chapter is concerned with the factors affecting both the demand for net additions to capital stock and the replacement of capital assets, but ignoring the government sector and investment in housing and inventories. Alternative names for this gross investment are 'private sector non-dwelling gross fixed capital formation' or 'gross private fixed non-residential domestic investment'.

The purpose of this chapter is to illustrate the testing of various theories of investment behaviour within a unified framework. Problems of specification, especially of the time structure of investment, and of estimation are discussed. Empirical evidence on investment at the aggregate and also the company level is presented and summarised, and finally a brief guide to the literature on investment is included.

In order to introduce the principal issues which may help to explain an observed series of expenditures on investment, reference is made to the procedure adopted by Jorgenson and Siebert (1968). Thus to begin with it may be proposed that in each time period there is some desired level of capital stock K^*. This is, of course, likely to be different from the actual level of capital stock, K. If in any period the desired level of capital stock is greater than the actual level then the decision to add to the existing stock of capital may be taken. Since investment takes time only a part of the discrepancy between K^* and K will be removed within a single time period. The actual level of capital stock observed at the end of period t, K_t, which is composed of the sum of an initial stock of capital plus net additions to the stock, is related to the desired level of capital stock in all previous periods. In particular,

$$K_t = w_0 K_t^* + w_1 K_{t-1}^* + w_2 K_{t-2}^* + \ldots \tag{2.1}$$

where the w_i are weights attached to the value of K^* i periods ago. These weights reflect the speed of adjustment of the actual to desired capital stock. If the discrepancy between the desired and actual capital stock were always removed instantaneously then

$$w_0 = 1, w_i = 0 \text{ for } i > 0 \text{ so that}$$
$$K_t = K_t^*.$$

Otherwise some of the other weights will be different from zero. It is useful to define a *lag operator*, L, which has the effect of delaying a variable one time period. For example, with a general variable x,

$$Lx_t = x_{t-1}, L^2x_t = x_{t-2}, \ldots, L^ix_t = x_{t-i}. \tag{2.2}$$

Following from this (2.1) can be written

$$
\begin{aligned}
K_t &= w_0K_t^* + w_1LK_t^* + w_2L^2K_t^* + \cdots \\
&= (w_0 + w_1L + w_2L^2 + \ldots)K_t^* \\
&= w(L)K_t^* \tag{2.3}
\end{aligned}
$$

so that $w(L)$ is the polynomial in the lag operator and is known as a distributed lag function. The equation corresponding to (2.3) for the previous time period is

$$K_{t-1} = w(L)K_{t-1}^*$$

and subtracting this from (2.3) gives

$$K_t - K_{t-1} = w(L)(K_t^* - K_{t-1}^*) \tag{2.4}$$

i.e. the actual change in capital stock is related to past changes in the desired capital stock. But $K_t - K_{t-1}$ is net investment in period t, which by definition, is gross investment less replacement investment. Hence

$$I_t^N \equiv I_t - I_t^R = K_t - K_{t-1} \tag{2.5}$$

where I_t^N is net investment
I_t is gross investment
I_t^R is replacement investment.

From (2.4) and (2.5)

$$I_t = w(L)(K_t^* - K_{t-1}^*) + I_t^R \tag{2.6}$$

This function explains gross investment in terms of lagged changes in desired capital stock and replacement investment. The three elements – $w(L)$, K_t^* and I_t^R – need to be specified in more detail before the investment function can be tested by reference to data and this is done in the next three sections.

2.2 REPLACEMENT INVESTMENT

Replacement investment occurs when old capital goods are scrapped and new ones are installed to replace them. If no technical progress or economies of scale occur then the physical rate of replacement investment will be equal to the rate of scrapping (or depreciation) assuming the required level of capital is unchanged. Thus replacement investment depends on the level of capital stock and also on its age structure. Jorgenson (1965) has argued that since capital goods have a variable length of life an initial investment will generate replacement investments at different times in the future. Each of these replacement investments will generate new replacements, which will in turn generate more replacements. This process continues indefinitely. The result is that, mathematically, replacement investment is a recurrent event, and by reference to renewal theory, the level of replacement investment will be approximately a constant fraction of capital stock so that

$$I_t^R = \delta K_{t-1} \tag{2.7}$$

where δ is the proportion of capital stock replaced each time period. The ratio $1/\delta$ is the average life of capital goods measured in unit time periods.

Equation (2.7) is proved by Jorgenson and Stephenson (1967) pp. 178–9, in the special case of the distribution of replacements over time being geometric so that $\qquad I_t^R = \delta I_{t-1} + \delta(1-\delta)I_{t-2} + \ldots$

Reintroducing the lag operator, L,

$$I_t^R = \delta L I_t + \delta(1-\delta)L^2 I_t + \ldots$$

$$= \frac{\delta L}{1 - (1-\delta)L} I_t \quad \text{or} \quad I_t = \frac{(1 - (1-\delta)L)}{\delta L} I_t^R. \tag{2.8}$$

Since capital stock at the end of a period is the sum of all past net investments,

$$K_t = I_t^N + I_{t-1}^N + I_{t-2}^N + \ldots$$

$$= I_t - I_t^R + I_{t-1} - I_{t-1}^R + I_{t-2} - I_{t-2}^R + \ldots$$

$$= (1 + L + L^2 + \ldots)(I_t - I_t^R)$$

$$= \frac{I_t - I_t^R}{1 - L}$$

and from (2.8)

$$K_t = \frac{1}{1-L} \left[\frac{1 - (1-\delta)L}{\delta L} - 1 \right] I_t^R$$

$$= \frac{I_t^R}{\delta L}.$$

Hence $\qquad I_t^R = \delta L K_t = \delta K_{t-1}$

which is (2.7).

If technical progress or economics of scale occur, each physical unit of replacement investment may be more efficient than the corresponding scrapped capital stock. In this case the price of the replacement investment may be assumed to reflect the added efficiency and (2.7) would still apply in monetary erms.

2.3 DESIRED CAPITAL STOCK

Various theories have been suggested to determine the desired level of capital stock and some of these are now considered. The simplest, which is discussed by Chenery (1952), is obtained by assuming that there is an economically most profitable amount of capital required to produce a given level of output, X, so that the desired level of capital stock is

$$K^* = \beta X \quad \text{or} \quad \frac{K^*}{X} = \beta$$

where β is the most profitable, or desired, capital–output ratio. Since X measures output per unit of time the value of β will depend upon the unit time period. In particular β will be smaller for annual data than for quarterly data. The difference between two successive values of K^* is

$$K_t^* - K_{t-1}^* = \beta X_t - \beta X_{t-1} = \beta(X_t - X_{t-1})$$

and the investment function (2.6) is

$$I_t = w(L)\beta(X_t - X_{t-1}) + I_t^R. \tag{2.9}$$

Thus the level of investment is not related to the level of output but to the change of output, which gives the name 'accelerator'. The particular version presented above is known as the 'crude accelerator', since many modifications have been proposed to avoid some of the difficulties and limitations of this particular formulation. These have been reviewed by many authors including Eckaus (1953) and Smyth (1964) and give an indication of the background to other theories explaining the desired level of capital stock:

(*a*) The treatment of excess capacity. If there is no excess capacity in the firm then the level of output cannot be increased to meet an increase in demand so that the desired level of capital stock may not be directly proportional to the level of output. If there is excess capacity then output can increase without investment occurring.

(*b*) The symmetry of the accelerator mechanism. It is unlikely that a 10 per cent increase in output and a 10 per cent decrease in output will lead to exactly the same amount of capital stock being bought and scrapped.

(*c*) Transitory changes in output. Some fluctuations in output will be regarded as temporary and investment plans will depend on expected future output rather than actual past output. In an otherwise expanding market a decrease in output could be regarded as a temporary setback caused by special factors so that the predicted reduction in investment may not occur.

(*d*) The availability of finance. Lack of finance may prevent desired levels of capital stock being achieved.

(*e*) Prices are ignored. A change in the relative prices of capital and labour, unconnected with changes in output, may induce firms to amend their investment plans.

(*f*) Discontinuities or indivisibilities in the production process. The investment required according to the accelerator may not correspond to an exact number of machines so that either too much or too little investment must occur.

(*g*) The optimum capital–output ratio or acceleration coefficient may not be constant. If firms exhibit non-constant returns to scale, or if the technology is changing then the fixed accelerator will only be an approximation.

(*h*) Only output matters. Desired investment is determined solely by changes in output and other variables such as profits, expectations, liquidity and interest rates are ignored.

These limitations of the crude accelerator have led to various modifications which attempt to overcome some of the problems. Chenery (1952) considers two modifications, the flexible accelerator and the capacity principle. Here discussion is confined to the particular modification subsequently proposed by Jack (1966) along much the same lines. With reference to (*a*), (*b*) and (*c*) above Jack argues that a new variable, X' say, is relevant in determining whether a change in output is important, where X' takes the maximum value of X observed in, say, the previous three time periods, so that

$$X' = \text{maximum}\ (X_{t-1}, X_{t-2}, X_{t-3}).$$

The relevant change in output so far as the investment decision is concerned may then be

$$\Delta' X_t = X_t - X' \qquad \text{if } X_t > X'$$

$$= 0 \qquad\qquad \text{if } X_t < X'$$

so that if current output X_t is greater than the recent maximum X' then $\Delta' X_t$ is positive and investment will occur. If current output is less than X' then $\Delta' X_t$ will be zero and only replacement investment will occur. Thus this modified accelerator mechanism behaves asymmetrically to changes in output and reductions in output are treated as temporary fluctuations. The investment function is

$$I_t = w(L)\beta(\Delta' X_t) + I_t^R \tag{2.10}$$

where β is the acceleration coefficient in this modified equation.

One of the limitations of the crude accelerator model is that financial considerations are ignored. A shortage of funds may prevent the desired level of capital stock from being achieved. Lund (1971) p. 39, lists the possible sources of funds for a firm as (*a*) depreciation allowances, (*b*) net profits (that is, gross profits less taxes and depreciation allowances), (*c*) fixed interest borrowing, (*d*) preference shares, (*e*) equity issues. Of these (*a*) and (*b*) are internal to the firm whilst the remainder are external. The internally generated funds are available for dividends and investment. If dividends are assumed to be determined by factors not directly relevant to investment then internal funds less dividends determine the desired level of capital stock in the liquidity theory of investment, so that

$$K_t^* = \beta L_t$$

and the investment function is

$$I_t = w(L)\beta(L_t - L_{t-1}) + I_t^R. \tag{2.11}$$

Liquidity, L_t, may be measured as gross profits after tax plus depreciation less dividends paid.

The role of profits in arriving at the desired level of capital stock is rather complex. Many studies of investment use current or recent profits as measures of expectations about the future profitability of investment. Grunfeld (1960) p. 211, however, recognises that while profits generally perform extremely well as an explanatory variable, they are highly correlated with other variables which are the underlying determinants of investment. He argues that management will not base expectations of future profits solely on realised profits since both general business optimism and anticipated changes in supply and demand conditions are relevant. He therefore proposes the stock market valuation of a company as a measure of future expected profits. This is the assessment by stock-market investors of the present value of the future stream of earnings of the company. The particular formulation for determining the desired level of capital stock, which is known as the expected profits model of investment, is

$$K_t^* = \beta V_t$$

where V_t is a measure of the stock market valuation of the company. The investment function is

$$I_t = w(L)\beta(V_t - V_{t-1}) + I_t^R. \tag{2.12}$$

Grunfeld's study used data on individual corporations. At the aggregate level the stock market valuation of all companies is unlikely to be an adequate measure of expectation because the number of quoted companies is constantly changing. An alternative measure is an index of the level of share prices which it is likely will be correlated strongly with the stock market valuation of those companies included in the index.

Profits are also important in the theory of investment developed by Jorgenson (1963) which is based on a neoclassical theory of the optimal accumulation of capital. The main assumption is that entrepreneurs aim to maximise the net worth or discounted future profits, of the firm under conditions of perfect competition. This is done subject to two constraints: that net investment equals gross investment less replacement investment (i.e. (2.5)) and that the production function is a Cobb–Douglas one. By use of the marginal conditions for profit maximisation the desired level of capital stock is

$$K_t^* = \frac{\beta p_t}{c_t} X_t$$

where X_t = level of output
 $\quad\quad\; p_t$ = price of output
 $\quad\quad\; c_t$ = price of a unit of capital services.

The value of c_t depends upon the price of investment goods, the rate of depreciation and the rate of interest, as well as the various tax and depreciation allowances relating to investment goods. Jorgenson and Siebert (1968) pp. 696–7, consider two versions of the neoclassical model which differ in the treatment of capital gains. The first version assumes capital gains affect the investment decision with the result

$$c_t = \frac{q_t}{1 - u_t}\left[(1 - u_t w_t)\delta + r_t - \left(\frac{q_t - q_{t-1}}{q_t}\right)\right]$$

while in the second version capital gains are set equal to zero and

$$c_t = \frac{q_t}{1 - u_t}[(1 - u_t w_t)\delta + r_t]$$

where q_t = price index of capital goods
 $\quad\quad\; u_t$ = rate of taxation on corporate income
 $\quad\quad\; w_t$ = proportion of depreciation at replacement cost deductible from income for tax purposes
 $\quad\quad\; \delta$ = rate of replacement
 $\quad\quad\; r_t$ = cost of capital.

Notice that δ, the rate of replacement, is the same as the coefficient of lagged capital stock in (2.7). The investment function for both neoclassical models is

$$I_t = w(L)\beta\left(\frac{p_t X_t}{c_t} - \frac{p_{t-1} X_{t-1}}{c_{t-1}}\right) + I_t^R. \tag{2.13}$$

2.4 THE DISTRIBUTED LAG FUNCTION $w(L)$

The function $w(L)$ is defined in (2.1)–(2.3). In (2.1) the observed level of capital stock is explained by all previous values of the desired capital stock. It is therefore impossible to estimate any of the investment functions in their general form without having data on all previous values. Some assumptions about the w_i are needed to solve this problem. Two restrictions on the values of w_i which are generally made are, for all i,

$$w_i \geqslant 0 \quad \text{and} \quad \Sigma w_i = 1. \tag{2.14}$$

That is, all the weights are positive or zero and add up to 1. Additional assumptions are still required in order to determine the weights.

One simple scheme proposed by Koyck (1954) has the useful property of allowing all past values of the variables to have some effect and yet only requires one unknown parameter. Since recent values of desired capital stock are likely to have a more important effect than past values, Koyck proposed that the weights should decline geometrically. That is, each weight is a constant proportion, λ, of the previous weight and

$$w_0 = 1 - \lambda, \; w_1 = (1 - \lambda)\lambda, \; w_2 = (1 - \lambda)\lambda^2,$$

so that in general

$$w_i = (1 - \lambda)\lambda^i \quad \text{for } i = 0, 1, \ldots \quad (2.15)$$

If $0 < \lambda < 1$ then all the weights are positive and their sum is 1 with

$$w_0 > w_1 > w_2 > w_3 \ldots$$

The distributed lag function can be written

$$
\begin{aligned}
w(L) &= w_0 + w_1 L + w_2 L^2 \ldots \\
&= (1 - \lambda)(1 + \lambda L + \lambda^2 L^2 + \ldots) \\
&= \frac{(1 - \lambda)}{1 - \lambda L}
\end{aligned}
\quad (2.16)
$$

so that (2.6) is

$$I_t = \frac{(1 - \lambda)}{(1 - \lambda L)} (K_t^* - K_{t-1}^*) + I_t^R.$$

Taking replacement investment to the left-hand side and multiplying by $(1 - \lambda L)$ gives

$$(1 - \lambda L)(I_t - I_t^R) = (1 - \lambda)(K_t^* - K_{t-1}^*)$$

or, alternatively

$$
\begin{aligned}
I_t - I_t^R &= \lambda L(I_t - I_t^R) + (1 - \lambda)(K_t^* - K_{t-1}^*) \\
&= \lambda(I_{t-1} - I_{t-1}^R) + (1 - \lambda)(K_t^* - K_{t-1}^*)
\end{aligned}
$$

and hence

$$I_t = \lambda(I_{t-1} - I_{t-1}^R) + (1 - \lambda)(K_t^* - K_{t-1}^*) + I_t^R. \quad (2.17)$$

Thus the Koyck lag scheme results in an equation involving only one change in the desired capital stock and requires the estimation of only one parameter, λ. However, as indicated above, w_0 is the largest weight so that the most recent changes in the desired capital stock are assumed to be the most important. This may not be true with annual data and it certainly will not be true with quarterly data. Once the desired level of capital stock is determined delays will occur before the resulting investment takes place. Contracts have to be agreed. Work may not start immediately. More delays can occur at the production, delivery and installation stages. The result is that investment which is currently occurring is more likely to be the result of decisions made last year than those made this year.

A version of Koyck's lag scheme which avoids this difficulty allows the weights for the first few periods to be determined freely before the geometric decline commences. However, this is at the cost of having extra values of the independent variables in the final equation.

Solow (1960) p. 392, generalised Koyck's scheme to allow for r different stages in the decision and investment process. Assuming that a geometric scheme applies at each of r stages with the same parameter λ the resulting weights and lag function are given by the Pascal distribution

$$w_i = \binom{r + i - 1}{i}(1 - \lambda)^r \lambda^i, \quad w(L) = \frac{(1 - \lambda)^r}{(1 - \lambda L)^r}. \qquad (2.18)$$

This is a more flexible weighting scheme since the choice of r affects the shape of the lag function. If $r = 1$ then this is simply the Koyck scheme. If r is greater than 1 the weights increase to some peak before declining to zero. However, Solow's approach has the disadvantage of requiring estimation with non-linear constraints. Jorgenson (1966) provides an even more general lag scheme by proving that any arbitrary lag function can be approximated by the rational lag form

$$w(L) = \frac{u(L)}{v(L)} \qquad (2.19)$$

where $u(L)$ and $v(L)$ are polynomials in the lag operator, L. This includes the Koyck form (2.16) and the Pascal distribution (2.18) as special cases. The form (2.19) is completely general but in practice it is usual to limit $v(L)$ to being linear or quadratic in L. This then limits the number of lagged values of I_t to one or two. The case where $u(L)$ and $v(L)$ are both quadratic in L will be used as an illustration of how (2.19) is incorporated in the investment function. From (2.6) and (2.7),

$$I_t = w(L)(K_t^* - K_{t-1}^*) + \delta K_{t-1}.$$

Re-arranging and substituting (2.19) gives

$$v(L)(I_t - \delta K_{t-1}) = u(L)(K_t^* - K_{t-1}^*),$$

and hence

$$(v_0 + v_1 L + v_2 L^2)(I_t - \delta K_{t-1}) = (u_0 + u_1 L + u_2 L^2)(K_t^* - K_{t-1}^*)$$

which can be written

$$v_0(I_t - \delta K_{t-1}) = u_0(K_t^* - K_{t-1}^*) + u_1(K_{t-1}^* - K_{t-2}^*)$$
$$+ u_2(K_{t-2}^* - K_{t-3}^*) - v_1(I_{t-1} - \delta K_{t-2})$$
$$- v_2(I_{t-2} - \delta K_{t-3}).$$

Since division by v_0 only affects the values of the u_i and v_i, the value of v_0 can be set equal to 1 to give the equation to be estimated:

$$I_t = u_0(K_t^* - K_{t-1}^*) + u_1(K_{t-1}^* - K_{t-2}^*) + u_2(K_{t-2}^* - K_{t-3}^*)$$
$$-v_1(I_{t-1} - \delta K_{t-2}) - v_2(I_{t-2} - \delta K_{t-3}) + \delta K_{t-1}. \quad (2.20)$$

This equation can be estimated by regression methods. The parameter δ occurs three times in (2.20). Rather than estimating the equation restricting the different δ's to be the same, the method adopted by Jorgenson and his associates is to use data to obtain δ, evaluate a series of $I_t - \delta K_{t-1}$, and then substitute these in (2.20). The equation is estimated and the resulting coefficient of K_{t-1} is compared with the value of δ from the data. If the two differ, the coefficient of K_{t-1} is used as the new value of δ and the process is repeated until the two values are close together. The data give the initial value of δ since from (2.5) and (2.7),

$$I_t - I_t^R = K_t - K_{t-1}$$

or

$$I_t^R = \delta K_{t-1} = I_t - (K_t - K_{t-1})$$

and, by summing for $t = 1$ to N,

$$\delta \Sigma K_{t-1} = \Sigma I_t - (K_N - K_0).$$

Finally

$$\delta = \frac{\Sigma I_t - (K_N - K_0)}{\Sigma K_{t-1}} \quad (2.21)$$

where the summations are for $t = 1$ to $t = N$.

Since the rational lag function is completely general a criterion must be adopted to determine the most satisfactory specification of $w(L)$. The one adopted by Jorgenson and Siebert (1968) is to choose the lag structure which minimises the residual variance subject to the condition that the signs of the estimated parameters satisfy their *a priori* expectations. The residual variance is estimated by $\Sigma e_i^2/(N - K')$ and so their approach is equivalent to maximising $\bar{R}^2$ since

$$\bar{R}^2 = 1 - \frac{\Sigma e_i^2/(N - K')}{\Sigma(Y_i - \bar{Y})^2/(N - 1)}$$

and the denominator of the fraction is constant for each set of data considered.[1] Additional constraints on the weights w_i are $w_i \geqslant 0$ and $\Sigma w_i = 1$. By expanding (2.19) the first of these conditions can be used to obtain constraints on the values of the u_i and v_i (again it is assumed $v_i = 0$ and $u_i = 0$ for $i > 2$)

$$w_0 + w_1 L + w_2 L^2 + \ldots = \frac{u_0 + u_1 L + u_2 L^2}{1 + v_1 L + v_2 L^2}.$$

---

[1] To avoid confusion a slight change is made in the notation used in Chapter 1. Here K' is the number of parameters in the linear regression model and e_i is an observed residual.

Multiplying out gives

$$w_0 + (w_1 + w_0 v_1)L + (w_2 + w_1 v_1 + w_0 v_2)L^2 + \dots$$
$$= u_0 + u_1 L + u_2 L^2$$

and hence by equating the coefficients of the powers of L:

$$w_0 = u_0, w_1 + w_0 v_1 = u_1, w_2 + w_1 v_1 + w_0 v_2 = u_2.$$

If both v_1 and v_2 are zero, then the requirement $w_i \geqslant 0$ reduces to

$$u_0 \geqslant 0, u_1 \geqslant 0, u_2 \geqslant 0. \tag{2.22}$$

If v_2 is zero but v_1 is not, then the requirement $w_i \geqslant 0$ becomes

$$u_0 \geqslant 0, u_1 \geqslant v_1 u_0, u_2 \geqslant v_1(u_1 - v_1 u_0) \tag{2.23}$$

and if both v_1 and v_2 are different from zero then

$$u_0 \geqslant 0, u_1 \geqslant u_0 v_1, u_2 \geqslant (u_1 - u_0 v_1)v_1 + u_0 v_2. \tag{2.24}$$

Jorgenson (1966) p. 147, has shown that the condition $\Sigma w_i = 1$ is equivalent to

$$\Sigma u_i = \Sigma v_i. \tag{2.25}$$

As a standard of comparison for the different investment theories a naïve model is used with the form

$$I_t = \beta_0 + \beta_1 I_{t-1} + \beta_2 I_{t-2} + \beta_3 I_{t-3} \tag{2.26}$$

where extra lagged values of investment are included as long as the value of $\bar{R}^2$ is increased. A theory of investment may be judged to be satisfactory if the performance of the best equation is at least superior to that of the naïve model.

A major criticism which applies to the rational distributed lag scheme is that the lag structure is assumed to be fixed. This is unlikely to be true even at the micro-economic level for a particular investment good, since if a firm decides a particular investment good is essential and should be obtained urgently, meetings can re-arranged, overtime can be worked and the whole decision and production process can be speeded up. When this occurs some costs will be higher so that the speed of adjustment of capital stock depends on economic considerations as well as purely organisational ones.

A further difficulty with the rational distributed lag occurs when the random disturbance term, ε, is considered. If ε is added to (2.6) then the random term in the case of a quadratic $v(L)$ function (as in (2.20)) is $v(L)\varepsilon_t$ or $(\varepsilon_t + v_1\varepsilon_{t-1} + v_2\varepsilon_{t-2})$ so that second-order autocorrelation of the residuals is to be expected. A rather unsatisfactory way round this problem is to add ε to (2.20) and make the assumption that it is random and non-autocorrelated.

2.5 AGGREGATE INVESTMENT FUNCTIONS

In this section the alternative investment functions discussed above will be estimated using annual data for the United Kingdom for the post-war period. Data are available in a consistent form for 1955–70 giving 16 observations. To allow for up to three lagged values of variables to be included the investment functions will be fitted for 1958–70. The data are taken from the Blue Book: National Income and Expenditure 1971 and earlier, unless otherwise stated, and the monetary variables are expressed in 1963 prices. The variables are:

X_t – Index of industrial production (1963 = 100) from Table 15.

$\Delta' X_t$ – Defined as $X_t - \max(X_{t-1}, X_{t-2}, X_{t-3})$ if this is positive and otherwise zero.

I_t – Gross domestic fixed capital formation for companies (from Table 6) divided by a price index of fixed assets (from Table 16) (£ thousand millions).

K_t – End of year t net capital stock at current replacement cost for companies (from Table 64) divided by a price index of fixed assets (from Table 16) (£ thousand millions).

L_t – Undistributed income (after taxation) of companies (from Table 27) divided by a price index of fixed assets (from Table 16) (£ thousand millions).

S_t – Average value of *Financial Times* share index (1935 = 100) during year t from *Financial Statistics*, Table 96 and from the *Financial Times*.

r_t – Rate of interest on $2\frac{1}{2}$ per cent Consols (per cent) from *Financial Statistics*, Table 107, May 1972 and the *Monthly Digest of Statistics*.

p_t – Price index (1963 = 100) of total final output (from Table 16).

u_t – Rate of taxation on company income (from Table 27) being total U.K. taxes plus taxes paid abroad divided by total income for companies.

q_t – Price index (1963 = 100) of fixed assets (from Table 16).

The theory of investment outlined above refers to corporate behaviour and so the variables are defined for companies where possible. For the period considered, companies were responsible for about 40 per cent of investment, the remainder being attributed to the government and personal sectors. The measures of investment, capital and liquidity are deflated by a price index of fixed assets which includes the price of non-company capital formation goods such as housing, so that the resulting measures in 1963 prices are likely to be biased away from the true values. The index of industrial production is used to measure output. This includes the output of such public sector industries as gas, electricity and water and so is not ideally suited to measuring output of companies. The rate of interest is measured by the return on $2\frac{1}{2}$ per cent Consols since this is more sensitive to market pressures, and hence should reflect the market rate of discounting more adequately, than the bank rate. The index of share prices used has 30 constituent shares which are leading industrial and commercial companies. It is selected because of its easy availability and the long run of annual figures without a break. More representative indices, in the sense of including a larger number of shares, are only available from the early sixties. The data are presented in Table 2.1.

Table 2.1. Annual data for the United Kingdom used to estimate alternative aggregate investment functions

Year	X_t	$\Delta' X_t$	I_t	K_t	L_t	S_t	r_t	p_t	u_t	q_t
1952	70·5	0								
1953	74·5	2·4								
1954	79·1	4·6								80
1955	83·1	4·0	1·168	13·3	2·210	195·0	4·17	80·8	0·3073	84
1956	83·4	0·3	1·395	14·4	2·169	180·6	4·73	85·2	0·2655	88
1957	85·0	1·6	1·551	15·9	2·248	188·3	4·98	88·1	0·2787	91
1958	84·0	0	1·567	16·7	2·214	181·9	4·98	90·2	0·2863	93
1959	88·3	3·3	1·642	17·0	2·413	250·2	4·82	91·2	0·2714	93
1960	94·5	6·2	1·870	18·4	2·470	318·6	5·42	92·4	0·1939	93
1961	95·7	1·2	2·099	20·0	2·344	319·8	6·20	94·9	0·2162	95
1962	96·7	1·0	2·053	21·5	2·299	285·5	5·98	97·9	0·2502	98
1963	100·0	3·3	1·987	22·9	2·578	316·9	5·58	100·0	0·2057	100
1964	108·3	8·3	2·384	24·9	2·781	346·9	6·03	103·0	0·1753	102
1965	111·7	3·4	2·475	27·4	3·067	337·3	6·42	107·4	0·1630	106
1966	113·2	1·5	2·425	29·4	2·225	331·9	6·80	111·6	0·1685	110
1967	113·9	0·7	2·372	29·6	2·314	355·0	6·69	114·7	0·2016	111
1968	119·8	5·9	2·582	31·8	2·169	463·3	7·39	120·5	0·2070	115
1969	122·9	3·2	2·825	34·4	2·233	419·8	8·88	126·0	0·2139	120
1970	124·1	1·2	2·940	39·0	2·265	361·0	9·16	134·9	0·2533	129

Sources: see text.

Estimating the naïve model (2.26) for 1958–70 with lags of up to three years gives:

$$I_t = \underset{(0·2340)}{0·1678} + \underset{(0·1075)}{0·9715 I_{t-1}} \tag{2.27}$$

$$\bar{R}^2 = 0·8705, \qquad F = 81·7, \quad \text{c.d.} = 1$$

$$I_t = \underset{(0·2462)}{0·1660} + \underset{(0·3166)}{0·9462 I_{t-1}} + \underset{(0·3222)}{0·0276 I_{t-2}} \tag{2.28}$$

$$\bar{R}^2 = 0·8576, \qquad F = 37·1, \quad \text{c.d.} = 0·13$$

$$I_t = \underset{(0·2886)}{0·2740} + \underset{(0·3236)}{0·9548 I_{t-1}} - \underset{(0·9808)}{0·6782 I_{t-2}} + \underset{(0·8497)}{0·6491 I_{t-3}} \tag{2.29}$$

$$\bar{R}^2 = 0·8515, \qquad F = 23·9, \quad \text{c.d.} = 0·002.$$

These results are presented in the manner discussed in Chapter 1, Section 1.2, with the estimated standard errors in brackets below the corresponding coefficients and $\bar{R}^2$ and F being measures of goodness of fit. The correlation determinant (c.d.) is a measure of multicollinearity (see Chapter 1, Section 1.3) between the independent variables. If there is just one independent variable, as in (2.27), this is unity, otherwise it varies between 0 and 1. The value of c.d. is low in (2.99) where the correlation between I_{t-2} and I_{t-3} is 0·96, and here multicollinearity is likely to be a problem. For these equations the Durbin–Watson statistics are 1·98, 1·97 and 2·05 respectively and these imply that first-order autocorrelation is absent but as pointed out in Chapter 1, Section 1.3 d is biased towards 2 when lagged values of the independent variable are present. Durbin's alternative test, discussed in Chapter 1, Section 1.3, is not appropriate since it requires a large sample and here $N = 13$. However, as the naïve models are only being used for comparative purposes the possibility of autocorrelation will be ignored.

For (2.27) the degrees of freedom for the F-statistic are $K' - 1 = 1$ and $N - K' = 11$ so that the 5 per cent critical value of F is 4·84 which is below the observed value of 81·7 so the overall fit of (2.27) is significantly better than random at the 5 per cent level. This is also the case with (2.28) and (2.29). Comparing these equations the naïve model with the highest $\bar{R}^2$ is (2.27) and this will be used as a standard of comparison for the models of investment behaviour.

The initial value of δ for the data is given by (2.21) with the summations from 1958 to 1970:

$$\delta = \frac{\Sigma I_t - (K_N - K_0)}{\Sigma K_{t-1}} = \frac{29 \cdot 221 - (39 \cdot 0 - 15 \cdot 9)}{309 \cdot 90} = 0 \cdot 01975.$$

This implies an average length of life of capital of 1/0·01975 or 50·6 years, which appears rather high.

The detailed results for the crude accelerator model (2.9) are presented in Table 2.2. The values of the correlation determinant (which were all greater than 0·05), F and the Durbin–Watson statistic are omitted. The column labelled value of δ gives the value used in obtaining the $I - \delta K$ terms. For the naïve model (2.27) the value of $\bar{R}^2$ is 0·8705. All the equations in Table 2.2 perform more successfully than this. The highest $\bar{R}^2$ is for (2.38) where the Durbin–Watson statistic is 1·67, which suggests that autocorrelation is not a serious problem. The F value for this equation is 55·8, which is significant at the 5 per cent level. Examining the coefficients of (2.38), only the estimated parameters of ΔX_t and K_{t-1} are more than twice their standard errors. A comparison of (2.38) with (2.30) shows that the other variables do contribute to the value of $\bar{R}^2$. The estimate of δ is 0·0608 which implies an average life of capital of 16·4 years. The other parameter estimates can be obtained by using (2.25),

$$\Sigma \hat{u}_i = \Sigma \hat{v}_i$$

Table 2.2. Crude accelerator results

Equation	Constant term	ΔX_t $u_0\beta$	ΔX_{t-1} $u_1\beta$	ΔX_{t-2} $u_2\beta$	$I_{t-1}-\delta K_{t-2}$ $-v_1$	$I_{t-2}-\delta K_{t-3}$ $-v_2$	K_{t-1} δ	$\bar{R}^2$	Value of δ
(2.30)	0·6478 (0·1686)	0·0216 (0·0155)					0·0644 (0·0065)	0·8892	
(2.31)	0·6006 (0·1085)	0·0205 (0·0099)	0·0398 (0·0101)				0·0614 (0·0042)	0·9547	
(2.32)	0·5842 (0·0969)	0·0302 (0·0103)	0·0394 (0·0090)	0·0195 (0·0106)			0·0586 (0·0041)	0·9641	
(2.33)	0·1655 (0·2452)	0·0389 (0·0147)			0·6651 (0·2784)		0·0588 (0·0059)	0·9246	0·058
(2.34)	0·3419 (0·1814)	0·0431 (0·0106)			0·8574 (0·2054)	−0·5419 (0·1736)	0·0650 (0·0039)	0·9618	0·065
(2.35)	0·3808 (0·1966)	0·0291 (0·0115)	0·0323 (0·0113)		0·3147 (0·2386)		0·0602 (0·0042)	0·9581	0·061
(2.36)	0·3849 (0·1887)	0·0366 (0·0125)	0·0162 (0·0165)		0·6149 (0·3266)	−0·3473 (0·2687)	0·0626 (0·0043)	0·9614	0·062
(2.37)	0·5621 (0·2580)	0·3053 (0·0114)	0·0386 (0·0126)	0·0183 (0·0169)	0·0330 (0·3541)		0·0586 (0·0044)	0·9591	0·0585
(2.38)	0·5884 (0·2390)	0·0388 (0·0121)	0·0220 (0·0163)	0·0204 (0·0157)	0·3254 (0·3835)	−0·3776 (0.2584)	0·0608 (0·0043)	0·9648	0·0608

Variables and coefficients

or $\qquad \hat{u}_0 + \hat{u}_1 + \hat{u}_2 = 1 + \hat{v}_1 + \hat{v}_2$

Since $\quad \hat{v}_1 = -0.3254, \hat{v}_2 = 0.3776,$

and $\qquad \beta\hat{u}_0 + \beta\hat{u}_1 + \beta\hat{u}_2 = 0.0388 + 0.0220 + 0.0204$

$$= 0.0812.$$

Hence, $\qquad \hat{u}_0 + \hat{u}_1 + \hat{u}_2 = \dfrac{0.0812}{\hat{\beta}} = 1 - 0.3254 + 0.3776$

so that $\quad \hat{\beta} = 0.0772, \hat{u}_0 = 0.5023, \hat{u}_1 = 0.2848$ and $\hat{u}_2 = 0.2641.$

These estimates are all consistent with the *a priori* expectations in (2.24)

The version of the modified accelerator model (2.10) which has the highest $\bar{R}^2$ is

$$I_t = \underset{(0.1159)}{0.7199} + \underset{(0.0136)}{0.0290 \, \Delta'X_t} + \underset{(0.0120)}{0.0012 \, \Delta'X_{t-1}} - \underset{(0.0136)}{0.0258 \, \Delta'X_{t-2}}$$

$$+ \underset{(0.0051)}{0.0631 K_{t-1}} \tag{2.39}$$

$$\bar{R}^2 = 0.9468, F = 54.4, \text{c.d.} = 0.60, d = 1.34.$$

In this case the conditions (2.22) are not satisfied and so this equation is rejected as being inconsistent with the *a priori* assumptions about the weighting scheme. The equation with the highest $\bar{R}^2$ which is consistent with the *a priori* assumptions is

$$I_t = \underset{(0.1208)}{0.6656} + \underset{(0.0125)}{0.0424 \, \Delta'X_t} + \underset{(0.0049)}{0.0610 \, K_{t-1}} \tag{2.40}$$

$$\bar{R}^2 = 0.9383, F = 92.2, \text{c.d.} = 0.97, d = 2.06.$$

The parameter estimates are $\hat{\delta} = 0.061$ and $\hat{\beta} = 0.0424$, and both are significantly positive.

For the liquidity model of investment (2.11) the most successful equation is:

$$I_t = \underset{(0.1561)}{0.5598} + \underset{(0.1324)}{0.1495 \, (L_t - L_{t-1})} + \underset{(0.1401)}{0.3720 \, (L_{t-1} - L_{t-2})}$$

$$+ \underset{(0.1330)}{0.1561 \, (L_{t-2} - L_{t-3})} + \underset{(0.0064)}{0.0707 \, K_{t-1}} \tag{2.41}$$

$$\bar{R}^2 = 0.9133, F = 32.6, \text{c.d.} = 0.73, d = 1.42.$$

Using (2.25) the parameter estimates are $\hat{\delta} = 0.0707, \hat{\beta} = 0.6776, \hat{u}_0 = 0.2206, \hat{u}_1 = 0.5490, \hat{u}_2 = 0.2304$ which satisfy (2.22).

The profits theory of investment, which uses share prices as the measure of future profits, gives highest $\bar{R}^2$ for

$$I_t = \underset{(0\cdot3514)}{0\cdot2777} + \underset{(0\cdot0012)}{0\cdot0004}(S_t - S_{t-1}) + \underset{(0\cdot0009)}{0\cdot0021}(S_{t-1} - S_{t-2})$$

$$+ \underset{(0\cdot3854)}{0\cdot5297}\,(I_{t-1} - 0\cdot0649K_{t-2}) + \underset{(0\cdot0062)}{0\cdot0649}K_{t-1} \qquad (2.42)$$

$$\bar{R}^2 = 0\cdot9141,\ F = 32\cdot9,\ \text{c.d.} = 0\cdot38,\ d = 1\cdot90.$$

The parameter estimates are

$$\hat{\delta} = 0\cdot0649,\ \hat{\beta} = 0\cdot0053,\ \hat{u}_0 = 0\cdot0752,\ \hat{u}_1 = 0\cdot3951$$

which satisfy the *a priori* assumptions.

The empirical testing of Jorgenson's neoclassical model (2.13) is rather awkward since the cost of capital, c, depends upon the value of δ and so has to be calculated for each of the cycles described above with respect to (2.20). In evaluating c the proportion of depreciation at replacement cost deductible from income for tax purposes is assumed to be unity. As an illustration of calculating the desired capital stock for this model with capital gains, in 1960 with $\delta = 0\cdot06$

$$c = \frac{93}{(1 - 0\cdot1939)}\left[(1 - 0\cdot1939)0\cdot06 + 0\cdot0542 + \frac{93 - 93}{93}\right]$$

$$= 62\cdot05$$

and hence, $\qquad K^* = \dfrac{pX}{c} = \dfrac{(92\cdot4)(94\cdot5)}{62\cdot05} = 140\cdot7.$

When capital gains affect the cost of capital the version of this neoclassical model with the highest $\bar{R}^2$ and which satisfies the restrictions on the parameter estimates is

$$I_t = \underset{(0\cdot2767)}{1\cdot2904} + \underset{(0\cdot00018)}{0\cdot00057}(K_t^* - K_{t-1}^*) + \underset{(0\cdot00024)}{0\cdot00059}(K_{t-1}^* - K_{t-2}^*)$$

$$- \underset{(0\cdot3174)}{0\cdot3000}\,(I_{t-1} - \delta K_{t-2}) - \underset{(0\cdot2161)}{0\cdot2565}(I_{t-2} - \delta K_{t-3})$$

$$+ \underset{(0\cdot0053)}{0\cdot0587}\,K_{t-1} \qquad (2.43)$$

$$\bar{R}^2 = 0\cdot9494,\ F = 46\cdot0,\ \text{c.d.} = 0\cdot21,\ d = 2\cdot21,\ \delta = 0\cdot059.$$

The parameter estimates are $\hat{u}_0 = 0\cdot7652$, $\hat{u}_1 = 0\cdot7916$, $\hat{v}_1 = 0\cdot3000$, $\hat{v}_2 = 0\cdot2565$, $\hat{\beta} = 0\cdot00074$, $\hat{\delta} = 0\cdot0587$.

Without capital gains the best equation is

$$I_t = \underset{(0\cdot2293)}{0\cdot4734} + \underset{(0\cdot00137)}{0\cdot00044}(K_t^* - K_{t-1}^*) + \underset{(0\cdot0009)}{0\cdot0023}(K_{t-1}^* - K_{t-2}^*)$$

$$+ \underset{(0\cdot2808)}{0\cdot5381}(I_{t-1} - \delta K_{t-2}) - \underset{(0\cdot3247)}{0\cdot4557}(I_{t-2} - \delta K_{t-3})$$

$$+ \underset{(0\cdot0068)}{0\cdot0714}K_{t-1} \tag{2.44}$$

$$\bar{R}^2 = 0\cdot9335, \ F = 34\cdot7, \ \text{c.d.} = 0\cdot25, \ d = 2\cdot06, \ \delta = 0\cdot071.$$

The parameter estimates are $\hat{u}_0 = 0\cdot1497$, $\hat{u}_1 = 0\cdot7678$, $\hat{v}_1 = -0\cdot5381$, $\hat{v}_2 = 0\cdot4557$, $\hat{\delta} = 0\cdot0714$, $\hat{\beta} = 0\cdot00296$.

In Table 2.3 the $\bar{R}^2$ values for the different theories of investment are collected together. The naïve model is inferior to any of the other models. The crude accelerator has the highest $\bar{R}^2$ and accordingly is regarded as the

Table 2.3. Summary of annual investment function results

Theory of investment	*Equation*	$\bar{R}^2$	*Rank*
Naïve model	(2.27)	0·8705	7
Crude accelerator	(2.38)	0·9648	1
Modified accelerator	(2.40)	0·9383	3
Liquidity	(2.41)	0·9133	6
Profits	(2.42)	0·9141	5
Neoclassical with capital gains	(2.43)	0·9494	2
Neoclassical without capital gains	(2.44)	0·9335	4

most satisfactory of the models tested. The neoclassical models also perform well. Overall the variation in $\bar{R}^2$ is not great and, bearing in mind the problems associated with the data, if would be unwise to use these empirical results in support of any one theory of investment. One fairly definite conclusion is that the proportion of capital stock replaced each year, δ, is around 0·065 giving an average life of capital goods of about 15 years.

In each of the equations presented the estimated value of δ is significantly positive. This is claimed by Jorgenson (1965) as support for the theory of replacement investment in Section 2.2. Griliches (1968), however, disputes this because successive values of K are almost identical and the sum of all the coefficients on K is close to zero.

Jorgenson and Stephenson (1967) estimated the neoclassical model without capital gains using quarterly data on U.S. manufacturing industry. The best fit was obtained with

$$w(L) = \frac{u_4 L^4 + u_5 L^5 + u_6 L^6 + u_7 L^7}{1 + v_1 L + v_2 L^2}$$

for which the standard error of regression is $0.0915(\bar{R}^2 = 0.9591)$. However, the estimated weights of the distributed lag function did not satisfy the constraint $-4v_2 \geqslant -v_1^2$ (see Jorgenson (1966) p. 147). The constraint was therefore imposed as the equality $v_2 = v_1^2/4$ and the equation re-estimated to give

$$I_t = 0.00305(K_{t-4}^* - K_{t-5}^*) + 0.00153(K_{t-5}^* - K_{t-6}^*)$$
$$(0.00077) \qquad\qquad\qquad (0.00076)$$

$$+ 0.00190(K_{t-6}^* - K_{t-7}^*) + 0.00270(K_{t-7}^* - K_{t-8}^*)$$
$$(0.00070) \qquad\qquad\qquad (0.00080)$$

$$+ 0.02084K_t + 1.20525(I_{t-1} - \delta K_{t-1})$$
$$(0.00178)$$

$$- 0.36316(I_{t-2} - \delta K_{t-2}).$$

No measure of the goodness of fit of this equation is presented, but Jorgenson and Stephenson (p. 216) conclude that the results provide 'a very close fit to historical experience' and that there is no evidence of autocorrelation of residuals.

An important aspect of their study is that they also have data on the two components of total manufacturing – total durables and total non-durables, which in turn were disaggregated into 8 and 7 sub-industries respectively. The equations of the neoclassical theory of investment were estimated for all 18 of these groups so that some evidence of the effects of aggregation is available. For example, the error in aggregating from 15 sub-industries to total manufacturing is examined by comparing the residual sums of squares of the 15 separate industry regressions with the residual sums of squares of a regression for all 15 industries in which the parameters are constrained to be identical. Similar tests for components of total durables and total non-durables were also carried out. In each case the hypothesis of no aggregation error is rejected, so that the interpretation of the aggregate results for manufacturing industry quoted above is placed in doubt. There is, of course, no reason to believe that the 15 sub-industries used by Jorgenson and Stephenson represent an optimal level of disaggregation. In the next section a study by Jorgenson and Siebert using company data is discussed and, presumably, in that case aggregation errors are reduced.

2.6 MICROLEVEL INVESTMENT FUNCTIONS

Jorgenson and Siebert (1968) compare five of the investment theories discussed in the earlier part of this chapter using annual data on 15 U.S. corporations for the period 1949–63. The theories tested are the crude accelerator (2.9), liquidity (2.11), expected profits (2.12), and the two versions of the neoclassical theory (2.13). The naïve model (2.26) is also estimated. Each theory of investment is tried with each of the 15 corporations. The variables used are

$X_t = p_t X_t / p_t$ = value of output of firm deflated by the wholesale price index (p_t) for the firm's industry group.

L_t = profits after taxes plus depreciation less dividends paid, deflated by the investment goods price index (q_t).

V_t = market value of the firm deflated by the gross national product price index.

The remaining variables u, w and r are defined immediately before (2.13) above. Since annual data are used the distributed lag function $w(L)$ is limited to current and up to two lagged values of both the change in desired capital stock and net investment. The distributed lag scheme which minimises the residual variance subject to the weights w being positive is selected as the best of the alternatives. Jorgenson and Siebert, p. 698, quote in detail the results for General Motors. For the crude accelerator the best results occur with

$$w(L) = \frac{u_1}{1 - v_1}$$

and the estimated equation is

$$I_t = 0\cdot1963 + 0\cdot0666(X_{t-1} - X_{t-2}) + 0\cdot4780(I_{t-1} - \delta K_{t-2}) + 0\cdot1878K_{t-1}$$
$$\quad\;(0\cdot0327) \qquad\qquad\qquad (0\cdot2115) \qquad\qquad\qquad (0\cdot0593)$$

$$\bar{R}^2 = 0\cdot62,\; d = 2\cdot21,\; s = 0\cdot1920,$$

where $s^2 = \Sigma e_i^2 / (N - K')$ is the estimate of the residual variance, e_i are the observed residuals, N the number of observations and K' the number of parameters estimated.

Using the restriction $u_1 = 1 + v_1$ the estimates of the weights are $\hat{v}_1 = -0\cdot4780$ and $\hat{u}_1 = 0\cdot5220$ so that $\hat{\beta} = 0\cdot1276$. Also, $\hat{\delta} = 0\cdot1878$. The best estimated equation for the liquidity theory is

$$I_t = 0\cdot2345 + 0\cdot3032(L_t - L_{t-1}) + 0\cdot4941(L_{t-1} - L_{t-2})$$
$$\quad\;(0\cdot2710) \qquad\qquad\qquad (0\cdot2743)$$

$$+ 0\cdot3989(I_{t-1} - \delta K_{t-2}) + 0\cdot1712K_{t-1}$$
$$\;\;(0\cdot2279) \qquad\qquad\qquad (0\cdot0620)$$

$$R^2 = 0\cdot61,\; d = 2\cdot29,\; s = 0\cdot2037.$$

For the expected profits theory the best equation is

$$I_t = 0\cdot2793 + 0\cdot0858(V_t - V_{t-1}) + 0\cdot0610(V_{t-1} - V_{t-2}) + 0\cdot1493\,K_{t-1}$$
$$\quad\;(0\cdot0267) \qquad\qquad\qquad (0\cdot0268) \qquad\qquad\qquad (0\cdot0571)$$

$$R^2 = 0\cdot64,\; d = 1\cdot36,\; s = 0\cdot1852.$$

When capital gains are included in the neoclassical theory the best equation is

$$I_t = 0.2449 + \underset{(0.0063)}{0.0160}(K_t^* - K_{t-1}^*) + \underset{(0.0066)}{0.0150}(K_{t-1}^* - K_{t-2}^*)$$

$$+ \underset{(0.2061)}{0.3444}(I_{t-1} - \delta K_{t-2}) + \underset{(0.0540)}{0.1794}K_{t-1}$$

$$R^2 = 0.70, d = 2.03, s = 0.1765.$$

For the neoclassical theory with no capital gains the best equation is

$$I_t = 0.1231 + \underset{(0.0094)}{0.0411}(K_t^* - K_{t-1}^*) + \underset{(0.0105)}{0.0654}(K_{t-1}^* - K_{t-2}^*)$$

$$+ \underset{(0.0089)}{0.0202}(K_{t-2}^* - K_{t-3}^*) + \underset{(0.1311)}{0.3732}(I_{t-2} - \delta K_{t-3})$$

$$+ \underset{(0.0361)}{0.1826}K_{t-1}$$

$$R^2 = 0.89, d = 2.32, s = 0.1148.$$

The estimated equation for the naïve model is not quoted by Jorgenson and Siebert but the overall fit is given by $R^2 = 0.47$, with $s = 0.2072$ and the Durbin–Watson statistic $= 2.22$.

For General Motors the ranking of the different theories of investment, in increasing order of residual variance is: neoclassical without capital gains, neoclassical with capital gains, expected profits, crude accelerator, liquidity and the naïve model. This ranking also corresponds to a ranking by significance of estimated coefficients.

When the results for all 15 corporations are considered a problem arises in that for some theories of investment with some corporations no change in desired capital stock variable reduces the standard error of the regression so that in these cases investment becomes a distributed lag of net investment, and the residual variance is set at a very large value. The overall performance of the different theories is summarised in Table 2.4 where the number of times each theory obtains a particular rank is given. The rank 1 has the smallest residual variance and rank 6 the largest. Thus the profits theory has the smallest residual variance for 2 of the 15 corporations, the second smallest for 1 corporation and so on. With Dupont, three theories, expected profits, liquidity, and neoclassical without capital gains, result in distributed lags of net investment and so each is given a rank of 5. The column labelled 'overall' gives the ranking of the average performance of the theories. The naïve model is generally the worst, followed by the liquidity theory which in 5 of the 15 cases reduced to a distributed lag of net investment. Jorgenson and Siebert therefore conclude, that for the corporations in their sample, financial constraints play a minor role in explaining investment behaviour. Kuh (1963), p. 213, comes to a similar conclusion in a study of 60 smaller corporations.

The expected profits and accelerator theories perform almost equally well resulting in similar residual variances, and both being inferior to the neoclassical theories. Jorgenson and Siebert conclude that the expected profits and accelerator theories are indistinguishable from each other in that sales or output determine profits and the stock market valuation of the corporation. Kuh (1963), p. 208, arrives at the same conclusion.

Table 2.4. The relative performance of investment theories

Theory	Rank						Overall
	1	2	3	4	5	6	
Naïve	0	0	2	1	5	7	6
Crude accelerator	2	2	2	5	1	3	4
Expected profits	2	1	6	4	2	0	3
Liquidity	1	1	2	2	5	4	5
Neoclassical I	5	7	2	1	0	0	1
Neoclassical II	5	4	1	1	4	0	2

Source: Compiled from Jorgenson and Siebert (1968), Table 3.

As stated above, both versions of the neoclassical theory are superior to the other theories of investment. Neoclassical I (with capital gains) results in a smaller residual variance than the naïve model with all 15 corporations, in 14 of the 15 cases with the liquidity model, and in 12 cases with the crude accelerator and the expected profits models. Neoclassical II (with no capital gains) does not perform as well as neoclassical I but is superior to the other theories. When the two neoclassical theories are compared, I is superior to II in 8 of the 15 cases. Jorgenson and Siebert go on to compare predictions of turning points in investment over the period for which the equations are fitted. Again the results produce a ranking from best to worst of neoclassical I, neoclassical II, expected profits, crude accelerator, liquidity and the naïve model.

Thus the evidence they present is overwhelmingly in favour of the neoclassical model. It must be remembered, however, that only 15 annual observations (plus two lagged values) are used in the estimations, and that no predictions outside the period 1949–63 are quoted. A comparison of Table 2.3 (aggregate investment for the United Kingdom) with Table 2.4 (corporate investment for the United States) shows a surprising amount of agreement. The main difference (if the results of the modified accelerator theory are ignored) is the performance of the crude accelerator theory, which is superior to the neoclassical theories in Table 2.3 but inferior in Table 2.4. Given the evidence of errors of aggregation quoted by Jorgenson and Stephenson, the performance of the neoclassical theories is surprisingly consistent.

2.7 FURTHER READING

Further evidence of the superiority of the neoclassical approach is provided in two articles by Jorgenson, Hunter and Nadiri (1970*a*), (1970*b*), in which the quarterly data used by Jorgenson and Stephenson at the sub-industry level are used to compare four alternative investment theories. The theories are essentially dynamic versions of the neoclassical theory of the firm, with different specifications of the variables included and the time structure of the investment process. The formulations of Jorgenson and Stephenson (1967) and Eisner (1962) prove to be the most satisfactory in explaining investment behaviour within the data period. They are also subject to less structural change when estimated from two subsets of the data.

Eisner and Strotz (1963) provide a comprehensive review of the literature on investment functions up to 1961. They consider in detail various theories of the investment process and critically assess the empirical evidence for those theories. Their review ends with a bibliography by G. R. Post which lists over 670 publications relevant to investment and classifies them according to the type of study (e.g. theoretical, qualitative, econometric), the level of aggregation, the factors considered to affect investment, and also the type of investment. Since 1961 many more studies have been published. A summary and discussion of recent empirical work, intended for final year undergraduate students is contained in Chapter 4 of the book by Lund (1971). More difficult surveys of investment theory and published empirical results are provided by Bridge (1971) Chapter 4 and Jorgenson (1971).

Feldstein and Foot (1971) discuss the relationship between replacement expenditure and investment and conclude that the simple model (2.7) is inadequate as the replacement rate varies from year to year. They show that the replacement rate is related to the internal availability of funds, the utilisation rate of capital stock and the level of non-replacement investment.

An alternative approach to measuring expectations by the level of share prices is to use surveys of business opinion, such as those published in the U.S. Survey of Current Business. These are discussed in the National Bureau of Economic Research volume (1960) and an example of the use of such data is provided by Eisner (1965).

Criticisms of the neoclassical model are discussed by Bridge (1971), Section 4.6.9, and in a mathematically difficult article, Gould (1968) considers the problem of changing prices when the net worth approach is adopted. He concludes that this makes the theory inadequate since the desired capital stock changes with the prices.

Almon (1965) has proposed and used a distributed lag scheme which assumes only that successive weights lie on a polynomial. Griliches (1967) provides a survey of distributed lag schemes. Recent moves in the direction of allowing the weights to vary over the period of observations are summarised by Lund (1971), Section 4.5.

All the above studies use time-series data. Bridge (1971), Section 4.7, reviews the cross-section studies of Eisner (1967) and Dhrymes and Kurz (1967) in the United States. Two recent studies using cross-section data in the United Kingdom are by Jack (1966) and by Dimsdale and Glyn (1971).

Research on the investment function is still in process and for details of the most recent work the student is advised to consult the journals where earlier references occur.

2.8 REFERENCES

Almon, Shirley (1965), 'The Distributed Lag Between Capital Appropriations and Expenditures', *Econometrica*, vol. 33, 178–96.

Bridge, J. L. (1971), *Applied Econometrics* (Amsterdam: North-Holland).

Chenery, H. B. (1952), 'Overcapacity and the Acceleration Principle', *Econometrica*, vol. 20, 1–20.

Dhrymes, P. J. and Kurz, M. (1967), 'Investment, Dividend and External Finance Behaviour of Firms,' in *Determinants of Investment Behaviour*, ed. R. Ferber. (1967) (New York: NBER), 427–67.

Dimsdale, N. H. and Glyn, A. J. (1971), 'Investment in British Industry – A cross-sectional approach', *Bulletin of the Oxford University Institute of Economics and Statistics*, vol. 33, 163–80.

Eckaus, R. S. (1953), 'The Acceleration Principle Reconsidered', *Quarterly Journal of Economics*, vol. 67, 209–30.

Eisner, R. (1962), 'Investment Plans and Realisations', *American Economic Review*, vol. 52, 190–203.

Eisner, R. (1965), 'Realisation of Investment Anticipations', pp. 95–128 in J. S. Duesenberry *et al.*, *The Brookings Quarterly Econometric Model of the United States* (Chicago: Rand McNally).

Eisner, R. (1967), 'A Permanent Income Theory for Investment: Some Empirical Explorations', *American Economic Review*, vol. LVII, 363–90.

Eisner, R. and Strotz, R. (1963), 'Determinants of Business Investment' with bibliography by G. R. Post, pp. 59–337 in D. B. Suits *et al.*, *Commission on Money and Credit; Impacts of Monetary Policy* (Englewood Cliffs: Prentice-Hall).

Feldstein, M. S. and Foot, D. K. (1971), 'The Other Half of Gross Investment: Replacement and Modernisation Expenditures', *Review of Economics and Statistics*, vol. 53, 49–58.

Gould, J. P. (1968), 'Adjustment Costs in the Theory of Investment of the Firm', *Review of Economic Studies*, vol. XXXV, 47–55.

Griliches, Z. (1967), 'Distributed Lags: A Survey', *Econometrica*, vol. 35, 16–49.

Griliches, Z. (1968), 'The Brookings Model Volume: A Review Article', *Review of Economics and Statistics*, vol. 50, 215–34.

Grunfeld, Y. (1960), 'The Determinants of Corporate Investment', in *The Demand for Durable Goods*, ed. A. C. Harberger (Chicago: University of Chicago Press), pp. 211–66.

Jack, A. B. (1966), 'The Capital Expenditure Functions', *Manchester School*, vol. XXXIV, 133–58.

Jorgenson, D. W. (1963), 'Capital Theory and Investment Behaviour, *American Economic Review Proceedings*, vol. 53, 247–59.

Jorgenson, D. W. (1965), 'Anticipations and Investment Behaviour', in *The Brookings Quarterly Econometric Model of the United States*, ed. J. S. Duesenberry, E. Kuh, G. Fromm and L. R. Klein (Chicago: Rand McNally), 35–92.

Jorgenson, D. W. (1966), 'Rational Distributed Lag Functions', *Econometrica*, vol. 34, 135–49.

Jorgenson, D. W. (1971), 'Econometric Studies of Investment Behaviour: A Survey', *Journal of Economic Literature*, vol. IX, 1111–47.

Jorgenson, D. W., Hunter, J., Nadiri, M. I. (1970a), 'A Comparison of Alternative Econometric Models of Quarterly Investment Behaviour', *Econometrica*, vol. 38, 187–212.

Jorgenson, D. W., Hunter, J., Nadiri, M. I. (1970b), 'The Predictive Performance of Econometric Models of Quarterly Investment Behaviour', *Econometrica*, vol. 38, 213–24.

Jorgenson, D. W. and Siebert, C. B. (1968), 'A Comparison of Alternative Theories of Corporate Investment Behaviour', *American Economic Review*, vol. LVIII, 681–712.

Jorgenson, D. W. and Stephenson, J. A. (1967), 'Investment Behaviour in U.S. Manufacturing, 1947–1960, *Econometrica*, vol. 35, 169–220.

Koyck, L. M. (1954), *Distributed Lags and Investment Analysis* (Amsterdam: North-Holland).

Kuh, E. (1963), *Capital Stock Growth; A Micro-econometric Approach* (Amsterdam: North Holland).

Lund, P. J. (1971), *Investment; The Study of an 'Economic Aggregate* (Edinburgh: Oliver & Boyd).

National Bureau of Economic Research (1960), *The Quality and Economic Significance of Anticipations Data* (Princeton: Princeton University Press).

Smyth, D. (1964), 'Empirical Evidence on the Acceleration Principle', *Review of Economic Studies*, vol. 31, 185–202.

Solow, R. M. (1960), 'On a Family of Lag Distributions', *Econometrica*, vol. 28, 393–406.

3. The Production Function

3.1 THE THEORY OF PRODUCTION

This chapter is concerned with the economic and econometric analysis of production. The basic theory of production and the properties of the production function are developed in this section and this is followed by their application to the Cobb–Douglas and C. E. S. functions resulting in *a priori* restrictions on the values of certain parameters. The difficulties of observation of the production function at various levels of economic activity are next considered. The results of empirical work in a cross-section micro-economic study and a time series macro-economic study are then described, and a guide to further reading concludes the chapter.

A production function is a mathematical function which relates the quantities of inputs and the quantities of outputs within a production unit, which may be variously defined as an activity or process, a firm, an industry or a national economy. It is usually regarded as a technical relationship between the quantities of inputs and the maximum amount of output which can be produced with a given set of inputs. The approach adopted here to the theory of production follows Walters (1963) Section 2, and Allen (1967) Chapter 3. It is useful to consider two factors of production: the labour input (L) and the capital input (K), with the production function being

$$Q = f(K, L) \tag{3.1}$$

where Q measures the rate of output. Thus L measures the rate of labour input and K the amount of capital input. The classical theory of production assumes that the marginal products of capital and labour are positive but that they are diminishing so that the graph of output against capital or labour will have the general shape illustrated in Figure 3.1. It is assumed that (3.1) is a single valued continuous function which is twice differentiable so that the assumption of diminishing marginal products of capital and labour requires

$$\frac{\partial Q}{\partial K} = Q_K > 0, \; Q_{KK} < 0, \; \frac{\partial Q}{\partial L} = Q_L > 0, \; Q_{LL} < 0 \tag{3.2}$$

where Q_K and Q_L are the marginal products of capital and labour. A given level of output can be produced by different combinations of capital and labour and so $f(K,L) =$ constant traces out the isoquants. For variation along any isoquant

$$\frac{\partial f}{\partial K} dK + \frac{\partial f}{\partial L} dL = 0$$

i.e. $$Q_K dK + Q_L dL = 0$$

and hence $$-\frac{dK}{dL} = \frac{Q_L}{Q_K} = R > 0. \tag{3.3}$$

Therefore the isoquants have a negative slope and the absolute value of this is the marginal rate of substitution (R). This measures the rate at which one input can be substituted for the other input. It is normally assumed that as the

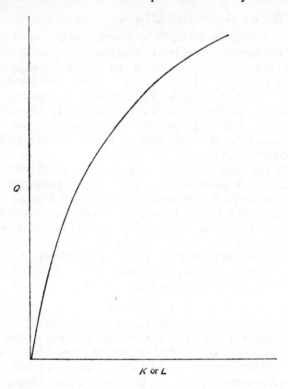

Figure 3.1

quantity of one of the inputs increases, the marginal rate of substitution decreases so that the reductions in the level of one variable made possible by increases in the level of the other variable become progressively smaller, i.e. by (3.3), dK/dL is increasing and so d^2K/dL^2 is positive. Hence the isoquants are assumed to be convex to the origin as in Figure 3.2. For a change from the point (K, L) along the constant product curve, $d(K/L)$ measures the change in the use of K compared with L and dR represents the corresponding change in the marginal rate of substitution. A measure of the rate of change of R is given by the elasticity of substitution between the factors K and L which is defined as the proportionate change in the ratio K/L expressed as a fraction of the proportionate change in R

$$\sigma = \frac{d(\ln (K/L))}{d (\ln (R))} = \frac{(L/K)d(K/L)}{dR/R}$$

where variation is along the constant product curve. It can be shown that alternative expressions for σ are

$$\sigma = \frac{R(LR + K)}{KL\left(R\dfrac{\partial R}{\partial K} - \dfrac{\partial R}{\partial L}\right)} = \frac{R(LR + K)}{KL\left(\dfrac{d^2K}{dL^2}\right)} \tag{3.4}$$

so that σ is inversely proportional to the curvature of the constant product curve (d^2K/dL^2) and measures the ease of substitution of L for K. If $\sigma = 0$ then

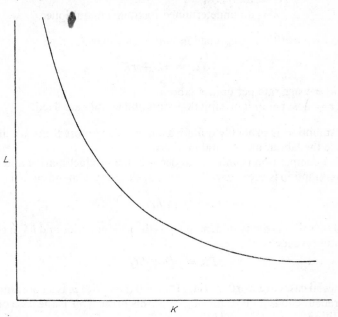

Figure 3.2

substitution is impossible since d^2K/dL^2 is infinite. If $\sigma = \infty$ then the constant product curve is a straight line since d^2K/dL^2 is zero. Since R, L, K and d^2K/dL^2 are all positive or zero, (3.4) shows that $\sigma \geqslant 0$.

Another property of the production function is whether or not there are constant returns to scale. That is, whether increasing the level of all inputs by a factor λ increases output by the same factor. If this is so,

$$f(\lambda K, \lambda L) = \lambda f(K, L) = \lambda Q$$

there are constant returns to scale and the production function is linear and homogeneous. Applying Euler's theorem gives

$$Q = Q_K K + Q_L L \qquad (3.5)$$

so that if the input factors are paid their marginal products then the total product Q is exhausted between them.

Further desirable properties of the production function can be developed by reference to profit maximising behaviour. It is assumed that the entrepreneur wants to choose values of Q, K and L which maximise net revenue (π) subject to the constraint imposed by the production function,

i.e. $\qquad\qquad \pi = TR - TC + \lambda(f(K, L) - Q) \qquad (3.6)$
where $\qquad\qquad TR =$ total revenue
$\qquad\qquad\quad TC =$ total cost
$\qquad\qquad\quad \lambda =$ an undetermined Lagrangian multiplier.

If perfect competition is assumed in both factor markets then

$$TC = wL + rK \qquad (3.7)$$

where $w =$ wage rate per unit of labour
$\qquad r =$ cost per unit of capital services and w and r are fixed.

This assumption is probably quite reasonable since most firms are unable to influence the labour and capital markets.

Perfect competition is unlikely to occur in the product market and so some other assumption is necessary. If a constant elasticity demand curve is assumed and

$$p = bQ^n$$

where $1/\eta$ is the elasticity of demand, p is the product price and b is a constant, then total revenue is

$$TR = pQ = bQ^{n+1}. \qquad (3.8)$$

Two special cases are worth noting. If $\eta = 0$ then price p, is a constant and the entrepreneur can sell all of his output at this price. This is the case of perfect competition.

If $\eta = -1$ then total revenue is a constant and is unaffected by changes in p or Q. In this case maximisation of π in (3.6) is effectively the minimisation of TC in (3.7). However, the minimum TC occurs when $L = 0$, $K = 0$, $Q = 0$, so that if $\eta = -1$ the level of output must take on some predetermined value Q° (say) so that Q is not a variable. The problem is to find the least cost combination of K and L which gives output Q°.

From (3.6), (3.7) and (3.8) the profit function can be written

$$\pi = bQ^{n+1} - wL - rK + \lambda(f(K, L) - Q).$$

The necessary conditions for maximum profits are

$$\frac{\partial \pi}{\partial L} = -w + \lambda f_L = 0$$

$$\frac{\partial \pi}{\partial K} = -r + \lambda f_K = 0$$

$$\frac{\partial \pi}{\partial \lambda} = f(K, L) - Q = 0$$

and when Q is a variable

$$\frac{\partial \pi}{\partial Q} = (\eta + 1)bQ^\eta - \lambda = 0$$

which give
$$w = \lambda f_L, r = \lambda f_K, \frac{w}{r} = \frac{f_L}{f_K} \tag{3.9}$$

and if
$$\left. \begin{array}{l} \eta \neq -1, \lambda = (\eta + 1)p, Q = f(K, L) \\ \eta = -1, Q^\circ = f(K, L) \end{array} \right\}. \tag{3.10}$$

Thus (3.9) states that the marginal rate of substitution equals the ratio of factor prices and (3.10) gives the value of the marginal products. The second-order conditions for a maximum are

$$\begin{vmatrix} \pi_{LL} & \pi_{LK} & f_L \\ \pi_{KL} & \pi_{KK} & f_K \\ f_L & f_K & 0 \end{vmatrix} > 0 \tag{3.11}$$

which becomes
$$D = 2f_{KL}f_L f_K - f_{LL}f_K^2 - f_{KK}f_L^2 > 0 \tag{3.12}$$

and when Q is a variable

$$\begin{vmatrix} \pi_{LL} & \pi_{LK} & \pi_{LQ} & f_L \\ \pi_{KL} & \pi_{KK} & \pi_{KQ} & f_k \\ \pi_{LQ} & \pi_{KQ} & \pi_{QQ} & -1 \\ f_L & f_K & -1 & 0 \end{vmatrix} < 0 \tag{3.13}$$

which reduces to
$$pD(\eta + 1)Q^{-1} - \lambda(f_{KK}f_{LL} - f_{KL}^2) < 0 \tag{3.14}$$

where D is given by (3.12). The case of perfect competition ($\eta = 0$) simplifies (3.14) to
$$f_{KK}f_{LL} - f_{KL}^2 > 0. \tag{3.15}$$

The relevance of these conditions will be discussed in the next section when particular production functions are considered.

This discussion of profit maximisation has assumed that a 'local' maximum occurs and profits decline once output passes the optimal value. If this is not the case then profits can always be increased by increasing the level of output and the maximum occurs when output is infinite. Then, however, the assumption of fixed values of r and w eventually becomes invalid and the framework of the analysis will need to be changed. The behaviour of other entrepreneurs will also become important.

3.2 THE COBB–DOUGLAS AND C.E.S. PRODUCTION FUNCTIONS

In this section the theory of production discussed above is applied to two well known functions, the Cobb–Douglas and the constant elasticity of substitution (or C.E.S.) function in order to examine the implications of the assumptions made. The theory will be used to provide *a priori* expectations about unknown parameters with a view to testing whether the theory is appropriate or not.

(a) The Cobb–Douglas function

The general form of the Cobb–Douglas production function for two factors is

$$Q = AK^\alpha L^\beta \tag{3.16}$$

where A, α and β are parameters. The value of A is determined partly by the units of measurement of Q, K and L and partly by the efficiency of the production process. The relevance of the efficiency of the process can be seen by considering two Cobb–Douglas production functions which differ only in the value of A. For given levels of K and L, the function with the higher value of A will have the larger value of Q and so will be the more efficient process. The function is single valued and continuous (for positive K and L) and the marginal products of capital and labour are

$$\frac{\partial Q}{\partial K} = Q_K = A\alpha K^{\alpha-1}L^\beta = \frac{\alpha Q}{K}$$

$$\frac{\partial Q}{\partial L} = Q_L = \frac{\beta Q}{L}.$$

By (3.2) these are positive so that assuming Q, L, K are positive, $\alpha > 0$ and $\beta > 0$. The second-order derivatives are

$$Q_{KK} = \frac{K\alpha Q_K - \alpha Q}{K^2} = \frac{\alpha(\alpha-1)Q}{K^2} \tag{3.17}$$

$$Q_{LL} = \frac{\beta(\beta-1)Q}{L^2} \tag{3.18}$$

so that $Q_{KK} < 0$ and $Q_{LL} < 0$ if α and β are both less than one. Hence, $1 > \alpha > 0, 1 > \beta > 0$. By (3.3) the marginal rate of substitution is

$$R = \frac{Q_L}{Q_K} = \frac{\beta Q/L}{\alpha Q/K} = \frac{\beta K}{\alpha L}$$

and the elasticity of substitution is given by (3.4) with

$$\frac{\partial R}{\partial K} = \frac{\beta}{\alpha L}, \frac{\partial R}{\partial L} = -\frac{\beta K}{\alpha L^2},$$

$$R(LR + K) = \frac{\beta K}{\alpha L}\left(\frac{\beta K}{\alpha} + K\right) = \frac{\beta K^2(\alpha + \beta)}{\alpha^2 L},$$

$$KL\left(R\frac{\partial R}{\partial K} - \frac{\partial R}{\partial L}\right) = KL\left(\frac{\beta^2 K}{\alpha^2 L^2} + \frac{\beta K}{\alpha L^2}\right) = \frac{\beta K^2(\alpha + \beta)}{\alpha^2 L}.$$

Hence,

$$\sigma = \frac{R(LR + K)}{KL\left(R\dfrac{\partial R}{\partial K} - \dfrac{\partial R}{\partial L}\right)} = 1.$$

That is, the elasticity of substitution is equal to 1 at every point on the Cobb–Douglas production function.

To examine the behaviour of the function when the scale of operations is changed, let the level of inputs increase by a factor λ, so that the new level of output Q^1 is given by

$$Q^1 = A(\lambda K)^\alpha (\lambda L)^\beta = \lambda^{\alpha+\beta} Q$$

and the degree of homogeneity is $\alpha + \beta$. If $\alpha + \beta = 1$ there are constant returns to scale. If $\alpha + \beta < 1$ there are decreasing returns to scale and for $\alpha + \beta > 1$ there are increasing returns to scale. Notice that these are independent of the values of K and L and apply at any point on the production function.

If profit maximising behaviour is assumed with a Cobb–Douglas production process then the conditions for maximum profits, from (3.9), are

$$w = \frac{\lambda \beta Q}{L}, r = \frac{\lambda \alpha Q}{K}, \frac{w}{r} = \frac{\beta K}{\alpha L} \tag{3.19}$$

and from (3.10) when $\eta \neq -1$, $\lambda = (\eta + 1)p$, so that

$$L = \frac{(\eta + 1)p\beta Q}{w}, K = \frac{(\eta + 1)p\alpha Q}{r}$$

and, provided $\alpha + \beta \neq 1$, the maximum level of output can be obtained from (3.16). When $\eta = -1$, (3.19) and (3.10) give

$$K = \frac{w\alpha L}{\beta r}, Q^\circ = AK^\alpha L^\beta = A\left(\frac{w\alpha}{\beta r}\right)^\alpha L^{\alpha+\beta}$$

and hence the values of K and L can be obtained. The second-order condition from (3.12) gives

$$D = \frac{\alpha\beta Q^3}{K^2 L^2}(\alpha + \beta)$$

which is greater than zero if α and β are positive. In the case of perfect competition, (3.15) gives

$$\frac{\alpha\beta Q^2}{K^2 L^2}(1 - \alpha - \beta) > 0$$

which is satisfied if $1 > \alpha + \beta$ so that for a unique maximum profit position to occur there must be decreasing returns to scale. This follows from the assumptions of perfect competition in the product and factor markets. If net revenue is positive and there are constant or increasing returns to scale it pays to increase the scale of operation.

With imperfect competition the second-order condition (3.14) gives

$$\frac{p(\eta + 1)\alpha\beta Q^2}{K^2 L^2}\{(\alpha + \beta)(\eta + 1) - 1\} < 0.$$

Since p, α, β, Q, K and L are positive, this inequality is satisfied if

$$(\eta + 1)[(\alpha + \beta)(\eta + 1) - 1] < 0$$

or both $\eta + 1 > 0$ and $(\alpha + \beta)(\eta + 1) < 1.$ (3.20)

This condition requires $-1 < \eta < 0$ and hence the demand for the product must be inelastic. The second part of (3.20) limits the maximum value of $\eta + 1$ to $1/(\alpha + \beta)$.

To summarise the results, profit maximisation occurs when (3.19) are satisfied and values of the labour and capital inputs can be obtained. The second-order condition requires there to be decreasing returns to scale for a maximum to occur when there is perfect competition. A more general result (3.20) applies when a constant elasticity demand curve is assumed but again the returns to scale behaviour of the Cobb–Douglas function may prevent profit maximisation from being achieved.

(b) The C.E.S. production function

The Cobb–Douglas production function is rather restrictive in that the elasticity of substitution is equal to 1 at every point on the function. A logical generalisation is to allow the elasticity of substitution to be a constant which may be different from 1. For two factors of production the general form of the constant elasticity of substitution (or C.E.S.) production function is

$$Q = \gamma[(1 - \delta)K^{-\rho} + \delta L^{-\rho}]^{-\nu/\rho}$$ (3.21)

where γ, δ, ρ and ν are parameters. The value of the parameter γ is dependent on the units of measurement used and is a measure of the efficiency of the process. For positive values of Q, K and L the function is single valued and continuous (subject to some restrictions on the values of the parameters). The marginal products of capital and labour are

$$Q_K = \left(\frac{-\nu}{\rho}\right) \gamma(1 - \delta)(-\rho)K^{-\rho-1}[(1 - \delta)K^{-\rho} + \delta L^{-\rho}]^{-(\nu/\rho)-1}$$

$$= \frac{\nu\gamma(1 - \delta)}{K^{1+\rho}} \left[\frac{Q}{\gamma}\right]^{1+\rho/\nu} = \frac{(1 - \delta)}{K^{1+\rho}} A Q^{1+\rho/\nu}$$

where $A = \dfrac{\nu}{\gamma^{\rho/\nu}}$

$$Q_L = \left(\frac{-\nu}{\rho}\right) \gamma(\delta)(-\rho)L^{-\rho-1}[(1 - \delta)K^{-\rho} + \delta L^{-\rho}]^{-(\nu/\rho)-1}$$

$$= \frac{\nu\gamma\delta}{L^{\rho+1}} \left[\frac{Q}{\gamma}\right]^{1+\rho/\nu} = \frac{\delta A Q^{1+\rho/\nu}}{L^{1+\rho}}.$$

These marginal products will be positive if

$$(1 - \delta)A > 0 \quad \text{and} \quad A\delta > 0 \tag{3.22}$$

so that[1]

$$1 > \delta > 0 \quad \text{and} \quad A > 0. \tag{3.23}$$

The second-order derivatives of (3.21) are

$$Q_{KK} = (1 - \delta)A \left[\frac{K^{1+\rho}(1 + \rho/\nu)Q^{\rho/\nu} Q_K - Q^{1+\rho/\nu}(1 + \rho)K^{\rho}}{K^{2+2\rho}}\right]$$

$$= \frac{Q^{1+\rho/\nu}(1 - \delta)A}{K^{2+2\rho}} [(1 + \rho/\nu)Q^{\rho/\nu}(1 - \delta)A - (1 + \rho)K^{\rho}]$$

$$Q_{LL} = \delta A \left[\frac{L^{1+\rho}(1 + \rho/\nu)Q^{\rho/\nu}Q_L - Q^{1+\rho/\nu}(1 + \rho)L^{\rho}}{L^{2+2\rho}}\right]$$

$$= \frac{Q^{1+\rho/\nu}\delta A}{L^{2+2\rho}} [(1 + \rho/\nu)Q^{\rho/\nu}\delta A - (1 + \rho)L^{\rho}].$$

These will be negative (given (3.22)) if

$$\frac{AQ^{\rho/\nu}(1 - \delta)}{K^{\rho}} < \frac{1 + \rho}{1 + \rho/\nu} \quad \text{and} \quad \frac{AQ^{\rho/\nu}\delta}{L^{\rho}} < \frac{1 + \rho}{1 + \rho/\nu}. \tag{3.24}$$

---

[1] These can easily be shown as follows. If $A > 0$ then (3.22) are satisfied if $(1 - \delta) > 0$ and $\delta > 0$ so that $1 > \delta > 0$. If $A < 0$, then (3.22) are satisfied if $(1 - \delta) < 0$ and $\delta < 0$, i.e. $1 < \delta$ and $\delta < 0$ which is a contradiction. Hence $A > 0$ and $1 > \delta > 0$.

Since $A, (1 - \delta), Q, L, K, \delta$ are all positive then

$$0 < \frac{1 + \rho}{1 + \rho/\nu}$$

so that either $\rho > -1$ and $\rho/\nu > 0$ or $\rho < -1$ and $\rho/\nu < -1$.

The marginal rate of substitution is

$$R = \frac{Q_L}{Q_K} = \left(\frac{\delta}{1 - \delta}\right)\left(\frac{K}{L}\right)^{1 + \rho} \tag{3.25}$$

and so depends upon δ and ρ as well as K and L. By partial differentiation of R,

$$\frac{\partial R}{\partial K} = \left(\frac{\delta}{1 - \delta}\right)\frac{(1 + \rho)K^\rho}{L^{1 + \rho}} = \frac{(1 + \rho)R}{K}$$

$$\frac{\partial R}{\partial L} = \left(\frac{\delta}{1 - \delta}\right)\frac{(-1 - \rho)K^{1 + \rho}}{L^{2 + \rho}} = -\frac{(1 + \rho)R}{L}$$

and the elasticity of substitution, from (3.4) is

$$\sigma = \frac{R(LR + K)}{KL\left(R\dfrac{\partial R}{\partial K} - \dfrac{\partial R}{\partial L}\right)} = \frac{R(LR + K)}{KL\left(\dfrac{R^2(1 + \rho)}{K} + \dfrac{(1 + \rho)R}{L}\right)}$$

$$= \frac{LR + K}{(1 + \rho)(LR + K)} = \frac{1}{1 + \rho}. \tag{3.26}$$

The parameter ρ is therefore related to the elasticity of substitution and so σ is a constant over the range of values of Q, K and L. This explains the name of the constant elasticity of substitution production function. Since $\sigma > 0$, ρ must be greater than -1, and from (3.24), $\rho/\nu > 0$.

The returns to scale behaviour of (3.21) can be examined by increasing the inputs K and L by a factor λ. The new level of output is

$$Q' = \gamma[(1 - \delta)\lambda^{-\rho}K^{-\rho} + \delta\lambda^{-\rho}L^{-\rho}]^{-\nu/\rho} = \lambda^\nu Q$$

and so if $\nu = 1$ there are constant returns to scale,
$\qquad\quad\ \nu > 1$ there are increasing returns to scale,
$\qquad\quad\ \nu < 1$ there are decreasing returns to scale.

Thus ν is the returns to scale parameter. As with the Cobb–Douglas function, for given values of the parameters, the same returns to scale behaviour occurs at all combinations of K and L.

If profit maximising behaviour is assumed with a C.E.S. function then (3.9) give

$$
\left.
\begin{aligned}
w &= \frac{\lambda\delta A Q^{1+\rho/\nu}}{L^{1+\rho}}, \quad r = \frac{\lambda(1-\delta)A Q^{1+\rho/\nu}}{K^{1+\rho}} \\[2mm]
\frac{w}{r} &= \frac{\delta}{(1-\delta)}\left(\frac{K}{L}\right)^{1+\rho}
\end{aligned}
\right\}.
\tag{3.27}
$$

This can be re-arranged to give

$$
\frac{wL}{rK} = \left(\frac{\delta}{1-\delta}\right)\left(\frac{K}{L}\right)^{\rho}
\tag{3.28}
$$

which shows that the ratio of the return to labour to the return to capital depends on δ, ρ and the capital–labour ratio. The parameter δ is known as the distribution parameter since an increase in δ increases the return to labour relative to capital. As with the Cobb–Douglas function the conditions (3.10) together with the production function (3.21) allow the profit maximising values of K and L to be determined. The second-order condition (3.12) does not add any extra information to (3.23)–(3.24). Again in the case of perfect competition a maximum can only occur if there are decreasing returns to scale, i.e. from (3.15) $\nu < 1$. With imperfect competition (3.14) gives a condition directly comparable to (3.20),

$$
\eta + 1 > 0 \quad \text{and} \quad \nu(\eta + 1) < 1.
\tag{3.29}
$$

Thus the results for profit maximisation with the C.E.S. function are all similar to those from the Cobb–Douglas function.

The *a priori* restrictions on the parameters of the C. E. S . function can now be summarised as follows

$$
\rho/\nu > 0, 1 > \delta > 0, \rho > -1, \gamma > 0.
\tag{3.30}
$$

The last of these arises because in (3.21) γ will have the same positive sign as Q.

3.3 DATA PROBLEMS AND AGGREGATION

The properties of two particular production functions have been discussed and the question arises as to whether the production function can be observed. At first sight this would appear possible if data on a particular firm were available. Consider a single observation of values of Q, K and L. This would not, of course, allow the parameters or form of a production function to be determined. But, more importantly, there would be no guarantee that the particular value of Q observed is the maximum level of output for the given values of K and L. That is, the observed point may not be on the production frontier. It has also been assumed that the firm has the desired usage of K and L which are the profit maximising values. If this is not so then the observed values will relate to a disequilibrium position and the correct model to explain them will have a dynamic form.

As indicated above, extra observations are required if the parameters and form of the function are to be identified. Two types of data are frequently available – time-series and cross-section. The former refers to observations in different time periods on the same firm, whilst the latter refers to observations in the same time period on different firms.

Time-series data on a firm. If time-series data are available, say successive annual observations on the same firm, problems additional to those associated with a single observation arise. Relative prices change over time and hence the optimal combinations of the factor inputs will also change. Observations are therefore much more likely to refer to disequilibrium positions because of lags in the adjustment process. The quality of entrepreneurial skill will also change with longer experience and staff changes so that there may be a movement from sub-optimal to optimal utilisation of given factor inputs. However, the major problem with time-series data is technical progress. That is, as knowledge increases processes which are technologically more efficient become available and the skill and quality of the labour force improves. The result is that factor input rates, substitutability between factors, efficiency parameters and the economies of scale behaviour can all change. Thus the parameters, and even the mathematical form, of the production function change over time.

Two methods of allowing for this have been suggested. One assumes that technical progress can be measured by adding a time trend, t, to the production function to give

$$Q_t = f(t, K_t, L_t)$$

and for example in the case of the Cobb–Douglas function

$$Q_t = A\, e^{\theta t} K_t^{\alpha} L_t^{\beta}.$$

Here θ is the exponential rate of technical progress, and implies that output rises at a rate of θ per cent per annum independently of changes in the factor inputs, and in particular, independently of new investment. This type of technical progress is not associated with the measures of capital or labour and is known as disembodied technical progress. Further, it is *Hicks-neutral* since the marginal rate of substitution of capital for labour is unchanged by technical progress. This formulation is, to some extent, unrealistic in that intuitively old machines are unchanged by new discoveries and technological progress will only have an effect on output through investment.

The second approach to technical progress assumes that new investment embodies technical advances and that only after investment occurs can technical progress have any effect. This is known as embodied technical progress and gives rise to a *vintage model* because a different production function applies for each vintage (or age) of capital. For example

$$Q_t(v) = f(v, L_t(v), K_t(v))$$

where $Q_t(v)$ = output at time t from machines of vintage v
$L_t(v)$ = labour used at time t on machines of vintage v
$K_t(v)$ = capital of vintage v in use at time t.

The term v in the production function measures technical progress and, for example, with the Cobb–Douglas function

$$Q_t(v) = A\, e^{\theta v} K_t(v)^\alpha L_t(v)^\beta.$$

The production function at time t is

$$Q_t = f(L_t, K_t)$$

with

$$Q_t = \int_{-\infty}^{t} Q_t(v)dv$$

$$L_t = \int_{-\infty}^{t} L_t(v)dv$$

$$K_t = \int_{-\infty}^{t} K_t(v)dv$$

being the measures of total output, labour input and capital input at time t. Some progress can be made with these expressions, if assumptions are made about the rate of depreciation of capital, but these will not be pursued here (see Brown (1966) Chapter 6).

Cross-section data on a firm. With cross-section data different problems arise. Since all the observations occur in the same time period relative prices will be constant. Technical progress can be ignored. The observations now refer to different firms and again it must be assumed, if the production function is to be observed, that each firm has its equilibrium capital and labour input requirements. Additionally, the use of data from different firms implies that all the firms considered have the same production function and therefore belong to the same industry. Once firms from different industries are included the interpretation of the production function is difficult. If the firms are from the same industry so that a common range of production possibilities is available then all firms should, theoretically, be at the same profit maximising position. However, differences in entrepreneurial ability will result in some sub-optimal observations and may give misleading estimates of efficiency parameters or returns to scale behaviour. If all firms adopt the equilibrium capital–labour ratio but make mistakes in the choice of output level, constant returns to scale may be implied. There will be a high correlation between the values of K and L. Any estimated production function is therefore likely to be misleading.

Industry level. The theoretical production function relates to the unit of production, the firm, and yet published data are generally only available for industries or industrial sectors. The problem thus arises of whether a particular production relationship which exists for a firm can be observed at the level of the industry. For this to be so, two conditions are generally necessary. Firstly all the firms within an industry are assumed to have the same form of production function, and secondly the production function must be additively separable.[1] That is, it must be possible to write the general function in the form

$$f(K, L) = g(K) + h(L).$$

The first of these conditions is imposed for simplicity since the only alternative is to assume that some of the firms have different production functions, which complicates the derivation of the function for the industry. The condition that the function is additively separable is satisfied by the two functions considered above. For the Cobb–Douglas function, taking logarithms gives

$$\log Q = \log A + \alpha \log K + \beta \log L,$$

so that

$$g(K) = \log A + \alpha \log K, \quad h(L) = \beta \log L,$$

and for the C.E.S. function, from (3.21),

$$Q^{-\rho/v} = \gamma^{-\rho/v}(1 - \delta)K^{-\rho} + \gamma^{-\rho/v} \delta L^{-\rho}$$

so that

$$g(K) = \gamma^{-\rho/v}(1 - \delta)K^{-\rho}, \quad h(L) = \gamma^{-\rho/v}\delta L^{-\rho}.$$

Thus the functions considered may be observed at the industry level. It remains necessary, however, to examine each function in turn to see the conditions imposed by the estimation of the industry level functions on the parameters and on the measures of the capital and labour inputs.

Considering the Cobb–Douglas production functions for two firms and expressing them in logarithmic form gives

$$\log Q_1 = \log A_1 + \alpha_1 \log K_1 + \beta_1 \log L_1$$
$$\log Q_2 = \log A_2 + \alpha_2 \log K_2 + \beta_2 \log L_2$$
$$\log (Q_1 Q_2) = \log (A_1 A_2) + \log (K_1^{\alpha_1} K_2^{\alpha_2}) + \log (L_1^{\beta_1} L_2^{\beta_2})$$

so that at the aggregate level the measure of Q is the logarithm of the product of Q_1 and Q_2, or twice the logarithm of the geometric mean of Q_1 and Q_2.[2] If the parameters are assumed to be the same for each firm then $\alpha_1 = \alpha_2$ and $\beta_1 = \beta_2$ so that the aggregate function may be written

$$\log (Q_1 Q_2) = \log (A_1 A_2) + \alpha \log (K_1 K_2) + \beta \log (L_1 L_2)$$

and again the aggregate measures of capital and labour are related to geometric rather than arithmetic averages.

Q [1] For a brief discussion see Walters (1963) pp. 9–10.

[2] The geometric mean of Q_1 and Q_2 is $(Q_1 Q_2)^{\frac{1}{2}}$ and in general the geometric mean of $Q_1, Q_2, Q_3 \ldots, Q_n$ is $(Q_1 Q_2 \ldots Q_n)^{1/n}$.

The situation is rather more complex for the C.E.S. function. Expressing (3.14) in logarithmic form for two firms gives

$$\log Q_1 = \log \gamma_1 - \frac{\nu_1}{\rho_1} \log [(1 - \delta_1)K_1^{-\rho_1} + \delta_1 L_1^{-\rho_1}]$$

$$\log Q_2 = \log \gamma_2 - \frac{\nu_2}{\rho_2} \log [(1 - \delta_2)K_2^{-\rho_2} + \delta_2 L_2^{-\rho_2}]$$

and even assuming $\nu_1 = \nu_2$, $\delta_1 = \delta_2$ and $\rho_1 = \rho_2$ does not allow the sum of $\log Q_1$ and $\log Q_2$ to be expressed in terms of sums or geometric means of capital and labour inputs. That is, if all the firms in an industry had C.E.S. production functions with identical parameters then (except for very special cases such as $\delta_1 = \delta_2 = 0$) the usual form of data which are available for an industry would not allow the parameters to be estimated by this method.

To summarise the results of aggregation from the firm to the industry level, in the case of the Cobb–Douglas function the imposition of identical parameters for all the labour inputs, and also for the all the capital inputs, allows the aggregate functions to be estimated provided the data are geometric averages. This is not so for the C.E.S. function.

There are also more general problems when industry data are considered. External economies, which can be ignored at the firm level, may be important at the industry level. As with data on firms, time-series and cross-section observations each have their own disadvantages. With the former, technical progress is again a major problem and the same two approaches discussed above are available. With cross-section data on different industries interpretation of the production function is the major problem. The estimated function cannot provide information about the substitutability of factors. Any returns to scale behaviour observed would depend on the statistical definition of the industries used. For example, if industry 1 has $Q = 12$ for $K = 8$, $L = 8$ and industry 2 has $Q = 32$ for $K = 16$, $L = 16$, then there are apparently increasing returns to scale. But if industry 2 is redefined as four small industries each with $Q = 8$ for $K = 4$, $L = 4$ then there are decreasing returns to scale.

Cross-section data need not refer to observations on different industries in one country. It could consist of observations on a particular industry for a range of countries in a particular year. In this case the assumption of a common production function is probably reasonable. However, even though cross-section data are used, technical progress may be a problem in that there may not be a common range of possible techniques available in each country. Definitions of industries vary and problems occur in measuring Q, K and L in common units, especially when international exchange rates do not accurately reflect the value of a currency. Relative prices are likely to vary, as are the factor and product market conditions. The size of the industry in different countries will vary so that in the statistical estimation heteroscedasticity may be a problem.

An alternative view of the production function solely as a macro-economic relationship has some attractions. The argument is that to reject the production function as a valid macro-economic concept because of the difficulties in the process of aggregation is to give too much emphasis to micro-economic theory. If this is accepted then it is legitimate to use aggregate data to estimate the parameters of production functions and to interpret these as average values for the data used. The estimated function is then a statistical description of the relationship between the macro-economic variables Q, K and L. It is not concerned with efficient techniques or with possible substitutions between the factors, but it may still provide useful information about an economy.

3.4 EMPIRICAL ESTIMATION

In this section the measurement of the variables in the aggregate production function is discussed and the empirical implications of the various forms of the different production functions are considered. The main variables are labour and capital input and the level of output. The theory of production implies all units of each of these variables are homogeneous. This is obviously not so. Aggregation of statistics requires some common unit of measurement and the ones commonly adopted are money for the value of output and capital input, and man-hours for the labour input. Aggregate series are generally weighted arithmetic averages of the data. For the capital services input, the valuation is determined by its expected rate of profit, and hence recent rates of profit. Thus the cost of capital, r, and the capital input K are interdependent variables. A further problem is that the level of capital stock and the utilisation of capital stock differ. Problems also occur with the measurement of the labour input. Crude measures are the number of employees or the number of man-hours worked. More satisfactory though is some measure which reflects the quality of labour supplied, using such weights as education level and age/sex categories. Output is generally measured in value-added terms by a weighted index number. Alternative weighting schemes would, of course, result in different output measures.

All the production relationships considered are deterministic and do not allow for random effects. A stochastic term u must be added to each equation for which the parameters are to be estimated. This term will represent all factors effecting the production process which have not been explicitly considered.

Thus the general production function is

$$Q = f(K, L, u).$$

In this formulation K and L are the independent (predetermined) variables and Q is the dependent variable. This implies that the entrepreneur chooses K and L and then Q is determined by the production function. However, it is more likely that the entrepreneur makes a joint decision about Q, K and L so that they are determined simultaneously. In this case the estimation of a single equation will give misleading results and the correct specification will require equations explaining the levels of K and L. Reference should be made to Griliches and Ringstad (1971) and Hildebrand and Liu (1965) for further discussion of this.

The Cobb–Douglas production function (3.16) is not in a convenient form for direct estimation by least squares methods and it is usually converted into a logarithmic form

$$\log Q = \log A + \alpha \log K + \beta \log L + u \qquad (3.31)$$

so that the residual u, is added to (3.16) in the multiplicative form e^u. *A priori* the values of α and β satisfy $1 > \alpha > 0$ and $1 > \beta > 0$, and if constant returns to scale are present then $\alpha + \beta = 1$. Alternatively, constant returns to scale can be imposed by putting $\beta = 1 - \alpha$ so that

$$Q = AK^\alpha L^{1-\alpha} e^u = A \left\{\frac{K}{L}\right\}^\alpha L e^u$$

or

$$\frac{Q}{L} = A \left(\frac{K}{L}\right)^\alpha e^u$$

and taking logarithms of both sides,

$$\log (Q/L) = \log A + \alpha \log (K/L) + u. \qquad (3.32)$$

This second form avoids multicollinearity between $\log K$ and $\log L$ and also reduces heteroscedasticity if the variance of u is correlated with L.[1]

The C.E.S. function (3.21) is difficult to estimate directly and it is not even possible to make a simple transformation to an estimatable form. Estimation of the C.E.S. function has therefore generally been limited to either examining whether the conditions for profit maximisation, (3.27), are satisfied or making some approximation to the function. From the first part of (3.27)

$$\left(\frac{Q}{L}\right)^{1+\rho} = \frac{w}{p\delta A} Q^{\rho - \rho/\nu} e^u$$

or

$$\log \left(\frac{Q}{L}\right) = \log C + \frac{1}{1+\rho} \log \left(\frac{w}{p}\right) + \frac{\rho(\nu - 1)}{\nu(1 + \rho)} \log Q + u \qquad (3.33)$$

where C is a constant. Thus if perfect competition and decreasing returns to scale exist the coefficient of $\log (w/p)$ yields an estimate of ρ and the coefficient of $\log Q$ can therefore be used to obtain an estimate of ν. This should be less than 1 for decreasing returns to scale. If $\rho = 0$ then (3.33) becomes

$$\log (Q/L) = \log C + \log (w/p) + u.$$

[1] See Chapter 1, Section 1.3.

A similar equation can be obtained from the profit maximising equations for the Cobb–Douglas function, (3.19),

$$\frac{Q}{L} = \frac{w}{p_\beta}\, e^u$$

or
$$\log(Q/L) = -\log\beta + \log(w/p) + u. \tag{3.34}$$

Thus if (3.33) is estimated for a Cobb–Douglas process the coefficient of $\log(w/p)$ should be about 1 and the estimated coefficient of $\log Q$ should not be significantly different from zero. Other values would imply a C.E.S. function. It will be apparent that the C.E.S. function and the Cobb–Douglas function are closely related. For example, it can be shown from further mathematical analysis that the C.E.S. function approaches a Cobb–Douglas function as $\rho \to 0$, and that the returns to scale behaviour indicated by the two functions is always the same.[1] That is, if the C.E.S. function has decreasing returns to scale then the Cobb–Douglas function also has decreasing returns to scale.

The corresponding equations for capital are obtained from (3.27) for the C.E.S. function to give

$$\log\left(\frac{Q}{K}\right) = \log C' + \frac{1}{1+\rho}\log\left(\frac{r}{\rho}\right) + \frac{\rho(v-1)}{v(1+\rho)}\log Q + u \tag{3.35}$$

where C' is a constant, and from (3.19),

$$\log(Q/K) = -\log\alpha + \log(r/p) + u \tag{3.36}$$

and the corresponding empirical tests can be made. In the case of the C.E.S. function the scale parameter γ and the distribution parameter δ do not occur explicitly in the maximising equations and so cannot be estimated by this approach.

Kmenta (1967) suggests an approximation to the C.E.S. which allows the parameters to be estimated. Writing (3.21) as

$$Q/L = e^u \gamma L^{v-1}[\delta + (1-\delta)(K/L)^{-\rho}]^{-v/\rho}$$

and taking logarithms gives

$$\log(Q/L) = \log\gamma + (v-1)\log L - (v/\rho)f(\rho) + u$$

where
$$f(\rho) = \log[\delta + (1-\delta)(K/L)^{-\rho}].$$

The expression $f(\rho)$ can be approximated by the use of Taylor's expansion

$$f(\rho) = f(0) + \rho f'(0) + \frac{\rho^2}{2!}f''(0) + \cdots$$

---

[1] See Evans (1969) p. 258.

since $\qquad\qquad f(0) = 0,$

$$f'(\rho) = \frac{(1 - \delta)(K/L)^{-\rho}(-\log(K/L))}{\delta + (1 - \delta)(K/L)^{-\rho}}$$

and $\qquad\qquad f'(0) = -(1 - \delta)\log(K/L)$

$$f''(\rho) = \frac{\delta(1 - \delta)(\log(K/L))^2}{\delta + (1 - \delta)(K/L)^{-\rho}} \text{ and } f''(0) = \delta(1 - \delta)(\log(K/L))^2$$

then, approximately

$$f(\rho) = -\rho(1 - \delta)\log(K/L) + \frac{\rho^2}{2}\delta(1 - \delta)(\log(K/L)^2$$

and hence,

$$\log(Q/L) = \log\gamma + (v - 1)\log L + v(1 - \delta)\log(K/L)$$
$$- 0{\cdot}5v\delta\rho(1 - \delta)(\log(K/L))^2 + u. \qquad (3.37)$$

The equivalent equation for the Cobb–Douglas function is found by rewriting (3.31) as

$$\log(Q/L) = \log A + (\beta - 1 + \alpha)\log L + \alpha\log(K/L) + u. \qquad (3.38)$$

Thus the only difference between these is the extra term which occurs in the C.E.S. form. The approximation used is closer when σ is close to 1, and if $\sigma = 1$ then $\rho = 0$ and (3.37) and (3.38) are the same. The estimated coefficient of $\log(K/L)^2$ therefore provides a test for a Cobb–Douglas or C.E.S. form. If the function is Cobb–Douglas then the estimated coefficient of $\log(K/L)^2$ should not be significantly different from zero. If this coefficient is significantly different from zero the Cobb–Douglas form is rejected but since the approximation to the C.E.S. required ρ to be close to zero the approximation is invalid. Therefore a rejection of the Cobb–Douglas form does not imply the function is C.E.S. An additional problem is that the coefficient of $\log(K/L)^2$ depends on ρ, v and δ. Since $0 < \delta < 1$ and ρ is likely to be small, the product $\rho v\delta(1 - \delta)$ will also be small, and therefore a large sample is required to estimate the coefficient with precision.

3.5 EMPIRICAL EVIDENCE

In this section two recent studies of the Cobb–Douglas and C.E.S. functions are discussed. Griliches and Ringstad (1971) use cross-section data on establishments in the manufacturing sector whilst Woodfield (1972) uses time series data for the whole manufacturing sector. These studies are selected because in each case different functions are estimated from the same basic data allowing a meaningful comparison of the results.

(a) A cross-section study

Griliches and Ringstad (1971) use data from the 1963 Norwegian Census of Manufacturing Establishments to estimate different production functions. They point out that much work on production functions uses highly aggregative data which cannot measure economies of scale. Their data is cross-sectional on 19,824 manufacturing establishments arranged into industry groups and does not include prices (other than wage rates) or details of the age/sex/skill characteristics of the labour force. They therefore do not attempt to construct and estimate a complete system of supply, demand and production equations but instead they concentrate on single equation estimation and examine in detail the biases which may arise. The main variables are

Q – Gross production less raw material consumption (i.e. value added)
K – Capital services
L – Hours worked.

Observation on these variables are all subject to errors. For example, gross production is measured in value terms but prices vary between establishments even within an industry. Capital services are calculated from the fire insurance value of capital goods, which may differ from the replacement value. The labour variable includes an allowance for work by proprietors and their families. There are therefore overwhelming grounds for expecting errors in variables problems[1] to be present and thus the parameter estimates will be biased. Griliches and Ringstad consider these biases in detail and also recognise the biases arising from the simultaneous nature of the relationship between output, capital and labour. For total manufacturing industry they estimate the Cobb–Douglas scale parameter $(\alpha + \beta - 1)$ to be 0·064, with a bias of 0·012 due to errors in variables and a bias of 0·0115 because of simultaneity. These biases are not independent and are thought to add up to 0·016, or 25 per cent of the estimated scale coefficient.

As an example of their results the estimates of the Cobb–Douglas form (3.38) and the C.E.S. Kmenta approximation form (3.37) for the industry 'suits, coats and dresses' (185 observations) are[2]

$$\log(Q/L) = 1.429 + \underset{(0\cdot025)}{0\cdot142 \log L} + \underset{(0\cdot052)}{0\cdot186 \log(K/L)}$$

$$\bar{R}^2 = 0\cdot1648, \ F = 19\cdot2$$

$$\log(Q/L) = 1\cdot431 + \underset{(0\cdot025)}{0\cdot142 \log L} + \underset{(0\cdot055)}{0\cdot183 \log(K/L)}$$

$$+ \underset{(0\cdot044)}{0\cdot008 \ (\log K/L)^2}$$

$$\bar{R}^2 = 0\cdot1602, \ F = 12\cdot7$$

[1] See Koutsoyiannis (1973) Chapter 12.
[2] Griliches and Ringstad (1971) p. 142, Table A.10.

In both equations the F values indicate an overall fit which is significantly better than random. The Cobb–Douglas estimates of α and β are 0·186 and 0·956 with $\hat{\alpha} + \hat{\beta} = 1·142$. For the C.E.S. approximation $\hat{\delta} = 0·8398$, $\hat{v} = 1·142$ and $\hat{\rho} = -0·104$ but the coefficient of $(\log L/K)^2$ is not significantly different from zero. Slightly increasing returns to scale are suggested in each case and the elasticity of substitution appears to be close to 1. The Cobb–Douglas function is also estimated with three additional variables to represent the location and the age of the establishment. Since the effects of these variables are difficult to quantify Griliches and Ringstad represent them by a special type of variable known as a *dummy* or *binary* variable.

A simple example of the use of a dummy variable is provided by the case of a Cobb–Douglas production function in which the parameter A (or 10^a) is thought to differ between the two regions of a country but the parameters α and β are thought to be the same over the two regions,

$$\text{i.e. Region } 1: Q = 10^{a_1}K^{\alpha}L^{\beta}$$
$$\text{Region } 2: Q = 10^{a_2}K^{\alpha}L^{\beta}.$$

The difference in the A values could be a result of different levels of efficiency in the utilisation of the capital and labour inputs. These two functions could be estimated independently with the probable result that two different estimates of α and two different estimates of β occur, each relying only on data for one region. An alternative approach is to estimate the function

$$Q = 10^{\gamma_0 + \gamma_1 R_1}K^{\alpha}L^{\beta}$$

where R_1 is a dummy variable which takes the values

$$R_1 = 0 \text{ for observations in region 2}$$
$$= 1 \text{ for observations in region 1.}$$

The effect of this is that the term $\gamma_0 + \gamma_1 R_1$ has the value $\gamma_0 + \gamma_1$ for observations in region 1, the value γ_0 for observations in region 2 and that estimates of α and β are based on all the observations rather than on the observations for one region. This procedure assumes that there are *a priori* reasons for expecting common values of α and β for the two regions. If there are grounds for expecting say, only a common value of α and hence different values of β a dummy variable can allow for this by writing the production function as

$$Q = 10^{\gamma_0 + \gamma_1 R_1}K^{\alpha}L^{\beta_0 + \beta_1 R_1}$$

which is estimated as

$$\log Q = \gamma_0 + \gamma_1 R_1 + \alpha \log K + \beta_0 \log L + \beta_1 R_1 \log L.$$

In this case the coefficient of $\log L$ is $\beta_0 + \beta_1$ for region 1 ($R_1 = 1$) and β_0 for region 2 ($R_1 = 0$).

The variables used by Griliches and Ringstad are

$R_1 = 1$ for establishments in the more industrialised districts outside the Oslo region,

$R_1 = 0$ otherwise.

$R_2 = 1$ for establishments in the less industrialised districts outside the Oslo region,

$R_2 = 0$ otherwise.

$F_1 = 1$ for establishments founded before 1953,

$F_1 = 0$ for establishments founded in 1953 or later.

The formulation of the Cobb–Douglas function estimated is

$$\log (Q/L) = \gamma_0 + \gamma_1 R_1 + \gamma_2 R_2 + \gamma_3 F_1 + \alpha \log (K/L) + (\alpha + \beta - 1) \log L.$$

Thus the constant term is allowed to vary between three regions:

$R_1 = 0$, $R_2 = 0$ – Oslo region,

$R_1 = 0$, $R_2 = 1$ – less industrialised districts outside the Oslo region,

$R_1 = 1$, $R_2 = 0$ – more industrialised districts outside the Oslo region,

and also with the age of the establishment. The estimated equation[1] for suits, coats and dresses is

$$\log (Q/L) = 1 \cdot 630 - 0 \cdot 184 R_1 - 0 \cdot 208 R_2 + 0 \cdot 035 F_1$$
$$\qquad\qquad (0 \cdot 077) \qquad (0 \cdot 068) \qquad (0 \cdot 079)$$

$$+0 \cdot 155 \log (K/L) + 0 \cdot 127 \log L$$
$$\quad (0 \cdot 052) \qquad\qquad (0 \cdot 025)$$

$$\bar{R}^2 = 0 \cdot 1982, \; F = 10 \cdot 1.$$

The overall fit is still significantly better than random and the $\bar{R}^2$ is increased by the addition of the dummy variables. The coefficients of R_1 and R_2 are significantly negative, showing that regional differences are important, but that of F_1 is not significantly different from zero. The effect of including the dummy variables on the estimates of α and β is that the new estimate of α is $0 \cdot 155$ compared with $0 \cdot 186$ and that of β is $0 \cdot 972$ compared with $0 \cdot 956$. The returns to scale estimate is $\hat{\alpha} + \hat{\beta} = 1 \cdot 127$ which is lower than the previous value.

Griliches and Ringstad estimated these equations for 27 industries and found that in 23 cases there are indications of economies of scale being present, which are significant for 17 industries. Only for 6 out of the 27 industries are the coefficient of $\log (K/L)^2$ significantly different from zero. They therefore conclude that only in a few industries is the Cobb–Douglas form found to be inadequate. They suggest this could be the result of errors in the data. Other results indicate that the returns to scale parameters ($\alpha + \beta$ for the Cobb–Douglas form and v for the C.E.S. form) are not constant but decrease with the scale of the industry.

[1] Griliches and Ringstad (1971) p. 142, Table A.10.

There is also a discussion of the results of estimating the C.E.S. function (3.21) more directly by writing it as

$$\log Q = \log \gamma + \nu \log F \qquad (3.39)$$

where $\qquad\qquad F = (\delta L^{-\rho} + (1 - \delta)K^{-\rho})^{-1/\rho}.$

Given values of δ and ρ, F can be evaluated and hence γ and ν can be estimated by least squares. Values of δ from 0·1 to 0·9 in steps of 0·1 are combined with values of ρ from 0·1 to 1·5 in steps of 0·2 to give values of F. The 'best' pair of γ and ρ values is selected as being the pair that minimises the residual sum of squares in (3.39) and hence estimates of δ, ρ, ν and γ are obtained. These are to some extent dependent on the size of the steps used in the iterations over δ and ρ. For the industry quoted above, i.e. suits, coats and dresses, the estimate of σ by this method is 0·9, compared with 1·12 for the Kmenta approximation.

(b) A time-series study

In a study of the New Zealand manufacturing sector, Woodfield (1972) estimated various production functions incorporating Hicks-neutral technical progress. The data are annual observations 1926–68 and the variables are

Q = real net value added in 1955 dollars
L = man-hours of labour
K = capital stock in use.

Attempts to estimate the Cobb–Douglas function

$$Q = AK^{\alpha}L^{\beta}\,e^{\theta t}$$

in the form

$$\log Q = \log A + \alpha \log K + \beta \log L + \theta t$$

failed because of multicollinearity. Woodfield therefore assumes cost minimisation by producers to give the ratio of factor shares

$$\frac{\alpha}{\beta} = \frac{(rK)}{(wL)}\,u = \Omega\,\text{(say)}.$$

A multiplicative error term u is included to allow the ratio of factor shares to deviate from the cost minimisation level. Then $\alpha = \Omega\beta$ and an estimate of Ω can be obtained by the method of maximum likelihood. Since it is assumed $\log u$ is normally distributed with mean 0 and variance σ^2 (say), and

$$\log \Omega = \log (rK/wL) + \log u$$

then, for the first observation,

$$p\,(\log \Omega_1) = \frac{1}{\sqrt{2\pi\sigma^2}}\exp\left\{-\frac{(\log \Omega_1 - \log (rK/wL))^2}{2\sigma^2}\right\}$$

and so the likelihood function for n observations is

$$L = \frac{1}{(2\pi\sigma^2)^{n/2}} \exp\left(-\frac{\Sigma\,(\log \Omega_1 - \log\,(rK/wL))^2}{2\sigma^2}\right)$$

and hence

$$\log L = -\frac{n}{2}\,\log\,(2\pi\sigma^2) - \frac{1}{2\sigma^2}\,\Sigma\left(\log \Omega - \log\frac{(rK)}{(wL)}\right)^2.$$

Maximising with respect to Ω gives

$$0 = \Sigma\,(\log \hat{\Omega} - \log\,(rK/wL))$$

or,

$$\hat{\Omega} = \text{antilog}\left\{\frac{1}{n}\,\Sigma\,\log\,(rK/wL)\right\}.$$

Woodfield finds $\hat{\Omega} = 1\cdot401$ and the estimated Cobb–Douglas function is

$$\log Q = 1\cdot382 + 0\cdot5879\,(\log L + \hat{\Omega}\log K)$$
$$(0\cdot1068)$$

$$+\ 0\cdot0228t$$
$$(0\cdot0045)$$

$$R^2 = 0\cdot9943.$$

The estimates of α and β are $\hat{\alpha} = 0\cdot2355$, $\hat{\beta} = 0\cdot5879$ so that there are indications of decreasing returns to scale with $\hat{\alpha} + \hat{\beta} = 0\cdot8234$. The estimated rate of technical progress is $2\cdot28$ per cent per annum and the coefficient is significantly positive. The estimated equation is therefore satisfactory.

The C.E.S. function with Hicks-neutral technical progress is

$$Q = \gamma\,e^{\theta t}[(1 - \delta)K^{-\rho} + \delta L^{-\rho}]^{-\nu/\rho}. \qquad (3.40)$$

Assuming cost minimisation, then

$$\frac{w}{r} = \frac{\delta}{1 - \delta}\left(\frac{K}{L}\right)^{1+\rho}$$

and hence

$$\log\,(w/r) = \log\,(\delta/(1 - \delta)) + (1 + \rho)\,\log\,(K/L).$$

This is estimated to give

$$\log\,(w/r) = 0\cdot9024 + 0\cdot7026\,\log\,(K/L)$$
$$(0\cdot1329)$$

$$R^2 = 0\cdot6819.$$

The estimates of the parameters are $\hat{\delta} = 0\cdot7114$ and $\hat{\rho} = 0\cdot2974$. Thus the estimated elasticity of substitution is 1·425, which is sufficiently different from 1 to indicate a C.E.S. function is preferable to a Cobb–Douglas one. Given the estimates of δ and ρ the variable

$$F = [(1 - \delta)K^{-\rho} + \delta L^{-\rho}]^{-1/\rho}$$

can be evaluated, (3.40) can be written as (c.f. (3.39))

$$Q = \gamma\, e^{\theta t} F^{\nu}$$

and this can be estimated as

$$\log Q = \log \gamma + \theta t + \nu \log F.$$

The resulting estimate is

$$\log Q = 1·414 + 0·0227t + 0·8265 \log F$$
$$\qquad\qquad (0·0045) \quad (0·1504)$$

$$R^2 = 0·9942.$$

The estimate of the returns to scale parameter ν is 0·8265 which is not significantly different from 1. The estimated rate of technical progress is similar to that for the Cobb–Douglas equation. The conclusion from these results is that the C.E.S. function is a satisfactory description of the data and is superior to the Cobb–Douglas function. However, in his conclusions, Woodfield notes that serial correlation is a problem in some of the regressions he presents. His results should therefore be regarded with caution.

Woodfield also considers the transcendental production function

$$Q = A\, e^{\theta t} K^{\alpha} L^{\beta} \exp \{\delta(K/L)\} \tag{3.41}$$

for which the elasticity of substitution is

$$\sigma = 1 - \frac{\delta(K/L)}{(\alpha + \delta(K/L))^2 - \alpha}$$

where $\alpha, \beta, \delta, \theta$ are parameters. The elasticity of substitution varies with the capital labour ratio and (3.41) is known as a variable elasticity of substitution (V.E.S.) function. If $\delta = 0$ it reduces to the Cobb–Douglas function and $\sigma = 1$. For a further discussion of the V.E.S. function and its properties see Woodfield (1972) and Lovell (1968).

3.6 FURTHER READING

For a detailed review of the theory and empirical work on production functions before 1963 see Walters (1963) where, as well as the Cobb–Douglas and C.E.S. functions, the linear activity analysis model of production is discussed. Since then an enormous number of studies have been published, most of which deal at an advanced level with particular functions or problems.

One of the more readable books is edited by Brown (1967) and includes discussions of recent developments in the theory of production (by R. M. Solow) and recent empirical studies of the C.E.S. function (by M. Nerlove).

Douglas (1948) collects together estimates of the Cobb–Douglas production function from a wide range of countries and for different time periods for both industry level and plant average data. The latter are obtained by dividing industry data on labour, capital and output by the number of plants in that industry. Nerlove (1965) discusses the Cobb–Douglas function in detail and examines the problems involved in estimating it from cross-section data and also from a time series of cross-section data. In his final chapter Nerlove derives a dynamic model of production where profit maximisation over time is assumed. Feldstein (1967) changes the specification of the input variables in the Cobb–Douglas function by allowing the elasticity of output with respect to the number of employees to differ from the elasticity with respect to the average number of hours per man. He discusses the problems of estimating such a Cobb–Douglas function and concludes that a cross-section study will avoid difficulties of autocorrelation and multicollinearity. From cross-section data for the United Kingdom he finds that the output elasticity with respect to hours per man is about twice the output elasticity with respect to the number of employees.

Arrow *et al.* (1961) popularised the C.E.S. function. They estimate the marginal productivity equation for labour ((3.33) with $v = 1$) to obtain the elasticity of substitution for an international cross-section of three-digit manufacturing industries, and find that σ is significantly different from 1 in 14 out of the 24 industries used. Zarembka (1970) provides a criticism of their results. Bodkin and Klein (1967) explore the assumptions about the form of the error term with the Cobb–Douglas function (with and without constant returns to scale) and the C.E.S. function. Both additive and multiplicative errors are assumed and the resulting estimates, from U.S. time-series data, are surprisingly close together.

Hildebrand and Liu (1965) use cross-section data on two-digit U.S. industries to estimate several versions of a simultaneous model consisting of a production function in which the labour input is split into production and non-production employees' man-hours, and in which technical progress is embodied in the capital measure; a demand function for output, and an adjustment equation for each type of employee. A summary and criticism of their work is provided by Bridge (1971), pp. 381–93.

Clemhout (1968) proposes a class of homothetic isoquant production functions which can be written

$$Q = F(f(K, L)) = F(z)$$

where F is monotonic in $f(K, L)$ and z is homogeneous of first degree in K and L. This class of functions allows returns to scale behaviour to vary at different output levels as well as the elasticity of substitution. A variable elasticity of substitution (V.E.S.) production function was mentioned at the end of the previous section. Sato and Hoffman (1968) derive a function for which the elasticity of substitution is a linear function of the capital–labour ratio. They estimate the marginal productivity conditions using time series data for the United States and Japan, and conclude that their V.E.S. specification is more realistic than the C.E.S.

Allen (1967) discusses the various forms of technical progress and vintage models. Brown (1966) provides a comprehensive discussion of the role of technical progress with the Cobb–Douglas and the C.E.S. functions. He uses different epochs (time periods) to quantify the effect on economic growth in the United States, of neutral and non-neutral technical progress. Green (1964) considers the general theoretical problems of aggregation and relates them to aggregate production functions and technical progress.

Fisher (1969) reviews production models in which capital goods are specific to firms and cannot be used interchangeably. He concludes that this raises doubts on the existence of aggregate measures of capital, labour and output, and hence on the existence of the aggregate production function.

3.7 REFERENCES

Allen, R. G. D. (1967), *Macro-economic Theory* (London: Macmillan), chapter 13.

Arrow, K. J., Chenery, H. B., Minhas, B. S. and Solow, R. M. (1961), 'Capital–Labour Substitution and Economic Efficiency', *Review of Economics and Statistics*, vol. 43, 225–50.

Bodkin, R. G. and Klein, L. R. (1967), 'Non-linear Estimation of Aggregate Production Functions', *Review of Economics and Statistics*, vol. 49, 28–44.

Bridge, J. L. (1971), *Applied Econometrics* (Amsterdam: North-Holland).

Brown, M. (1966), *On the Theory and Measurement of Technological Change* (Cambridge: Cambridge University Press).

Brown, M. (ed.) (1967), *The Theory and Empirical Analysis of Production* (New York: National Bureau of Economic Research), vol. 31 of *Studies in Income and Wealth*.

Clemhout, S. (1968), 'The Class of Homothetic Isoquant Production Functions', *Review of Economic Studies*, vol. 35, 91–104.

Douglas, P. H. (1948), 'Are there Laws of Production?', *American Economic Review*, vol. 38, 1–14.

Evans, M. K. (1969), *Macroeconomic Activity* (New York: Harper & Row).

Feldstein, M. S. (1967), 'Specification of the Labour Input in the Aggregate Production Function', *Review of Economic Studies*, vol. 34, 375–86.

Fisher, F. M. (1969), 'The Existence of the Aggregate Production Function', *Econometrica*, vol. 37, 553–77.

Green, H. A. J. (1964), *Aggregation in Economic Analysis* (Princeton: Princeton University Press).

Griliches, Z. and Ringstad, V. (1971), *Economies of Scale and the Form of the Production Function* (Amsterdam: North-Holland).

Hildebrand, G. H. and Liu, T. C. (1965), *Manufacturing Production Functions in the United States, 1957* (New York: New York State School of Industrial and Labour Relations).

Kmenta, J. (1967), 'On the Estimation of the C.E.S. Production Function', *International Economic Review*, vol. 8, 180–9.

Koutsoyiannis, A. (1973), *Theory of Econometrics* (London: Macmillan).

Lovell, C. A. K. (1968), 'Capacity Utilisation and the Production Function Estimation in Postwar American Manufacturing', *Quarterly Journal of Economics*, vol. 82, 218–39.

Nerlove, M. (1965), *Estimation and Identification of Cobb–Douglas Production Functions* (Amsterdam: North-Holland).

Sato, R. and Hoffman, R. F. (1968), 'Production Functions with Variable Elasticity of Factor Substitution: Some Analysis and Testing', *Review of Economics and Statistics*, vol. 50, 453–60.

Walters, A. A. (1963), 'Production and Cost Functions: An Econometric Survey', *Econometrica*, vol. 31, 1–65.

Woodfield, A. (1972), 'Estimates of Hicks-neutral Technical Progress, Returns to Scale and the Elasticity of Substitution in New Zealand Manufacturing 1926–68', *New Zealand Economic Papers*, vol. 6, 73–92.

Zarembka, P. (1970), 'On the Empirical Relevance of the C.E.S. Production Functions', *Review of Economics and Statistics*, vol. 52, 47–53.

4. Wage–Price Models

4.1 THE WAGE-CHANGE EQUATION

In this chapter the factors relating wages, prices, unemployment and other variables are discussed. Various explanations of the percentage change in wages are presented in the first two sections and empirical evidence is examined in Section 4.3. Since it is clear that prices and wages are interdependent a simple two-equation model of this relationship is presented in Section 4.4 and estimated in Section 4.5. These sections also serve as a prelude to Chapters 5 and 6 where larger systems of equations are considered.

Phillips (1958) suggested that in the United Kingdom a relationship exists between the percentage rate of change of money wage rates and the percentage of the labour force unemployed, and provided evidence that this curve had remained stable for the period 1861–1957. This relationship has become known as the *Phillips curve*. However, it was Lipsey (1960) who first attempted to provide a theoretical explanation of the observed relationship. Starting with the demand and supply curves for labour, with W (or wages) for the price of labour and Q the quantity supplied or demanded, he obtained Figure 4.1. The intersection of the two curves may be considered to define an equilibrium wage, W_E. Above this there is excess supply while if the wage rate is below this there is excess demand. For wage rates different from W_E there will be a tendency for the wage rate to move towards W_E. Phillips postulated that the rate of the adjustment of W is non-linearly related to the level of excess demand in such a way that the greater the excess demand the more rapid the adjustment towards the equilibrium point. Thus if d and s are the quantities demanded and supplied then the rate of change of wages, $\dot{w}$, may be given by

$$\dot{w} = f\left(\frac{d-s}{s}\right) \tag{4.1}$$

$$= \alpha\left(\frac{d-s}{s}\right)$$

if a simple proportional relationship between $\dot{w}$ and $(d-s)$ relative to s is assumed. The graph of this function is given in Figure 4.2. As Lipsey points out the advantage of Figure 4.2 over 4.1 is that even if the demand and supply curves are shifting because of exogenous factors, the relation in Figure 4.2 may be observed if the adjustment mechanism is unchanging because $\dot{w}$ depends only on the proportionate excess demand and not on the levels of d

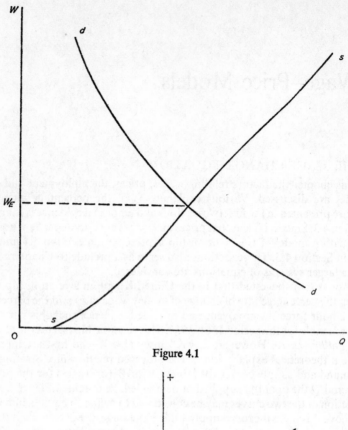

Figure 4.1

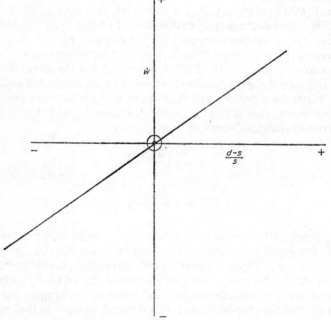

Figure 4.2

and s. Next, the relationship between excess demand and the percentage unemployment (u) is considered. At the equilibrium wage rate W_E (Figure 4.1) it is assumed that u is not zero because of the presence of frictional unemployment. If excess demand is positive then u will be below the frictional level while if excess demand is negative u will be above the frictional level. But no matter how high excess demand is, the value of u will never be zero. Thus the relationship between excess demand and u is as shown in Figure 4.3. Finally, combining

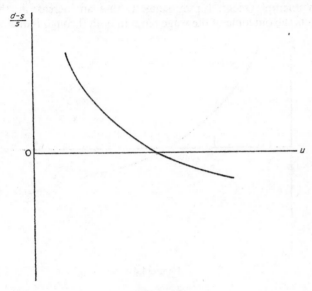

Figure 4.3

Figures 4.2 and 4.3 gives the observable relationship between $\dot{w}$ and u shown in Figure 4.4 which is the Phillips curve

$$\dot{w} = g(u). \tag{4.3}$$

One possible functional form for $g(u)$ is

$$g(u) = \gamma + \beta u^{-1} \tag{4.4}$$

which must have $\beta > 0$ for the curve to be downward sloping and must have $\gamma < 0$ if point c in Figure 4.4 occurs for a positive value of u. That is, the *a priori* restrictions on β and γ are

$$\beta > 0, \quad \gamma < 0. \tag{4.5}$$

Other possible functional forms for $g(u)$ are the linear form

$$g(u) = \gamma + \beta u \qquad (\gamma > 0, \beta < 0)$$

and the quadratic

$$g(u) = \gamma + \beta_1 u + \beta_2 u^2 \qquad (\gamma > 0, \beta_1 > 0, \beta_2 \lessgtr 0).$$

Phillips did not suggest that u explains all the variation observed in $\dot{w}$. Other variables judged to be relevant are the change in the cost of living and the change in unemployment. Lipsey suggests that an increase in the cost of living affects the outcome of the wage bargain both through inducing workers

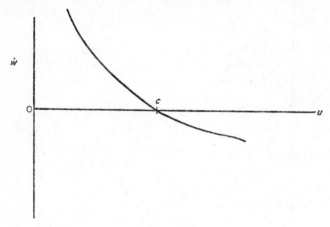

Figure 4.4

to be more aggressive in demanding wage increases and through making employers more willing to grant increases (which can be passed on as price increases). Similarly, a decrease in the cost of living acts as a damper on wage increases. If the percentage change in the cost of living is $\dot{p}$ then (4.3) is modified to

$$\dot{w} = g(u) + k\dot{p} \qquad (4.6)$$

where k is a positive constant. If k is exactly equal to unity then (4.6) is equivalent to setting the percentage change in real wages as a function of u, in contrast to (4.3) where money wages are used. If k is less than unity then workers are not fully compensated for price increases and their real wages decline.

However, Friedman (1968) argues that the Phillips curve should relate anticipated real wages and unemployment. Anticipated real wages depend on both money wages and also the expected price change $\dot{p}^*$ so that (4.6) is modified to

$$\dot{w} = g(u) + k\dot{p}^*. \qquad (4.7)$$

Turnovsky (1972) uses several assumptions about how the expected price change is determined. The simplest is

$$\dot{p}_t^* = \dot{p}_t \tag{4.8}$$

where the expected price change is the current price change. Hence (4.6) is seen to be a special case of the general Phillips curve (4.7) with expected prices determined by (4.8). To some extent (4.8) is unrealistic in that a lag occurs between a price change being recorded, indices being computed and the figures being published, so that an alternative specification is

$$\dot{p}_t^* = \dot{p}_{t-1}. \tag{4.9}$$

A third determination of expectations is provided by the *extrapolative* hypothesis

$$\dot{p}_t^* = \dot{p}_t + \theta(\dot{p}_t - \dot{p}_{t-1}) \tag{4.10}$$

which relates expected price changes to past changes, with an adjustment for recent trends. The parameter θ will be positive if the trend is extrapolated or negative if past trends are expected to be reversed. If θ is zero, (4.8) is obtained and if θ is minus one (4.9) is obtained. Since (4.10) can be written

$$\dot{p}_t^* = (1 + \theta)\dot{p}_t - \theta\dot{p}_{t-1}$$

it can be seen to be a special case of

$$\dot{p}_t^* = \lambda_0\dot{p}_t + \lambda_1\dot{p}_{t-1} + \lambda_2\dot{p}_{t-2} + \ldots \tag{4.11}$$

where the λ_i are weights which sum to unity if expectations are realised. As in Chapter 2, Section 2.4, some further assumption about the weights is necessary before (4.11) can be used. Rather than consider the various distributed lag schemes in Chapter 2, here all values of λ_i except λ_0, λ_1, and λ_2 will be always set equal to zero so that expectations about price changes will be determined by recent experience only, which seems intuitively reasonable. The general function is

$$\dot{p}_t^* = \lambda_0\dot{p}_t + \lambda_1\dot{p}_{t-1} + \lambda_2\dot{p}_{t-2} \tag{4.12}$$

with
$$\lambda_0 + \lambda_1 + \lambda_2 = 1. \tag{4.13}$$

Before considering other variables which may be included in the Phillips curve it is important to clarify the definitions of the variables $\dot{w}$ and $\dot{p}$. Lipsey (1960) argues that since theoretically $\dot{w}$ is a continuous derivative the best approximation to it using discrete observations is the *first central difference*

$$\dot{w}_t = \frac{W_{t+1} - W_{t-1}}{2W_t}. \tag{4.14}$$

Lipsey illustrates this by a diagram (see Figure 4.5) showing a continuous variable which is observed at regular intervals. The best estimate of the derivative at point 2 is the slope of the line joining 1 and 3, since the slope of the line joining 1 and 2 gives an estimate of the derivative somewhere between 1 and 2. Lipsey therefore estimates functions of the form

$$\frac{W_{t+1} - W_{t-1}}{2W_t} = g(u_t) + k\left[\frac{p_{t+1} - p_{t-1}}{2p_t}\right]. \tag{4.15}$$

Bowen and Berry (1963), however, argue that such functions introduce both a lead and a lag into the relationships between W and u. This can be shown by rewriting (4.14) as

$$\dot{w}_t = \frac{W_{t+1} - W_t + W_t - W_{t-1}}{2W_t} = \tfrac{1}{2}\left[\frac{W_{t+1} - W_t}{W_t} + \frac{W_t - W_{t-1}}{W_t}\right] \tag{4.16}$$

and from (4.15) both the wage changes from t to $t+1$ and from $t-1$ to t are affected by u_t. Therefore (4.15) is mis-specified in that the measure of unemployment, u_t, is incorrect and a more appropriate measure might be the

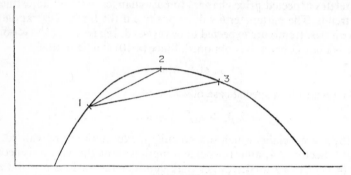

Figure 4.5

sum of u_{t+1}, u_t and u_{t-1}. As (4.16) indicates that the first central difference can be regarded as (approximately) the average of two simple differences, an alternative formulation which is suggested is

$$\frac{W_t - W_{t-1}}{W_{t-1}} = g(u_{t-1}) + k\left[\frac{p_t - p_{t-1}}{p_{t-1}}\right]. \tag{4.17}$$

In this case the wage change from $t-1$ to t is related to the value of u at time $t-1$, thus avoiding the difficulty of including a wage variable timed before u. However, (4.17) does imply a lag of one time period between W_t and u_{t-1}, or an average lag of half a period between the wage change and the unemployment measure. It has been implicitly assumed that no such lag exists, and therefore Bowen and Berry measure unemployment by the average of u_t and u_{t-1} to avoid introducing the lag. Thus (4.17) is rewritten

$$\frac{W_t - W_{t-1}}{W_{t-1}} = g\left[\frac{u_t + u_{t-1}}{2}\right] + k\left[\frac{p_t - p_{t-1}}{p_{t-1}}\right]. \tag{4.18}$$

This equation includes $(u_t + u_{t-1})$ and the question arises: does this cause statistical problems which make (4.18) more prone to autocorrelated residuals than (4.15)? The answer is that this is unlikely since only one variable, u, is averaged in (4.18) whilst in (4.15) the dependent variable and an independent variable are averaged. For brevity the variables in (4.18) are now redefined by

$$\dot{w}_t = \frac{W_t - W_{t-1}}{W_{t-1}}, \quad \bar{u}_t = \frac{u_t + u_{t-1}}{2}, \quad \dot{p}_t = \frac{p_t - p_{t-1}}{p_{t-1}} \qquad (4.19)$$

and hence (4.18) can be written

$$\dot{w}_t = g(\bar{u}_t) + k\dot{p}_t$$

or, replacing $\dot{p}$ by $\dot{p}^*$ as in (4.7),

$$\dot{w}_t = g(\bar{u}_t) + k\dot{p}_t^*. \qquad (4.20)$$

Phillips suggests that the rate of change of the demand for labour, and hence of unemployment, influences the rate of change of money wages. That is, for any given level of unemployment, if unemployment is decreasing (so that the rate of change of unemployment, $\dot{u}$, is negative), then employers will bid more for the available labour than if unemployment is increasing (and $\dot{u}$ is positive). Lipsey also suggests that Phillips implicitly considers expectations about future labour market conditions, in that employers vary the strength of their bidding according to their expected future requirements. Since the employer can adjust the employment level more easily than the wage level (and in either direction), $\dot{u}$ will be relevant. The expectations of employees will also be affected by $\dot{u}$. Thus (4.20) is modified to

$$\dot{w}_t = g(\bar{u}_t) + k\dot{p}_t^* + e\dot{u}_t \qquad (4.21)$$

where $e < 0$ and $\dot{u}$ is defined in the same way as $\dot{w}$. (In fact Lipsey himself rejects the need for $\dot{u}$ by arguing that employers can adjust immediately to the expected position by moving along the curve (4.20), and he explains deviations from (4.20) as the result of aggregation over different employment markets.)

4.2 THE EFFECTS OF DIFFERENT LABOUR MARKETS

Initially two equal sized employment markets are considered with the same form of unmodified Phillips curve (4.3)

$$\dot{w}_1 = g(u_1), \quad \dot{w}_2 = g(u_2)$$

where the subscripts refer to the markets. If u_1 and u_2 are equal then $\dot{w}_1$ and $\dot{w}_2$ are equal and the aggregate curve relating $\dot{w} = (\dot{w}_1 + \dot{w}_2)/2$ and $u = (u_1 + u_2)/2$ is $\dot{w} = g(u)$, which is the same as the curve for each market. However, suppose u_1 is greater than u_2, as in Figure 4.6, then while $u = (u_1 + u_2)/2$, the aggregate wage change is

$$\dot{w} = \frac{\dot{w}_1 + \dot{w}_2}{2} = \frac{g(u_1) + g(u_2)}{2} > g(u)$$

because of the non-linearity in the curve. Thus the aggregate wage change is greater for a given aggregate level of unemployment than if the unemployment levels in each market are the same.

Thomas and Stoney (1971) generalised the above analysis to the case of n distinct labour markets with unemployment rates $u_1, u_2, \ldots, u_n$. If the proportion of the total labour force employed in labour market i is α_i then, summing for $i = 1$ to n,

$$\Sigma\alpha_i = 1 \quad \text{and} \quad \Sigma\alpha_i u_i = u$$

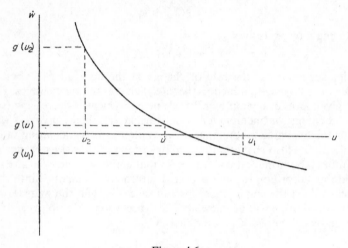

Figure 4.6

where u is the aggregate unemployment rate. For each labour market it is assumed that the local unemployment rate u_i and the aggregate expected price change p^* determine $\dot{w}_i$. Hence

$$\dot{w}_i = g(\bar{u}_i) + k\dot{p}^* \tag{4.22}$$

where time subscripts have dropped from (4.20) and where the function g and constant k are assumed to be the same for all markets. The aggregate wage change is

$$\dot{w} \equiv \Sigma\alpha_i \dot{w}_i = \Sigma\alpha_i g(\bar{u})_i + k\dot{p}^* \tag{4.23}$$

and this function could be estimated. However, Thomas and Stoney go on to consider the effects of a wage transfer mechanism between different labour markets. They argue that when trade unions are bargaining for higher wages one factor which is important is the existence of recent wage increases for comparable employees in different labour markets. They consider a transfer mechanism whereby the pressure of demand for labour in one 'leading'market causes large wage changes for that market through the Phillips curve and then spills over to other, non-leading, markets where the demand for labour is not as high. In the non-leading markets the wage change is therefore the result of two factors, the demand for labour within these markets, and an additional wage change which depends on the outcome of bargaining, in the leading market. Thus for the leading market (market *l*, say) the wage change is given by (4.22)

$$\dot{w}_l = g(\bar{u}_l) + k\dot{p}^* \tag{4.24}$$

and for the non-leading markets

$$\dot{w}_i = g(\bar{u}_i) + k\dot{p}^* + h_i(\dot{w}_l - g(\bar{u}_i) - k\dot{p}^*) \tag{4.25}$$
$$i \neq l, i = 1, \ldots, n$$

where $\dot{w}_l$ measures the wage change in the leading market and h_i is a constant. If h_i is zero then there is no transfer mechanism operating. If h_i is unity then the wage changes in the leading and non-leading markets are the same. Values of h_i between zero and unity are normally expected. The aggregate wage change will be

$$\dot{w} \equiv \Sigma\alpha_i\dot{w}_i = \Sigma\alpha_i g(\bar{u}_i) + k\dot{p}^* + \Sigma\alpha_i h_i(g(\bar{u}_l) - g(\bar{u}_i)) \tag{4.26}$$

where all the summations are for $i = 1$ to n (since $g(\bar{u}_l) - g(\bar{u}_i)$ is zero when $i = l$). Given the form of the function g, (4.26) can be estimated once the leading market is identified. Thomas and Stoney define the leading market as that market which consistently has the lowest rate of unemployment and the highest rate of wage change. All other markets are non-leading.

Thomas and Stoney develop a more general model with m leading markets in the leading sector. These markets are the ones which at some time or other have the lowest level of unemployment. If it is assumed that no transfer mechanism applies within the leading sector then the wage change equations are

$$\dot{w}_i = g(\bar{u}_i) + k\dot{p}^* \qquad (i = 1, \ldots, m) \tag{4.27}$$

for the m leading markets, with the aggregate change for these markets of

$$\dot{w}_L = \Sigma\alpha_i'\dot{w}_i = \Sigma\alpha_i'g(\bar{u}_i) + k\dot{p}^* = g(\bar{u}_L) + k\dot{p}^* \qquad (i = 1, \ldots, m) \tag{4.28}$$

where α_i' are the proportions of the labour force of the leading sector employed in market i. For the non-leading markets

$$\dot{w}_i = g(\bar{u}_i) + k\dot{p}^* + h_i(\dot{w}_L - g(\bar{u}_i) - k\dot{p}^*) \qquad (i = m + 1, \ldots, n). \tag{4.29}$$

If the transfer mechanism is assumed to operate with equal strength in each of the non-leading markets so that $h_i = h$ then (4.29) simplifies to

$$\dot{w}_i = g(\bar{u}_i) + k\dot{p}^* + h(g(\bar{u}_L) - g(\bar{u}_i)) \tag{4.30}$$

where $i = m + 1, \ldots, n$. The aggregate wage change equation is from (4.27) and (4.30)

$$\dot{w} \equiv \Sigma\alpha_i\dot{w}_i = \Sigma_1^n\alpha_i g(\bar{u}_i) + k\dot{p}^* + h\Sigma_{m+1}^n\alpha_i(g(\bar{u}_L) - g(\bar{u}_i)). \tag{4.31}$$

Comparing (4.31) and (4.23) the effect of the transfer mechanism is to add a term measuring the variation between the leading and non-leading markets to the wage change equation. Equation (4.31) can be used to obtain the estimates of the unknown parameters k and h once the form of g is specified.

The various Phillips curves discussed are listed in Table 4.1. It can be seen that the basic curve (4.7) is modified by the addition of the unemployment change variable and also by a consideration of separate labour markets. The latter version is also modified to allow for a transfer mechanism.

Table 4.1. Summary of the alternative specifications of the Phillips curves

---

(i) Basic curve:

$$\dot{w}_t = g(\bar{u}_t) + k\dot{p}_t^* \tag{4.7}$$
$$(k > 0)$$

(ii) Unemployment change version:

$$\dot{w}_t = g(\bar{u}_t) + k\dot{p}_t^* + e\dot{u}_t \tag{4.21}$$
$$(e < 0) \qquad (k > 0)$$

(iii) Several markets version:

$$\dot{w}_t = \Sigma\alpha_i g(\bar{u}_{it}) + k\dot{p}_t^* \tag{4.23}$$
$$(k > 0)$$

(iv) Several markets plus transfer mechanism:

$$\dot{w}_t = \Sigma\alpha_i g(\bar{u}_{it}) + k\dot{p}_t^* + h\Sigma^n_{m+1} \quad \alpha_i(g(\bar{u}_L) - g(\bar{u}_i)) \tag{4.31}$$

where
$$g(\bar{u}_L) = \Sigma_1^m \quad \alpha_i' g(\bar{u}_i)$$

Specification of g: $g(\bar{u}_i) = \gamma + \beta(\bar{u}_i)^{-1}$ $\qquad$ (4.32)

A priori restrictions: $\beta > 0, \gamma < 0$ $\qquad$ (4.5)

$$0 < h < 1, k > 0, e < 0,$$
$$\lambda_1 + \lambda_2 + \lambda_3 = 1 \tag{4.13}$$

4.3 THE EMPIRICAL ESTIMATION OF PHILLIPS CURVES

In this section the various wage change functions presented above are estimated using annual data for the United Kingdom. The effects of severe wage restraint by the U.K. Government were not considered and so data for 1950–66 are used, avoiding the pre-1950 and post-1966 periods of restraint, and the regressions cover 1953–66 (14 observations) to allow for lags. Another problem is the definition of the labour market. At first sight it would appear appropriate to define each industry as a labour market, since wage negotiations in the United Kingdom are generally on an industry basis. However, Archibald (1969) points out that industrial unemployment data refer to the industry of previous employment rather than the industry where employment is sought.

An alternative, which is adopted here, is to regard different geographical regions as different labour markets. This will be a better measure of the demand for labour if mobility between regions is less than mobility between industries. The variables used[1] are all annual averages of monthly data and are centred at the end of June in year t

> W – index of hourly wage rates, from *Ministry of Labour Gazette (M.L.G.)* (February 1967) p. 182, and earlier, transformed to 1955 = 100.
>
> p – index of retail prices, from *M.L.G.* (February 1967) p. 186, and earlier, transformed to 1950 = 100.
>
> u – percentage of the total labour force unemployed from *The British Economy, Key Statistics*, 1900–1966, Table E.
>
> α_i – percentage of the total labour force employed in region i, from *M.L.G.* (February 1967) and earlier.
>
> u_i – percentage of the labour force in region i which is unemployed, from *M.L.G.* (February 1967) and earlier.

The definitions of the regions are

1. London–Southern–Eastern.
2. Midlands.
3. Yorkshire–Lincolnshire.
4. South-Western.
5. North-Western.
6. Northern.
7. Scotland.
8. Wales.
9. Northern Ireland.

There are three regions – London–Southern–Eastern, Midlands and Yorkshire–Lincolnshire – which have the minimum level of unemployment at some time over the period covered and these will be regarded as the leading sectors for estimating (4.31). The data are presented in Table 4.2. For the period 1953–66 $\dot{w}$ ranges from 2·71 to 8·00 and u ranges from 1·2 to 2·6 (or $\bar{u}$ from 1·25 to 2·35), so that, if Figure 4.4 is the correct relationship between $\dot{w}$ and u, all the observations lie to the left of point c. It is therefore unlikely that point c, the level of u for which $\dot{w}$ is zero, will be determined with precision. The *a priori* constraint on (4.32) that $\gamma < 0$ may not be satisfied and yet the general shape of Figure 4.4, the basic Phillips curve, may occur.

The graph of $\dot{w}$ and $\bar{u}$ is presented in Figure 4.7. Preliminary regressions of $\dot{w} = g(\bar{u})$ suggested that the best form of the function g is (4.4)

$$g(\bar{u}_t) = \gamma + \beta(\bar{u}_t^{-1}).\tag{4.32}$$

---

[1] We are grateful to Mr P. J. M. Stoney of the University of Liverpool for giving us access to the data used by Thomas and Stoney (1971), some of which is published in their article.

Table 4.2. Data for Phillips curves estimation

	P_t	w_t	u_t	$\dot{p}_t$	$\dot{w}_t$	$\bar{u}_t^{-1}$	$\tilde{u}_t$	C_t	D_t
1950	100	73·0	1·6	—					
1951	109·1	79·2	1·3	9·10					
1952	119·1	85·7	2·2	9·17					
1953	122·8	89·7	1·8	3·11	4·67	0·500	−18·2	0·634	0·186
1954	125·1	93·6	1·5	1·87	4·35	0·606	−16·7	0·774	0·225
1955	130·7	100·0	1·2	4·48	6·84	0·741	−20·0	0·988	0·302
1956	137·2	108·0	1·3	4·97	8·00	0·800	8·3	1·033	0·292
1957	142·2	113·6	1·6	3·64	5·19	0·690	23·1	0·840	0·197
1958	146·5	117·9	2·2	3·02	3·79	0·526	37·5	0·619	0·146
1959	147·3	121·1	2·3	0·55	2·71	0·444	4·5	0·540	0·146
1960	148·8	126·3	1·7	1·02	4·29	0·500	−26·1	0·633	0·185
1961	154·0	134·3	1·6	3·49	6·33	0·606	−5·9	0·737	0·195
1962	160·4	140·5	2·1	4·16	4·62	0·541	31·3	0·624	0·156
1963	163·7	145·7	2·6	2·06	3·70	0·426	23·8	0·497	0·129
1964	169·1	153·2	1·7	3·30	5·15	0·465	−34·6	0·565	0·153
1965	177·1	162·9	1·5	4·73	6·33	0·625	−11·8	0·786	0·233
1966	184·0	173·7	1·6	3·90	6·63	0·645	6·7	0·793	0·207

Table 4.2 (*cont.*). Regional unemployment rates (u_{it})

Region

	1	2	3	4	5	6	7	8	9
1952	1·30	1·3	1·3	1·5	3·6	2·6	3·3	2·9	10·4
1953	1·25	1·0	1·0	1·6	2·1	2·4	3·1	3·0	8·1
1954	1·05	0·7	0·7	1·5	1·5	2·3	2·8	2·5	7·0
1955	0·75	0·6	0·6	1·1	1·4	1·8	2·4	1·8	6·8
1956	0·85	0·8	0·8	1·3	1·3	1·5	2·4	2·0	6·4
1957	1·10	1·1	1·1	1·8	1·6	1·7	2·6	2·6	7·3
1958	1·40	1·7	1·7	2·2	2·7	2·4	3·8	3·8	9·3
1959	1·30	1·6	1·6	2·1	2·8	3·3	4·4	3·8	7·8
1960	1·00	1·1	1·1	1·7	1·9	2·9	3·7	2·7	6·8
1961	1·05	1·2	1·2	1·4	1·6	2·5	3·2	2·6	7·5
1962	1·35	1·6	1·7	1·7	2·6	3·8	3·8	3·1	7·5
1963	1·60	1·9	2·1	2·2	3·1	5·0	4·8	3·7	8·0
1964	1·05	0·9	1·3	1·5	2·1	3·4	3·7	2·6	6·6
1965	0·90	0·9	1·1	1·6	1·6	2·6	3·0	2·6	6·1
1966	1·00	1·2	1·2	1·8	1·5	2·6	2·9	2·9	6·1

Table 4.2 (*cont.*). Regional unemployed. Weights ($100\alpha_{it}$)

Region

	1	2	3	4	5	6	7	8	9
1952	34·1	15·3	9·4	5·0	13·9	5·9	9·9	4·3	2·2
1953	34·2	15·2	9·3	5·1	13·9	5·8	9·9	4·3	2·2
1954	34·0	15·3	9·8	4·9	13·8	5·7	9·9	4·3	2·2
1955	35·0	15·1	9·7	5·3	13·2	5·6	9·7	4·4	2·2
1956	34·3	15·2	9·7	4·9	13·8	5·9	9·8	4·4	2·1
1957	35·0	15·1	9·7	5·0	13·3	5·7	9·8	4·3	2·2
1958	35·3	14·9	9·5	5·2	13·4	5·8	9·5	4·3	2·1
1959	35·7	14·7	9·4	5·5	13·0	5·8	9·6	4·3	2·1
1960	35·8	14·9	9·5	5·3	13·3	5·6	9·3	4·2	2·1
1961	34·8	15·2	9·7	5·6	13·5	5·7	9·4	4·2	2·1
1962	34·1	15·4	9·3	5·7	12·8	5·7	9·5	4·3	2·1
1963	35·3	15·7	9·3	5·5	13·0	5·6	9·4	4·2	2·1
1964	35·3	15·9	9·3	5·8	12·7	5·5	9·2	4·2	2·1
1965	35·3	15·9	8·8	5·6	12·9	5·6	9·3	4·3	2·2
1966	36·5	16·2	8·7	5·6	12·4	5·5	9·0	4·1	2·1

This form produced a higher $\bar{R}^2$ (0·69) than the linear form ($\bar{R}^2 = 0·66$) or the quadratic form ($\bar{R}^2 = 0·66$). Using (4.32) with (4.7) and (4.21) gives

$$\dot{w}_t = \gamma + \beta(\bar{u}_t)^{-1} + k\dot{p}_t^* \qquad (4.33)$$

$$\dot{w}_t = \gamma + \beta(\bar{u}_t)^{-1} + k\dot{p}_t^* + e\dot{u}_t. \qquad (4.34)$$

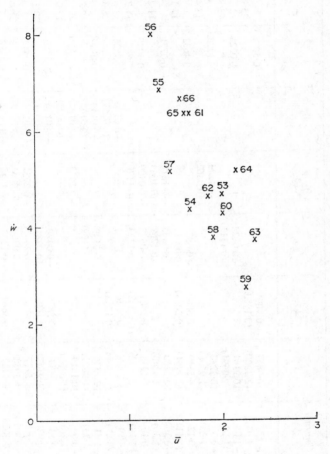

Figure 4.7. $\dot{w}$ and $\bar{u}$

Similarly, from (4.23) and (4.32),

$$\Sigma\alpha_i g(\bar{u}_{it}) = \Sigma\alpha_i(\gamma + \beta(\bar{u}_{it})^{-1}) = \gamma + \beta\Sigma\alpha_i(\bar{u}_{it})^{-1} = \gamma + \beta C_t \quad (4.35)$$

where $\qquad\qquad C_t = \Sigma\alpha_i(\bar{u}_{it})^{-1}$ for $i = 1$ to n

and hence in (4.23),

$$\dot{w}_t = \gamma + \beta C_t + k\dot{p}_t^*. \qquad (4.36)$$

Table 4.3. Estimates of (4.33) and (4.34)

Independent variables

Estimates of	Constant γ	$\bar{u}_t^{-1}$ β	$\dot{p}_t$ $k\lambda_1$	$\dot{p}_{t-1}$ $k\lambda_2$	$\dot{p}_{t-2}$ $k\lambda_3$	$\dot{u}_t$ e	k	F	$\bar{R}^2$	d
(4.39)	−0·27 (1·03)	6·6857 (2·3280)	0·5001 (0·1953)				0·5001	25·4	0·822	1·70
(4.40)	−1·06 (1·28)	10·9161 (2·0691)		−0·0224 (0·1117)			−0·0224	13·9	0·666	1·34
(4.41)	−0·33 (1·26)	10·3238 (1·9508)			−0·1223 (0·0862)		−0·1223	17·4	0·716	1·32
(4.42)	0·12 (1·11)	6·2649 (2·3791)	0·5509 (0·2033)	−0·0878 (0·0922)			0·4631	17·1	0·788	1·83
(4.43)	−0·36 (1·30)	10·1260 (2·0240)		0·0845 (0·1269)	−0·1616 (0·1063)		−0·0771	11·2	0·701	1·39
(4.44)	0·19 (1·18)	6·4938 (2·5672)	0·5001 (0·2542)	−0·0547 (0·1324)	−0·0409 (0·1120)		0·4045	11·7	0·768	1·77
(4.45)	−0·19 (0·83)	6·2061 (1·8865)	0·5626 (0·1593)			−0·0176 (0·0067)	0·5626	28·3	0·863	1·99
(4.46)	−1·21 (1·23)	10·9526 (1·9821)		0·0149 (0·1102)		−0·0144 (0·0102)	0·0149	10·8	0·693	1·31
(4.47)	−0·09 (1·10)	10·1819 (1·6902)			−0·1623 (0·0769)	−0·0184 (0·0085)	−0·1623	17·0	0·787	1·55
(4.48)	0·03 (0·92)	5·9966 (1·9747)	0·5876 (0·1691)	−0·0490 (0·0781)		−0·0166 (0·0071)	0·5386	20·1	0·854	2·24
(4.49)	−0·0680 (0·8910)	9·5427 (1·3953)		0·2437 (0·0980)	−0·2951 (0·0821)	−0·0273 (0·0078)	−0·0514	21·0	0·860	2·35
(4.50)	0·3025 (0·7724)	6·9462 (1·6891)	0·3667 (0·1708)	0·1233 (0·1000)	−0·1912 (0·0846)	−0·0242 (0·0067)	0·2988	24·4	0·900	2·93

From (4.31) and (4.32),

$$\Sigma\alpha_i(g(\bar{u}_{Lt}) - g(\bar{u}_{it})) = \Sigma\alpha_i\beta((\bar{u}_{Lt})^{-1} - (\bar{u}_{it})^{-1})$$

$$= \beta\Sigma\alpha_i((\bar{u}_{Lt})^{-1} - (\bar{u}_{it})^{-1}) = \beta D_t \qquad (4.37)$$

where $\qquad D_t = \Sigma\alpha_i((\bar{u}_{Lt})^{-1} - (\bar{u}_{it})^{-1})$ for $i = m + 1, \ldots, n,$

so with (4.35), (4.31) becomes

$$\dot{w}_t = \gamma + \beta C_t + k\dot{p}_t^* + h\beta D_t. \qquad (4.38)$$

The estimates of (4.33) and (4.34) are given in Table 4.3 for different forms of $\dot{p}^*$. As previously the standard errors are in brackets below the estimated coefficients. The estimates of k are from the estimated coefficients of $\dot{p}_t$, $\dot{p}_{t-1}$ and $\dot{p}_{t-2}$ with $\lambda_0 + \lambda_1 + \lambda_2 = 1$. None of the estimates of γ are significantly different from zero, but in each case the estimate of β is significant with the expected sign. The estimates of k, which *a priori* should be positive, vary considerably, but the negative values are associated with insignificant coefficients. If the negative k values are rejected, the best estimates of (4.33) are (4.39) and (4.42) of which (4.39) has the highest $\bar{R}^2$ and (4.42) the most satisfactory Durbin–Watson statistic. Multicollinearity is not a problem with these equations since the lowest correlation determinant is 0.2 (for (4.44)) and the standard errors are small relative to the estimated coefficients. Many of these points apply to the estimates of (4.34), also presented in Table 4.3. In terms of $\bar{R}^2$, F and the Durbin–Watson statistic the best estimate of (4.34) is (4.45). Comparing (4.45) and (4.39) the inclusion of $\dot{u}$ reduces the standard errors of the estimates of β and $k\lambda_1$, improves the Durbin–Watson statistic, and increases $\bar{R}^2$. The estimate of e is significantly negative in agreement with the *a priori* expectation. Equation (4.45) implies that if prices rise by 1 per cent then wages increase by 0.56 per cent, or price increases are not fully reflected in wage increases. Similarly for a given level of unemployment and price change, if $\dot{u}$ increases by 1 per cent then $\dot{w}$ reduces by 0.0176 per cent. As mentioned in Chapter 1, Section 1.3, autocorrelation can appear to occur if there is a specification error in the equation (such as use of the wrong mathematical form or the exclusion of an important variable). Alternatively, the disturbances may be truly non-random. With (4.50) a possible mis-specification is the omission of a variable measuring the dispersion of unemployment between markets. If this possibility is ignored (for the moment) and the residuals are assumed to be first-order autocorrelated then Durbin's method can be applied. The transformed equation is

$$\dot{w}_t = \gamma(1 - \rho) + \rho\dot{w}_{t-1} + \beta(\bar{u}_t)^{-1} - \beta\rho(\bar{u}_{t-1})^{-1} + k\lambda_0\dot{p}_t$$

$$+ (k\lambda_1 - \rho k\lambda_0)\dot{p}_{t-1} + (k\lambda_2 - \rho k\lambda_1)\dot{p}_{t-2}$$

$$- \rho k\lambda_2\dot{p}_{t-3} + e\dot{u}_t - \rho e\dot{u}_{t-1} + \varepsilon_t$$

where ρ is the first-order autocorrelation coefficient. When this equation is estimated the coefficient of $\dot{w}_{t-1}$ is -0.72 so that the transformed variables are

$$\dot{w}_t' = \dot{w}_t + 0.72\dot{w}_{t-1}, \; (\bar{u}_t^{-1})' = \bar{u}_t^{-1} + 0.72\bar{u}_{t-1}^{-1}, \text{ etc.}$$

The equation to be estimated is

$$\dot{w}_t' = \gamma(1 - \rho) + \beta(\bar{u}_t^{-1})' + k\lambda_0 \dot{p}_t' + k\lambda_1 \dot{p}_{t-1}' + k\lambda_2 \dot{p}_{t-2}' + e\dot{u}_t'$$

and the estimate is

$$\dot{w}_t' = 0.8282 + 6.3978(\bar{u}_t^{-1})' + 0.3852\dot{p}_t'$$
$$\quad\;\; (0.5775) \quad (0.8291) \qquad\quad (0.1002)$$

$$+0.1938\dot{p}_{t-1}' - 0.2355\dot{p}_{t-2}' - 0.0290\dot{u}_t'$$
$$\quad (0.0929) \qquad\;\; (0.0574) \qquad\;\; (0.0044)$$

$$\bar{R}^2 = 0.978, \; d = 3.09, \; F = 107.0.$$

This equation is no better than (4.50) since the Durbin–Watson statistic is not improved. The assumption of first-order autocorrelation of the residuals of (4.50) must be rejected and a mis-specification of the function is suspected. It should be noted that there are only 14 observations and that the removal of autocorrelation with a small sample is generally difficult.

The several markets version of the Phillips curve (4.23) and the version with the transfer mechanism were also estimated with the same $\dot{p}^*$ definitions as in Table 4.3. In each case where $\dot{p}_t$ was absent from an equation the estimate of k became negative and so these equations are not reported. The remaining equations are in Table 4.4. Again the estimate of γ is not significantly different from zero, and the estimate of β, the coefficient of C, which measures the variation of unemployment between the different markets, is positive. Considering (4.51)–(4.53) the estimates of k are $0.5230, 0.4824$ and 0.3756 which satisfy the *a priori* expectations, and the estimates of β are significantly positive. Multicollinearity is not a problem and the most satisfactory equation is (4.52), with $\bar{R}^2 = 0.813$ and the Durbin–Watson statistic $= 1.87$. Comparing this with the basic Phillips curve with the same $\dot{p}^*$, (4.42), the slightly higher $\bar{R}^2$ of (4.52) is the only important difference. The conclusion is that the several markets version of the Phillips curve is a small improvement on the basic Phillips curve. However, when the several markets version and the unemployment change version are compared, the latter is superior in each case in terms of $\bar{R}^2$ and is therefore preferred.

The inclusion of the transfer mechanism as in (4.54)–(4.56) produces disappointing results. The only significant coefficients are those of $\dot{p}_t$. Multicollinearity is serious since the correlation determinants are low ($0.05, 0.05$ and 0.02) with the correlation between C_t and D_t being 0.95, and the estimate of β changes dramatically when D_t is included in the equation. The $\bar{R}^2$ values are no improvement on (4.52). The estimates of h, from $h\beta \div \beta$ are all greater than 10 instead of satisfying $0 < h < 1$, and they imply that non-leading

Table 4.4. Estimates of (4.36) and (4.38)

Independent variables

Estimates of	Constant γ	C_t β	$\hat{p}_t$ $k\lambda_1$	$\hat{p}_{t-1}$ $k\lambda_2$	$\hat{p}_{t-2}$ $k\lambda_3$	D_t $h\beta$	F	$\bar{R}^2$	d
(4.51)	0·12 (0·81)	4·7399 (1·4508)	0·5230 (0·1732)				29·3	0·813	1·66
(4.52)	0·47 (0·88)	4·4792 (1·4734)	0·5690 (0·1791)	−0·0866 (0·0863)			19·9	0·813	1·87
(4.53)	0·59 (0·92)	4·8257 (1·5957)	0·4755 (0·2289)	−0·0273 (0·1238)	−0·0725 (0·1055)		14·2	0·803	1·80
(4.54)	0·45 (0·87)	1·0942 (3·9167)	0·5638 (0·1779)			11·0255 (11·0027)	19·9	0·813	1·82
(4.55)	0·74 (0·94)	1·1479 (3·9506)	0·6028 (0·1845)	−0·0797 (0·0874)		10·1377 (11·1394)	14·9	0·810	2·07
(4.56)	0·99 (0·97)	0·6457 (3·9925)	0·4769 (0·2252)	0·0089 (0·1259)	−0·1056 (0·1078)	13·2027 (11·5946)	12·0	0·809	2·24

markets have larger wage increases than leading markets, in contradiction to the definitions of leading and non-leading markets. Thomas and Stoney (1971) found their estimates of h were greater than 1 and suggest this may reflect data inadequacies, particularly in the measures of dispersion by labour markets.

When the various Phillips curves are compared the best one is probably (4.45), the unemployment change equation with expected price changes measured by $\dot{p}_t$. A problem which arises is the interdependence of $\dot{w}$ and $\dot{p}$. The discussion has ignored the possibility of wages and prices having a two-way causality. That is, wage changes causing price changes which cause wage changes. This similtaneity of prices and wages is the subject matter of the rest of this chapter.

4.4 WAGE–PRICE SYSTEMS

A price equation at the macro-economic level is now considered. The approach adopted is based on Lipsey and Parkin (1970), and it is assumed that, per unit of output

$$\text{price} = \text{costs} + \text{profit}.$$

Costs can be allocated to three components: labour, capital and imported materials. Other material costs will be reflected in labour and capital costs at the macro-economic level. If profits are a proportionate mark-up on price then

$$P = WL + RK + MT + AP \qquad (4.57)$$

where
P = price per unit of output
W = wages per unit of labour
L = labour input per unit of output
R = cost per unit of capital services
K = capital services per unit of output
M = price per unit of imported materials
T = imported materials input per unit of output
A = proportionate mark-up for profits.

It will be assumed that K, T and A are constants, so that techniques are fixed and no technical progress occurs, and also the mark-up is fixed. If the *ex ante* expectations about W, L, R and M are W^*, L^*, R^* and M^* then

$$P_t = W_t^* L_t^* + R_t^* K + M_t^* T + AP_t$$

and differentiating with respect to time gives

$$\dot{P}_t = \dot{W}_t^* L_t^* + W_t^* \dot{L}_t^* + \dot{R}_t^* K + \dot{M}_t^* T + A\dot{P}_t$$

or, dividing by P_t and re-organising the right-hand side,

$$\frac{\dot{P}_t}{P_t} = \frac{\dot{W}_t^*}{W_t^*}\left[\frac{L_t^* W_t^*}{P_t}\right] + \frac{\dot{L}_t^*}{L_t}\left[\frac{W_t^* L_t^*}{P_t}\right] + \frac{\dot{R}_t^*}{R_t}\left[\frac{R_t K}{P_t}\right] + \frac{\dot{M}_t^*}{M_t^*}\left[\frac{TM_t^*}{P_t}\right] + \frac{A\dot{P}_t}{P_t}.$$

If small letters are used to represent proportional rates of change then

$$(1 - A)\dot{p}_t = \left[\frac{L_t^* W_t^*}{P_t}\right] \dot{w}_t^* + \left[\frac{W_t^* L_t^*}{P_t}\right] \dot{i}_t^* + \left[\frac{KR_t^*}{P_t}\right] \dot{r}_t^* + \left[\frac{TM_t^*}{P_t}\right] \dot{m}_t^*.$$

Let

$$a_1' = \frac{L_t^* W_t^*}{P_t}, \quad a_1' = \frac{KR_t^*}{P_t}, \quad a_3' = \frac{TM_t^*}{P_t}$$

which are the proportion of price consisting of labour costs, capital costs and imported material costs. It is now assumed that these are constants, and if a_i are defined by

$$a_i = a_i'/(1 - A) \text{ for } i = 1, 2, 3,$$

then

$$\dot{p}_t = a_1 \dot{w}_t^* + a_1 \dot{i}_t^* + a_2 \dot{r}_t^* + a_3 \dot{m}_t^*.$$

Finally, $\dot{i}_t^*$ which is the proportionate change in labour input per unit of output, can be replaced by $-\dot{q}_t^*$, the negative of the proportionate change in output per head, and a constant term, a_0, can be included to allow for differences in units of measurement of the variables so that

$$\dot{p}_t = a_0 + a_1 \dot{w}_t^* + a_2 \dot{r}_t^* + a_3 \dot{m}_t^* + a_4 \dot{q}_t^* \tag{4.58}$$

where $a_4 = -a_1$. The expectations about the a_i values are

$$a_1 > 0, \, a_2 > 0, \, a_3 > 0, \, a_4 < 0, \, a_4 = -a_1. \tag{4.59}$$

It is now assumed that

$$\dot{r}_t^* = \dot{r}_{t-1}, \, \dot{m}_t^* = \dot{m}_{t-1}, \, \dot{q}_t^* = \dot{q}_{t-1} \tag{4.60}$$

so that expectations on these variables are based on the immediate past values. For $\dot{w}^*$, two alternative forms are considered. The first is

$$\dot{w}_t^* = \dot{w}_{t-1} \tag{4.61}$$

which is the same as (4.60), and the second is

$$\dot{w}_t^* = \dot{w}_t \tag{4.62}$$

in which expectations are determined by the current rate of change, or, expectations are fully realised. The two alternatives (4.61) and (4.62) result in different price change equations and these are taken in turn with a wage change equation.

From (4.58), (4.60) and (4.61),

$$\dot{p}_t = a_0 + a_1 \dot{w}_{t-1} + a_2 \dot{r}_{t-1} + a_3 \dot{m}_{t-1} + a_4 \dot{q}_{t-1} \tag{4.63}$$

in which the current rate of price change depends on past values of the other variables. The wage change equation to be used is the general form of (4.45),

$$\dot{w}_t = b_0 + b_1(\bar{u}_t)^{-1} + b_2\dot{p}_t + b_3\dot{u}_t \tag{4.64}$$

where the expected signs of the b_i are

$$b_1 > 0, \ b_2 > 0, \ b_3 < 0. \tag{4.65}$$

The equations (4.63) and (4.64) are now assumed to involve two endogenous variables, $\dot{p}_t$ and $\dot{w}_t$, and six predetermined variables consisting of one lagged endogenous variable, $\dot{w}_{t-1}$, and five exogenous variables. If this assumption is not made and, for example, it is assumed that u and $\dot{u}$ are jointly determined with $\dot{p}$ and $\dot{w}$, then more equations are required to explain wage-price behaviour.

Equations (4.63) and (4.64) represent a special case of simultaneous equation systems in which the equations are said to be *recursive*.[1] The pattern of causation between the endogenous variables can be traced:

$$\dot{w}_{t-1} \rightarrow \quad \dot{p}_t \quad \rightarrow \dot{w}_t$$
$$\quad\quad (4.63) \quad\quad (4.64)$$

and so it is in order to estimate (4.63) and (4.64) by ordinary least squares (OLS). The structural parameters can therefore be estimated.

When wage change expectations are determined by (4.62), then with (4.58) and (4.60),

$$\dot{p}_t = a_0 + a_1\dot{w}_t + a_2\dot{r}_{t-1} + a_3\dot{m}_{t-1} + a_4\dot{q}_{t-1}. \tag{4.66}$$

Taking this with (4.64) it can be seen that $\dot{p}_t$ depends on $\dot{w}_t$ and also $\dot{w}_t$ depends on $\dot{p}_t$. The two equations are closely interrelated and estimation of each equation by OLS will result in biased estimates of the parameters. This is because one of the assumptions of OLS is that the independent variables and the error terms should be uncorrelated, and this is not the case here. For example, if ε_1 and ε_2 are the error terms in (4.64) and (4.66), from (4.66) $\dot{p}$ and $\dot{w}$ are correlated. Similarly, from (4.64) $\dot{w}$ and ε_1 are correlated and hence $\dot{p}$ (an independent variable) and ε_1 in (4.64) are correlated. The resulting OLS estimates will be biased and inconsistent.

An alternative method of estimation to OLS is indirect least squares (ILS). If (4.66) is substituted into (4.64) then

$$\dot{w}_t = \frac{1}{(1 - a_1b_2)} \{b_0 + b_2a_0 + b_1(\bar{u}_t)^{-1} + a_2b_2\dot{r}_{t-1} + a_3b_2\dot{m}_{t-1}$$
$$+ a_4b_2\dot{q}_{t-1} + b_3\dot{u}_t\} \tag{4.67}$$

and substituting from (4.64) into (4.66) gives

$$\dot{p}_t = \frac{1}{(1 - a_1b_2)} \{a_0 + a_1b_0 + a_1b_1(\bar{u}_t)^{-1} + a_1b_3\dot{u}_t + a_2\dot{r}_{t-1}$$
$$+ a_3\dot{m}_{t-1} + a_4\dot{q}_{t-1}\}. \tag{4.68}$$

---

[1] See Johnston (1972), pp. 377–80 for a discussion of recursive systems and their estimation. See also Chapter 5, Section 5.3.

These are the *reduced form* equations, in which the current endogenous variables depend only on exogenous variables. The method of ILS involves estimating the reduced form equations by OLS. The problem, however, is that even if (4.67) and (4.68) are estimated by OLS it is not possible to use the estimated coefficients to determine the structural parameters in (4.64) and (4.66). This is because the system of equations is overidentified (see Chapter 5, Section 5.3).

A third method of estimation of (4.64) and (4.66) is two-stage least squares (2SLS). The problem of the simultaneity between $\dot{p}_t$ and $\dot{w}_t$ is resolved by obtaining the reduced form equations (4.67) and (4.68) and estimating them by OLS as the first stage. The second stage then uses the predicted value of $\dot{p}_t$, $\hat{\dot{p}}_t$ from (4.68) in (4.64), and the predicted value of $\dot{w}_t$, $\hat{\dot{w}}_t$, from (4.67) in (4.66) to give

$$\dot{w}_t = b_0 + b_1(\bar{u}_t)^{-1} + b_2\hat{\dot{p}}_t + b_3\dot{u}_t \qquad (4.69)$$

$$\dot{p}_t = a_0 + a_1\hat{\dot{w}}_t + a_2\dot{r}_{t-1} + a_3\dot{m}_{t-1} + a_4\dot{q}_{t-1} \qquad (4.70)$$

and these are estimated by OLS as the second stage. This procedure is intended to remove the effect of the error terms on the endogenous variables. From (4.69) and (4.70) the structural parameters of the original equations are easily obtained. The 2SLS estimates are consistent but are biased in small samples.

Other methods of estimation are available which allow for the interdependence of systems of equations and references to them are included in Section 4.6 of this chapter and also Chapter 5, Section 5.3. It is also possible to impose the restriction $a_4 = -a_1$ in the estimation of the price change equation. This is not done here, but the estimates of a_4 and a_1 are to be compared in the next section as a check on whether this restriction is satisfied.

4.5 EMPIRICAL ESTIMATION OF THE WAGE–PRICE SYSTEMS

The wage–price systems discussed above are estimated in this section using annual data for the United Kingdom for 1953–66. The variables $\dot{w}$, $\dot{p}$, $\bar{u}$ and $\dot{u}$ are as defined in Section 4.3 and listed in Table 4.2. The additional variables for the price change equation are

Q – Industrial production per employee from *The British Economy: Key Statistics 1900–1966 (K.S.)*, Table C,

R – Rate of interest (per cent) on $2\frac{1}{2}$ per cent Consols from *K.S.*, Table M,

M – Index of the price of imports of goods and services (1958 = 100), from the *Blue Book 1967*, Table 16.

and these are presented in Table 4.5, together with their percentage changes and two variables required in the 2SLS estimation. The yield on Consols measures the general level of interest rates and is assumed to be correlated with the user of cost of capital. It was not thought necessary to adjust this for tax allowances, depreciation and capital gains (as in Chapter 2, Section 2.3). The

Table 4.5 Additional Data Required for Estimation of a Price Change Equation

	Q_t	R_t	M_t	$\hat{q}_t$	r_t	$\hat{m}_t$	$\hat{w}_t$	$\hat{p}_t$
1951	89	3·78	112					
1952	88	4·23	110	-1·12	11·90	-1·79		
1953	92	4·08	99	4·55	-3·55	-10·00	4·60	2·71
1954	96	3·75	99	4·35	-8·09	0·00	4·23	1·46
1955	98	4·17	102	2·08	11·20	0·00	6·91	3·96
1956	98	4·73	103	0·00	13·43	3·03	7·73	5·40
1957	99	4·98	105	1·02	5·29	0·98	6·08	4·34
1958	100	4·98	100	1·01	0·00	1·94	4·25	3·08
1959	105	4·82	100	5·00	-3·21	-4·76	3·01	1·33
1960	109	5·42	101	3·81	12·45	0·00	4·89	2·51
1961	109	6·20	101	0·00	14·39	1·00	5·97	3·82
1962	111	5·98	101	1·83	-3·55	0·00	4·40	3·17
1963	116	5·58	104	4·50	-6·69	0·00	3·11	1·84
1964	123	6·03	107	6·03	8·06	2·97	5·05	2·71
1965	125	6·42	108	1·63	6·47	2·88	6·51	4·13
1966	124	6·80	110	-0·80	5·92	1·85	5·86	3·86

measure of import prices includes goods and services and so does not correspond directly with the cost of imported materials.

For the recursive system (4.63) and (4.64) the OLS estimates are

$$\dot{p}_t = -1.71 + 0.7427\dot{w}_{t-1} + 0.0017\dot{r}_{t-1} + 0.1781\dot{m}_{t-1} + 0.3921\dot{q}_{t-1}$$
$$\quad\; (1.44)\;\; (0.2401) \qquad (0.0427) \qquad (0.0684) \qquad (0.1453)$$
$$\tag{4.71}$$
$$\bar{R}^2 = 0.648,\; F = 6.97,\; \text{c.d.} = 0.20,\; d = 2.04$$
$$\dot{w}_t = -0.19 + 6.2061(\bar{u}_t)^{-1} + 0.5626\dot{p}_t - 0.0176\dot{u}_t \quad (4.72)$$
$$\quad\;\; (0.83)\;\; (1.8865) \qquad\quad (0.1593) \qquad (0.0067)$$
$$\bar{R}^2 = 0.863,\; F = 28.3,\; \text{c.d.} = 0.49,\; d = 1.99.$$

The price change equation (4.71) is satisfactory in terms of $\bar{R}^2$, autocorrelation and multicollinearity, but when conditions (4.59) are considered, the estimated coefficient of $\dot{q}_{t-1}$ is significantly positive, whereas it is expected to be significantly negative. That is, (4.71) implies an increase in output per employee leads to an increase in prices. Also the estimated coefficient of $\dot{r}_{t-1}$ is not significantly different from zero. The wage change equation is identical to (4.45) and is acceptable. The recursive system (4.63) and (4.64) does not therefore result in estimates which can be accepted.

When expected wage changes are given by (4.61) the OLS estimate of the wage change equation is (4.72), and the corresponding estimate of the price change equation (4.66) is

$$\dot{p}_t = -0.20 + 0.6714\dot{w}_t + 0.0222\dot{r}_{t-1} + 0.0829\dot{m}_{t-1} - 0.0788\dot{q}_{t-1}$$
$$\quad\; (0.87)\;\; (0.1883) \qquad (0.0359) \qquad (0.0689) \qquad (0.1312)$$
$$\tag{4.73}$$
$$\bar{R}^2 = 0.699,\; F = 8.53,\; \text{c.d.} = 0.34,\; d = 1.80.$$

As with (4.71), this equation is satisfactory in so far as $\bar{R}^2$, autocorrelation and multicollinearity are concerned, but here only the estimated coefficient of $\dot{w}_t$ is significantly positive. The other estimated coefficients have the correct signs but are also close to zero. It is clear that the restriction $a_4 = -a_1$ is not satisfied. Since the estimated coefficients are all subject to bias and inconsistency these OLS estimates of the structural equations (4.64) and (4.66) are not acceptable.

As shown above, the ILS estimates of (4.64) do not allow the structural parameters to be estimated and so ILS is an inappropriate method of estimation. However, since the reduced form equations (4.67) and (4.68) are required for 2SLS they are now presented:

$$\dot{w}_t = -0.45 + 9.4501(\bar{u}_t)^{-1} + 0.0231\dot{r}_{t-1} + 0.1454\dot{m}_{t-1}$$
$$\quad\;\; (0.88)\;\; (1.6094) \qquad\quad (0.0281) \qquad (0.0504)$$
$$\quad\quad + 0.03676\dot{q}_{t-1} - 0.0192\dot{u}_t \tag{4.74}$$
$$\quad\quad\;\; (0.1110) \qquad\; (0.0096)$$
$$\bar{R}^2 = 0.841,\; F = 14.8,\; \text{c.d.} = 0.27,\; d = 1.52$$

$$\dot{p}_t = -0.81 + 6.7374(\bar{u}_t)^{-1} - 0.0039\dot{u}_t + 0.0314\dot{r}_{t-1}$$
$$(1.30)\ (2.3858)\qquad\qquad (0.0142)\quad (0.0416)$$

$$+\ 0.1719\dot{m}_{t-1} - 0.0105\dot{q}_{t-1} \qquad\qquad (4.75)$$
$$(0.0747)\qquad (0.1646)$$

$$\bar{R}^2 = 0.591,\ F = 4.76,\ \text{c.d.} = 0.27,\ d = 1.10.$$

Equations (4.74) and (4.75) show the predicted values, $\hat{w}_t$ and $\hat{p}_t$ for the 2SLS estimates, and these are included in Table 4.5. The 2SLS estimates are, from (4.69) and (4.70):

$$\dot{w}_t = -0.26 + 4.0124(\bar{u}_t)^{-1} + 0.8226\hat{\dot{p}}_t - 0.0192\dot{u}_t \qquad (4.76)$$
$$(1.24)\quad (3.3116)\qquad\qquad (0.3239)\quad\ (0.0095)$$

$$\dot{p}_t = -0.17 + 0.6650\hat{\dot{w}}_t + 0.0227\dot{r}_{t-1} + 0.0838\dot{m}_{t-1} - 0.0764\dot{q}_{t-1}$$
$$(0.94)\quad (0.2077)\qquad (0.0366)\qquad (0.0700)\qquad\ (0.1347)$$
$$(4.77)$$

In (4.76) the estimated coefficients of $\hat{\dot{p}}$ and $\dot{u}$ are significant and have the correct sign whilst the estimated coefficient of $\bar{u}^{-1}$ has the correct sign but is not significant. Comparing the equation with the OLS estimate (4.72) the coefficients and standard errors are different suggesting that the OLS results are misleading. Equation (4.77) is less satisfactory since only the coefficient of $\hat{\dot{w}}$ is significant and the restriction $a_4 = -a_1$ is not satisfied. This result is very similar to the OLS estimate (4.73) except that the 2SLS standard errors are larger.

Of these systems estimates, the best one is the 2SLS. However, even for this the price change equation is not completely satisfactory and it may be that different assumptions in the mark-up equation (4.57) would produce better results. It is also important to remember that, while the 2SLS estimates are consistent and OLS are not, consistency is a large sample property and does not imply anything about the small sample properties of the estimator.

4.6 FURTHER READING

There has been an enormous volume of material published in recent years relating to wage-price models. The main references are mentioned in the preceding sections and only a selection of the more important omissions are included here.

The basic Phillips curve has been subjected to many criticisms. Corry and Laidler (1967) argue that the trade-off between unemployment and inflation is not necessarily of the form shown in Figure 4.3. This is because unemployment depends on both the number of quits per time interval and the average time spent between jobs. If the excess demand for labour is high there may be a movement towards more congenial jobs so that the number of quits increases with the excess demand for labour. Thus unemployment may *increase* with the excess demand for labour.

Peston (in Johnson and Nobay, 1971) finds the Phillips curve a difficult relationship to explain, particularly at the micro-economic level. He also points out that Phillips's original curve which was estimated for 1861–1913 gave a close fit for both 1913–48 and 1948–57, and is therefore remarkably stable in the face of the changes in the United Kingdom economy over that period. Holt (1969), however, derives a Phillips curve from considering the behaviour of individual workers. Each unemployed worker is assumed to have an acceptance wage which is the minimum he will accept. As the length of time he is unemployed increases, the acceptance wage declines. By making assumptions about productivity and expectations, the change in wages is related to the level of unemployment. The most comprehensive discussion of the micro-economic theory of inflation is in the volume edited by Phelps (1970).

More general reviews of wage–price models are provided by Perry (1966), Bowen (1960) and Bodkin *et al.* (1966). Perry develops the wage-change equation term by term and examines the predictive ability of his final equation. He also estimates a five-equation wage–price–profit sub-system and considers its dynamic properties. Bowen's study is particularly strong on the discussion of the theoretical role of productivity, excess demand, profits, prices and wage comparisons in the wage equation. Bodkin *et al.* provide an international comparison of empirical results as well as a discussion of the implications of the Phillips curve for Canada.

The definition of the variables is a major problem in wage–price model estimation. Bowen and Berry (1963) discuss the problem of the correct alignment of observations with respect to three possible methods – the wage-lag method, using u_t, $u_t - u_{t-1}$ and $(w_{t+1} - w_t)/w_t$, the first central difference method, using u_t, $(u_{t+1} - u_{t-1})/2$, and $(w_{t+1} - w_{t-1})/2w_{t-1}$, and the averaged unemployment method using $(u_t + u_{t+1})/2$, $u_{t+1} - u_t$ and $(w_{t+1} - w_t)/w_t$. They explain their preference for the last of these methods and present comparative results for that and the second method. Taylor (1970) shows that for the United States the recorded unemployment figures underestimate the amount of unemployment because of labour hoarding and hidden unemployment. Labour hoarding occurs when employed labour is underutilised, whilst hidden unemployment occurs when, for example, married women become unemployed and leave the labour force. Taylor concludes that labour hoarding is quantitatively important whereas hidden unemployment is not. Brownlie and Hampton (1967) estimate a Phillips curve for New Zealand and because of the low level of unemployment (below 0·1 per cent) and the high level of vacancies (greater than 2·2 per cent) the specified relationship is between $\dot{w}$ and the percentage of vacancies.

Other variables have been suggested for inclusion in the Phillips curve. Lipsey and Steuer (1961) consider the role of profits in the wage-change equation for the United Kingdom. When a profits variable is included with unemployment in the equation it is generally found to be insignificant at both the industry level and the aggregate level for 1949–58. Vanderkamp (1972) extends the Phillips curve to include a productivity variable which is the deviation in aggregate labour productivity from its trend value. This is thought to measure excess demand in the firm. Kuh (1967) argues that empirically the Phillips curves does not exist for the United States. He suggests that the level of wage rates is determined by the marginal value productivity of labour and develops a distributed lag model which is superior to the Phillips curve. Agarwala *et al.* (1972) also doubt the value of the Phillips curve. They are interested in the factors which determine wages and prices in the long run and which therefore determine the equilibrium point, rather than the adjustments towards the equilibrium point. They report equations explaining real wages and the money value of gross national product. Pierson (1968) splits data for the United States between those sectors with strong unions (which have a high percentage of unionisation of workers) and weak unions, and finds that there is an important spill-over effect from the strong to weak unions. Hines (1969) uses the change in trade union membership as a proxy for union pushfulness with U.K. data, and finds it is significant in equations explaining wage increases at the sector level.

Several studies have recognised the interdependence of wages and prices and have therefore dealt with systems of equations. Dicks-Mireaux (1961) estimates a two-equation model by 2SLS with the change in wages being dependent on price changes, productivity changes and a special variable measuring the level of the pressure of demand for labour. His price change equation has wage changes, productivity changes and past changes in import prices as explanatory variables. Klein and Ball (1959) estimate a four-equation wage–price system by the limited information maximum likelihood method. Their equations determine the change in weekly wage rates, the gap between weekly earnings and weekly wage rates, the hours worked and the consumers' price index. Hines (1964) uses OLS and 2SLS to estimate a three-equation system in which the change in wages is explained by past changes in prices, unemployment, and both the level and rate of change of union membership. The second equation explains price changes, and the third explains the change in union membership in terms of the level of union membership, past price changes and past profits. Black and Kelejian (1970) use 2SLS to estimate a five-equation model of the United States labour market. The demand for labour and the demand for man-hours are determined from profit maximisation subject to a C.E.S. production function. The wage change equation includes unemployment, price changes, the marginal productivity of labour (derived from the C.E.S. function), and a variable reflecting changes in the distribution of output between one-digit industries. The final two equations determine the supply of primary labour force workers and the supply of secondary labour force workers.

Finally, Laden (1972) discusses average cost (or mark-up) pricing and perfectly competitive pricing, and in an empirical study of United States manufacturing industry for 1954–66 finds that the results are consistent with average cost pricing but not with the perfectly competitive market model.

4.7 REFERENCES

Agarwala, R. *et al.* (1972), 'A Neoclassical Approach to the Determination of Prices and Wages', *Economica*, N.S., vol. 39, 250–63.

Archibald, G. C. (1969), 'The Phillips Curve and the Distribution of Unemployment', *American Economic Review Proceedings*, vol. 59, 124–34.

Black, S. W. and Kelejian, H. H. (1970), 'A Macro Model of the U.S. Labour Market', *Econometrica*, vol. 38, 712–41.

Bodkin, R. G. *et al.* (1966), 'Price Stability and High Employment: The Options for Canadian Economic Policy' (Ottawa: The Economic Council of Canada.)

Bowen, W. G. (1960), *The Wage–Price Issue: A Theoretical Analysis* (Princeton: Princeton University Press).

Bowen, W. G. and Berry, R. A. (1963), 'Unemployment Conditions and Movements of the Money Wage Level', *Review of Economics and Statistics*, vol. 55, 163–72.

Brownlie, A. D. and Hampton, P. (1967), 'An Econometric Study of Wage Determination in New Zealand', *International Economic Review*, vol. 8, 327–34.

Corry, B. and Laidler, D. (1967), 'The Phillips Relation: A Theoretical Explanation', *Economica*, N.S., vol. 34, 189–97.

Dicks-Mireaux, L. A. (1961), 'The Interrelationship Between Cost and Price Changes, 1946–59: A Study of Inflation in Post-war Britain', *Oxford Economic Papers*, vol. 13, 267–92.

Friedman, M. (1968), 'The Role of Monetary Policy', *American Economic Review*, vol. 58, 1–17.

Hines, A. G. (1964), 'Trade Unions and Wage Inflation in the U.K. 1893–1961', *Review of Economic Studies*, vol. 31, 221–51.

Hines, A. G. (1969), 'Wage Inflation in the U.K. 1948–1962: A Disaggregated Study', *Economic Journal*, vol. 79, 66–89.

Holt, C. C. (1969), 'Improving the Labour Market Trade Off between Inflation and Unemployment', *American Economic Review Proceedings*, vol. 59, 135–46.

Johnson, H. G. and Nobay, A. R. (eds.) (1971), *The Current Inflation* (London: Macmillan).

Johnston, J. (1972), *Econometric Methods*, 2nd ed. (New York: McGraw-Hill).

Klein, L. R. and Ball, R. J. (1959), 'Some Econometrics of the Determination of Absolute Prices and Wages', *Economic Journal*, vol. 69, 465–82.

Kuh, E. (1967), 'A Productivity Theory of Wage Levels: An Alternative to the Phillips Curve', *Review of Economic Studies*, vol. 34, 333–60.

Laden, B. E. (1972), 'Perfect Competition, Average Cost Pricing and the Price Equation', *Review of Economics and Statistics*, vol. 54, 84–8.

Lipsey, R. G. (1960), 'The Relation Between Unemployment and the Rate of Change of Money Wage Rates in the U.K. 1862–1957: A Further Analysis', *Economica*, N.S., vol. 27, 1–31.

Lipsey, R. G. and Parkin, J. M. (1970), 'Incomes Policy: A Reappraisal', *Economica*, N.S., vol. 37, 115–38.

Lipsey, R. G. and Steuer, M. D. (1961), 'The Relation Between Profits and Wage Rates', *Economica*, N.S., vol. 28, 137–55.

Perry, G. L. (1966), *Unemployment, Money Wage Rates and Inflation* (Boston: The M.I.T. Press).

Phelps, E. S. (1970), *Microeconomic Foundations of Employment and Inflation Theory* (New York: Norton).

Phillips, A. W. (1958), 'The Relationship Between Unemployment and the Rate of Change of Money Wage Rates in the U.K., 1861–1957', *Economica*, N.S., vol. 25, 283–99.

Pierson, G. (1968), 'The Effect of Union Strength on the U.S. Phillips Curve', *American Economic Review*, vol. 58, 456–67.

Taylor, J. (1970), 'Hidden Unemployment, Hoarded Labour and the Phillips Curve', *Southern Economic Journal*, vol. 37, 1–16.

Thomas, R. L. and Stoney, P. J. M. (1971), 'Unemployment Dispersion as a Determinant of Wage Inflation in the U.K., 1925–1966', *Manchester School*, vol. 39, 83–116.

Turnovsky, S. J. (1972), 'The Expectations Hypothesis and the Aggregate Wage Equation: Some Empirical Evidence for Canada', *Economica*, N.S., vol. 39, 1–17.

Vanderkamp, J. (1972), 'Wage Adjustment, Productivity and Price Change Expectations', *Review of Economic Studies*, vol. 39, 61–72.

5. Macro-economic Models I: The Specification Problem and Related Issues

5.1 INTRODUCTION

In Chapter 4, Section 4.4, a two-equation wage–price model is discussed which extends the single-equation models of the preceding sections, in which wage change is shown to be a function of price change and unemployment, to suggest that wage changes also contribute towards price changes so that prices and wages become *jointly dependent*. This reflects a belief that although it seems plausible to regard the general price level to be an important influence on wage rates whether at the micro- or macro-level, it also seems likely that the average wage rate at the macro-level has in turn a bearing on the general price level. Another instance of a joint dependence between variables which is associated with a transition from the level of micro-economic units to that of a macro-economy is found in the familiar notion that while aggregate consumption may be influenced by aggregate income the latter is also determined by total expenditure of which expenditure on consumption is an important part. It should be emphasised, however, that these examples of simultaneity are made necessary by aggregation over time as much as by aggregation over economic units. Thus, although it could be said that there must be finite lags between expenditure and its impact on incomes and between a wage change and its impact on price, while income has usually to be received before it can be spent and new wage rates often take time to negotiate, these lags are blurred, if they are not lost altogether, in the kind of data which are usually available in practice, much of which are available at best only quarterly. In other words, the interval to which each observation relates is often long enough to obscure lags between a change and at least some of its subsequent effects.

The specification of a model which has two or more jointly dependent variables means that the distinction drawn between dependent and independent variables in dealing with a single-equation model is inadequate. In particular, it is more appropriate to distinguish between jointly dependent variables, the behaviour of which is accounted for by the model as a whole, and those variables, other than disturbances, which are not accounted for in this way. The former are referred to as *endogenous variables* and the latter as *exogenous variables*. It is also necessary to add a third category of variables in differentiating between current and lagged terms in the endogenous variables of a model since the latter may be taken as having been established in advance when deciding which variables are determined in any given current period, t.

Together with exogenous variables, lagged or otherwise, they may be regarded as forming a wider class of 'independent' variables in period t which are more appropriately referred to as *predetermined variables*.

As implied in the alternative specifications of the two-equation wage–price models looked at in Chapter 4, a *simultaneous equation model* is one which is composed of two or more equations each of which has one of two alternative characteristics: either it expresses a relationship between two or more endogenous variables or it may include only a single endogenous variable providing this variable appears elsewhere in the model as an explanatory variable. If this is so then at least one of the endogenous variables of the model can only be expressed in terms of predetermined variables and disturbances alone by a solution of the model which involves all of the equations of which it is composed. This solution, which has already been referred to as the reduced form of a model, may be regarded as giving explicit expression to the dependence of each of the endogenous variables on predetermined variables and disturbances alone that is implied by the specification of as many equations as endogenous variables in the original, structural, form of a model.

The number and the scope of the equations used, together with the related classification of variables as either endogenous or exogenous, in specifying a macro-economic model depends essentially on the level of disaggregation adopted in seeking to account for the behaviour of different variables relating to the various activities and sectors of a macro-economy and on whether the model is to be used in the analysis of short- or long-term issues. The first of these matters is largely self-evident while the second has a bearing on whether it is necessary to account for variables such as the stock of capital, or the pressure of demand on existing capacity, and the distribution of income which may be avoided in a short-term income-determination model if it can be assumed that the supply of output can match the demand for output and that the distribution of income is not subject to change.

Further points of a general nature relating to the specification of a macro-economic model can be conveniently pursued with reference to a simple example. To begin with attention is focused on the stochastic consumption function,

$$C_t = \alpha + \beta Y_t + u_t \qquad (5.1)$$

where C_t and Y_t represent aggregate consumption and income. As noted earlier, however, the relationship between these two variables cannot be confined to a single function; in particular, if expenditure on consumer goods falls without spending elsewhere (Z_t) then income must fall. It seems necessary therefore to add to (5.1) the identity

$$Y_t = C_t + Z_t \qquad (5.2a)$$

The need to consider Y_t as an endogenous rather than an exogenous variable can be traced in econometric terms also since an exogenous variable must be determined outside the model, which means that it should not be related to any of the variables of the model, including disturbances. However, if C_t is one of the variables which combine to form Y_t, the latter is thereby related to u_t and an additional relationship is required to account for Y_t. In addition, it may be that aggregate consumption depends not only on the level of aggregate income but also its distribution. If this second factor is explicitly ignored in (5.1) then it becomes part of the disturbance variable while the income which determines C_t may itself be affected by matters, such as taxes and transfers, which have an important bearing on income distribution. Again, therefore, it seems unreasonable to assume that u_t and Y_t are uncorrelated and it may be concluded that Y_t cannot be regarded as an exogenous variable.

While an explanation of Y_t may be offered in the form of (5.2a), attention is now shifted to Z_t to see whether this can be regarded as an exogenous variable, which is so only if it is uncorrelated with u_t as well as Y_t and C_t. It may be argued, however, that it is unlikely that the various sources of income other than expenditure on consumer goods are uncorrelated with those variables which are correlated with consumption other than income. For example, investment (I_t) is one part of Z_t which may be thought to be correlated with u_t, bearing in mind that it covers prices, including the rate of interest, and the level and distribution of wealth. The result is a search for additional relationships which may be used to incorporate explanations of other constituent parts of income explicitly in the model. In the first place the autonomous expenditure component of income, Z_t, may be broken down into two components, private investment (I_t) and autonomous government expenditure (G_t) so that

$$Y_t = C_t + I_t + G_t. \tag{5.2b}$$

An explanation of the level of investment may now be added which takes account of both the need for investment to maintain a stock of capital which is in turn sufficient to maintain the output of the economy, Y_t, and the cost of borrowing in the form of the rate of interest, r

$$I_t = f(Y_t, r_t). \tag{5.3}$$

The rate of interest may not be considered to be exogenous but may rather be related to the level of real cash balances, M_t, which may perhaps be more appropriately considered exogenous, in such a way that M_t satisfies the speculative demand for money (which depends on the rate of interest) and the transactions demand for money (which depends on the level of income Y_t),[1]

$$M_t = g(Y_t, r). \tag{5.4}$$

The model now consists of four equations which together determine the levels of four endogenous variables (Y_t, C_t, I_t and r) given two exogenous variables, M_t and G_t. All the variables are assumed to be expressed in real terms so that the price level is implicitly determined exogenously. This is of

---

[1] This is in contrast with the crude version of the quantity theory of money of the classical approach whereby the nominal stock of money is directly proportional to income, the constant of proportionality being the reciprocal of the velocity of money.

course far from realistic, but the price level (p) can be included as an endogenous variable on adding three more relationships in the form of a production function and functions which also introduce the money wage rate (w_t) and the level of employment (L_t) as further endogenous variables. In the case of a Keynesian model of an economy with surplus capacity, the level of output, Y_t, may still be regarded as being determined by aggregate demand and not by the capacity to produce[1] so that the production function is included rather as a means of determining the level of employment that can be offered to labour given Y_t, the stock of capital assets (K_t) and the productivity of labour and capital (which may be assumed constant for the purposes of this exposition)

$$Y_t = h(L_t, K_t). \tag{5.5}$$

A correspondence between the marginal productivity of labour and the real wage rate, assuming that the conditions of perfect competition apply,

$$\frac{\partial Y}{\partial L} = \frac{w_t}{p_t}$$

may be used to determine the price level (rather than the demand for labour as in the classical system) if an explanation can be found for the money wage rate. Using Keynes's viewpoint that the money wage rate is inflexible below a given level, say the observed present rate, then two equations

$$p_t = p(w_t, L_t, Y_t) \tag{5.6}$$

$$w_t = w_0 \tag{5.7}$$

can be used to complete a system which simultaneously determines the seven jointly dependent variables Y_t, C_t, I_t, r, L_t, p_t and w_t given the exogenous variables G_t, M_t, and w_0. Full employment is not guaranteed but is determined by the level of real income and thereby by government policy operating on the variables G_t and M_t.

Although this exercise in identifying and relating the variables of a macroeconomic system has come a long way from the consumption function (5.1) above it is still far from adequate for the purposes of an empirical study of the relationship between these variables or for the purposes of forecasting or advising on policy. One problem is that only (5.1) and (5.2) have been given a specified mathematical form. It may be tempting to express the remaining equations as a set of linear functions for the sake of simplicity, but from what has been noted earlier in Chapters 2, 3 and 4 it can be concluded that this would be unsatisfactory, particularly in respect of the production function and the wage–price equations. Furthermore, even if the real balance equation and the investment function can be realistically specified as linear functions, say, in the form of a simple accelerator mechanism in the case of the latter (with the

---

[1] This again contrasts with classical theory in which available resources and the 'state of the arts' determine total output.

cost of capital, in the form of r, added on), it is necessary to modify the static system considered so far, which relates each endogenous variable to other endogenous variables for the period t alone without reference to the values of these variables established in previous periods. Thus in the case of the investment function it is necessary to express the income variable in terms of the first difference $\dot{Y}_t (\equiv Y_t - Y_{t-1})$ and to introduce a lagged term in the capital stock, in order to allow for expenditure on replacement. Other first difference variables are required in the wage–price equations. The effect of this second modification is to change the character of the model to one which is dynamic since changes in the values of the endogenous variables can then be accounted for in terms other than changes in the values of exogenous variables and disturbances or changes in the structure of the model.

Using a simplified version of (4.66) together with (4.64) in the place of (5.6) and (5.7) together with specifications of the investment and production functions which are roughly in line with some of the alternatives reviewed in earlier chapters, plus two additional identities defining (i) the level of unemployment, U_t, given the total labour force, N_t, and the level of employment, L_t, and (ii) the capital stock given K_{t-1} and net investment over period t, the model can now be written

$$C_t = \alpha_0 + \alpha_1 Y_t + u_{1t} \tag{5.8a}$$

$$I_t = \beta_0 + \beta_1 \dot{Y}_t + \beta_2 r_t + \beta_3 K_{t-1} + u_{2t} \tag{b}$$

$$M_t = \gamma_0 + \gamma_1 Y_t + \gamma_2 r_t + u_{3t} \tag{c}$$

$$Y_t = \delta_0 L_t^{\delta_1} K_t^{\delta_2} u_{4t} \tag{d}$$

$$\dot{p}_t = \theta_0 + \theta_1 \dot{w}_t + u_{5t} \tag{e}$$

$$\dot{w}_t = \psi_0 + \psi_1 \dot{p}_t + \psi_2 U_t^{-1} + \psi_3 \dot{U}_t + u_{6t} \tag{f}$$

$$Y_t = C_t + I_t + G_t \tag{g}$$

$$U_t = N_t - L_t \tag{h}$$

$$K_t = K_{t-1} + (I_t - \beta_3 K_{t-1}) = (1 - \beta_3) K_{t-1} + I_t. \tag{i}$$

In this form the model exhibits structural features which are not uncommon among larger simultaneous equation models in general. To begin with there are enough variables in the model and a small enough number of explanatory variables in each stochastic equation for there to be enough different variables missing from each of these equations for them to be distinguishable from each other. (If, for example, any two equations related the same set of variables then it would not be possible to say which was which, but this problem becomes more unlikely the more equations and the more variables there are. See Section 5.3).) Secondly, the model can be described as a segmental one since C_t, Y_t, I_t and r_t are jointly determined by equations (5.8a), (b), (c) and (g) while p_t and w_t are also jointly determined once Y_t, and thereby L_t and U_t, are established. The model is therefore made up of two sets of jointly dependent variables which are related but not in such a way that they are all mutually dependent (which would be so if either w_t or p_t were to have an influence on C_t, Y_t, I_t or r_t). The situation may be illustrated as follows in terms of a flow diagram, distinguishing between values of the variables relating to three periods of time (which thereby illustrates the dynamic character of the model and the variables via which values of endogenous variables in any given period influence the values of these variables in succeeding periods) and setting endogenous variables within squares and exogenous variables within circles (disturbances are omitted).

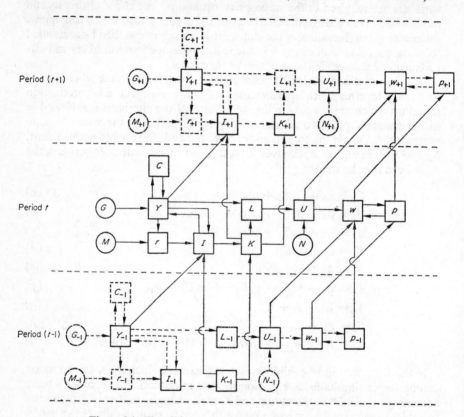

Figure 5.1. Flow-Diagrammatic Representation of Model (5.8)

Although the model is now expressed in such a way that it can be tested against observation and although it may seem reasonably realistic and comprehensive it still has two main shortcomings. In the first place it is noted that important gaps remain in the variables included in the model. These gaps will become more evident in later sections of this chapter but one or two omissions may already have been noticed. For example, no account has been taken of foreign trade and although government expenditure has been included the way in which government revenues affect, and are affected by, other variables has been overlooked. The first omission may be tackled by introducing components of GNP which relate to the foreign trade balance in the form of either exogenous or endogenous variables, whichever seems appropriate. So far as the second deficiency is concerned, one thing that needs to be done in particular is to replace the explanatory income variable in the consumption function by a measure of disposable income. Again there is a choice, which has to be decided in the light of the scope and objectives of the model, in the way in which this new variable is added. Thus disposable income might be obtained either by means of additional exogenous variables which account for the difference between total and disposable income or by adding an explanation of the level of taxation in terms of various categories of income (which would introduce the need to deal with profits, dividends, business income, etc.) as well as perhaps an explanation of transfer payments such as subsidies, pensions, unemployment benefits, etc.

Secondly, it may be considered more realistic to disaggregate other variables, and in particular the aggregates adopted so far for consumption and investment. For example, expenditures on different categories of consumption are influenced by different factors and a distinction should be made at least between durable goods and non-durable goods plus services. In the case of investment, different variables are needed to explain investment in plant and equipment as opposed to investment in housing or in inventories. Disaggregation may also be pursued by sector of production so that, for example, manufacturing industry, agriculture and other sectors of industry and commerce may be dealt with separately. These kinds of development may lead onto further extensions of a model in the form of equations which account for the behaviour of the deflators to be used for the different components of aggregate demand and production. The rate of interest must also be disaggregated to distinguish between long- and short-term interest rates.

Disaggregation is usually helpful because a model is thereby made more sensitive to peculiar factors which influence the behaviour of any given variable. In particular since many of the relationships adopted in the specification of a macro-economic model are based on micro-economic theory this theory is more likely to hold if the aggregates used are restricted to group micro-economic units which are as similar as possible. However, even if this advice is faithfully followed it remains necessary to ask if the relationships between certain variables suggested by micro-economic theory apply equally well to aggregates of the same variables, which is the subject of the section that follows.

5.2 THE AGGREGATION PROBLEM

Observations on aggregates which relate to an economy as a whole are simply the sum of observations which relate to individual micro-economic units. This suggests that one way of specifying a macro-economic model would be to express it as a series of relationships which refer in turn to each activity of each of these units. The behaviour of the economy as a whole with respect to these activities could then be obtained as the sum of the reactions of the individual micro-economic units subject to various accounting identities. The snag with this kind of approach is that although it is conceptually sound enough, after the fashion of a Walrasian system of simultaneous equations, it has the practical disadvantage of producing an extremely unwieldy result in the form of thousands upon thousands of equations. In order to have something of more manageable proportions it is therefore useful to restrict the variables used in the specification of a macro-economic model to measures like aggregate consumption without reference to all the items of expenditure of which this is composed.[1] The question then arises as to whether the relationship between consumption and income suggested by micro-economic theory applies equally well to consumers as a whole using variables like aggregate consumption and income.

The conditions under which a linear function can be said to apply equally well to both micro and macro-economic units may be summarised as follows:

(*a*) Where an explanatory variable is the same for all micro-economic units, e.g. a price, then it is the same variable in the linear function for the macro-economic unit while the macro-economic parameter is the sum of the parameters found in the individual micro-economic functions.

(*b*) Where the variable changes between different micro-economic units, e.g. the income of each unit, but the parameters in the individual micro-economic functions are all the same, then this parameter also applies in the case of the macro-economic function but the variable is now the sum of the different variables found in the micro-economic functions.

(*c*) If both the parameters and the variables change from one micro-economic function to another then both the parameters and the variables of the macro-economic function are also different. For a variable which takes on a different value in each micro-economic function, like the different prices found in a series of demand functions which relate to different commodities and services, a macro-economic variable may be formed, at least conceptually if not in practice, as a weighted sum using the parameters of the micro-economic functions as weights

$$\beta_1 X_{1i} + \beta_2 X_{2i} + \ldots + \beta_n X_{ni} = \beta' X_i'.$$

As noted in Chapter 3, Section 3.3, much the same conclusions apply to an additively separable log-linear function except that a summated variable takes the form of the logarithm of the product of the observations on the variable which relate to the micro-economic units, which is weighted or not depending on whether the parameters of the micro-economic functions are different or the same.

[1] For a discussion of the view that too much information is lost in using this kind of highly aggregated data and that full use should be made of sample survey techniques and modern computational facilities to minimise this loss by restricting levels of agregation and concentration on a 'microanalytic research strategy', see Orcutt (1962, 1967).

Thus the parameters and variables found in a function relating to a micro-economic unit have essentially the same interpretation as those found in a relationship of the same mathematical form but relating to a macro-economic unit only under special circumstances. Even where this correspondence in interpretation holds it may be that a variable that is required in theory is not available in practice. An aggregation error then arises which adds a further source of ambiguity in the interpretation of an estimated function. However, it might perhaps be argued in certain instances that a functional relationship between aggregates has the same form as is suggested by micro-economic theory and yet is a reasonable enough explanation in itself without assuming that it summarises precisely what happens at the micro-economic level. For example, a log-linear production function may be thought to apply to an industry or a sector as a whole for much the same reasons as to a firm, in particular it seems reasonable to continue to assume that factors may not be substituted for each other to the point where one factor could be used to the exclusion of another.

Wherever it is impossible to avoid aggregation errors it must be hoped that they are at least sufficiently small that the parameters of the aggregates used are reasonably stable. The conditions under which this objective may be met in theory underline the way in which aggregation errors are likely to be mini-mised in practice. For example, it has already been noted that the aggregation problem is a serious one even when using a linear function if both parameters and variables of the relationship change from one micro-economic unit to another. In this case summation across units produces terms like

$$\sum_{j=1}^{n} \beta_j X_{ji}$$

which may be rewritten in the alternative forms

$$\frac{\Sigma_j \beta_j X_{ji}}{\Sigma_j X_{j,i}} \cdot \Sigma_j X_{j,i} \text{ or } \frac{\bar{\beta} \Sigma_j \beta_j X_{ji}}{\bar{\beta}}.$$

These are interpretations proposed respectively by Klein (1950) and by Theil (1954). Klein's approach is the one which is more easily followed in practice, since aggregates like $\Sigma_j X_{ji}$ are published rather than $\Sigma_j \beta_j X_{ji}/\bar{\beta}$, and in this case the macro-economic parameter turns out to be the weighted sum of the micro-economic parameters using the share of each micro-economic unit, j, of the aggregate $\Sigma_j X_{j,}$ as weights. If this share changes between observations, i, on aggregates then the macro-economic parameter $(\Sigma_j \beta X_{ji})/(\Sigma_j X_{ji})$ must also be subject to change. This problem is avoided in the Theil approach which is based on an aggregation of the micro-economic parameters, in the form of their arithmetic mean, rather than an aggregation of the variable X_j, in the form of the sum $\Sigma_j X_{ji}$. The macro-economic variable is then a weighted sum of the X_{ji} using the ratio between each micro-economic parameter and the average of all of these parameters as weights. In this case the macro-economic parameters are unaffected by changes in the shares of the micro-economic units in the sum $\Sigma_j X_{ji}$ and they remain constant as long as the micro-economic parameters remain unchanged.

Apart from being ruled out on practical grounds by the kind of published data that are generally available at present, Theil's approach has the additional drawbacks of recommending that (i) different measures of the same variable be used in the different equations of a macro-economic model because the weights $\beta_j/\bar{\beta}$ change from one equation to another, and (ii) a macro-economic slope parameter should be a simple average of the relevant micro-economic parameters despite the different relative sizes of the variables to which these parameters relate. Thus Klein's method has much to commend it especially if changes in the relative shares, $X_{j,\,i}/\Sigma_j X_{ji}$, can be reduced to a minimum. It can also be seen that if it were possible to aggregate in such a way that all the micro-economic parameters relating to a variable were the same then the two interpretations would coincide. These conclusions emphasise the need to choose aggregates and to restrict the level of aggregation with the objective of grouping economic activities which are much the same and economic units which are subject to as little change as possible in their relative size or which are as similar as possible in their behaviour.

5.3 ESTIMATION AND OTHER ASPECTS OF STATISTICAL INFERENCE

The specification of a simultaneous model may give rise to special problems for econometric analysis some of which are reviewed briefly here. To begin with it is necessary to ask whether observations on a set of variables can be used to estimate more than one relationship between the variables. This is a problem which can be illustrated with reference to the exact part of a two-equation model

$$Y_1 = \beta_{10} + \beta_{12}Y_2 + \gamma_{11}X_1 + \gamma_{12}X_2 + \ldots + \gamma_{1K}X_K \qquad (5.9a)$$
$$Y_2 = \beta_{20} + \beta_{21}Y_1 + \gamma_{21}X_1 + \gamma_{22}X_2 + \ldots + \gamma_{2K}X_K \qquad (5.9b)$$

which although it can only account for the behaviour of two endogenous variables can be generalised to include any K exogenous variables. If each of the equations is indeed believed to relate all $(K + 2)$ variables as in (5.9a) and (5.9b) then they are indistinguishable from one another. It can be seen, for example, that an infinite number of equations of the same form as (5.9a) can be obtained from a linear combination of the two equations using the arbitrary weights λ_1 and λ_2

$$\lambda_1 Y_1 + \lambda_2 Y_2 = (\lambda_1\beta_{10} + \lambda_2\beta_{20}) + \lambda_1\beta_{12}Y_2 + \lambda_2\beta_{21}Y_1$$
$$+ (\lambda_1\gamma_{11} + \lambda_2\gamma_{21})X_1 + \ldots$$

$$Y_1 = \frac{1}{\lambda_1 - \lambda_2\beta_{21}}(\lambda_1\beta_{10} + \lambda_2\beta_{20}) + (\lambda_1\beta_{12} - \lambda_2)Y_2$$
$$+ (\lambda_1\gamma_{11} + \lambda_2\gamma_{21})X_1 + \ldots$$

The same conclusion applies to (5.9b) so that a fit of either equation to a set of data produces an ambiguous result. This is known as the *identification problem*, the solution of which requires that each equation be made different from the other(s) in some way. For example, this problem would not have arisen in the case of (5.9a) if one of the variables found in (5.9b) were missing from (5.9a). Thus, if a parameter restriction like $\gamma_{11} = 0$ applies so that the first equation is

$$Y_1 = \beta_{10} + \beta_{12}Y_2 + \gamma_{12}X_2 + \ldots + \gamma_{1K}X_K. \qquad (5.10)$$

then no linear combination of (5.10) and (5.9b) has the same form as (5.10) other than (5.10) itself, which is obtained on setting $\lambda_2 = 0$. The same applies to (5.9b) is this were to exclude a variable which is found in the first equation of a model. Both equations are then *identified* when without these restrictions they are said to be *underidentified*.

This reasoning can be developed to suggest a rule that to be identified an equation should have at least $(G - 1)$ linear parameter restrictions, where G is the number of equations and where the most obvious restriction of this kind is one which excludes certain variables from an equation. This is a rule, known as the *order condition for identification*, which is generally applicable to linear systems and which is a necessary but not sufficient condition for identification. In practice, however, it is an adequate guide to identifiability for all but certain special kinds of restriction.[1] It is also reasonably safe to say that identification is not usually a problem in models of more than three or four equations. As an illustration of this point consider a system of G equations, each of which includes two endogenous variables and up to three predetermined variables, only one of which, for the sake of argument, may be considered as being unique to each equation (e.g. a lagged term in the left-hand side endogenous variable or an exogenous variable) so that the model includes at least $(G + 2)$ predetermined variables. In this case the model has $2(G + 1)$ variables so that there are at least $(2G - 3)$ restrictions on the parameters of each equation which can be compared to the order condition requirement that they should have $(G - 1)$. The equations are therefore just identified under these not unrealistic circumstances even if $G = 2$ and there is room for another explanatory variable in each equation for every extra equation that is added to the model. Even in the case of a five-equation model, therefore, each equation may include up to three more explanatory variables on top of those accounted for by the above scheme and still be identified.

As noted in Section 4.4 of Chapter 4, the appearance of endogenous variables as explanatory variables in a multiple equation model must mean, except in the case of the special conditions reviewed below, that these explanatory

---

[1] The only exception which needs to be guarded against in practice is that which arises when one equation excludes the same explanatory variables, and perhaps more, as another equation. There are other distributions of missing variables and more subtle parameter restrictions which can be formulated for which the order condition is ineffective, although these are unlikely to be encountered in any but the smallest models.

variables are correlated with disturbances. The result of this particular violation of the assumptions of the classical linear regression model is that OLS estimators are no longer unbiased while this biasedness persists no matter how large the sample is so that these estimators are also said to be inconsistent.[2] Before reviewing what can be done about this it is useful to examine the possibility of building models for which this estimation problem does not arise. To begin it is noted that not all the equations of a simultaneous equation system necessarily have explanatory variables which are correlated with disturbances if only because all the explanatory variables of some equations may be exogenous variables. (Lagged endogenous variables may also be added providing the disturbances are not auto-correlated.) In view of this it must also be possible to build models for which *all* the equations have this property even though some may have endogenous variables on the right-hand side. This is because any endogenous variable (Y_1) which is related only to exogenous variables must itself be uncorrelated with current disturbances of all the other equations of the model if these current disturbances are also uncorrelated with one another. It follows that any endogenous variable (Y_2) which is related to Y_1 and exogenous variables alone must share this property and this also applies to a third endogenous variable (Y_3) which is related to Y_1, Y_2 and exogenous variables alone, and so on. The two characteristics thereby identified, in the form of a diagonal variance–covariance matrix of current structural form disturbances and a triangular array of structural form parameters of current endogenous variables

$$
\Sigma = \begin{bmatrix} \sigma_{11} & 0 & \cdots & 0 \\ 0 & \sigma_{12} & \cdots & 0 \\ \cdot & \cdot & \cdot & \cdot \\ \cdot & \cdot & \cdot & \cdot \\ \cdot & \cdot & \cdot & \cdot \\ 0 & 0 & \cdots & \sigma_{GG} \end{bmatrix} \qquad \mathbf{B} = \begin{bmatrix} 1 & 0 & 0 & \cdots & 0 \\ \beta_{21} & 1 & 0 & \cdots & 0 \\ \beta_{31} & \beta_{32} & 1 & \cdots & 0 \\ \cdot & \cdot & \cdot & \cdot & \cdot \\ \cdot & \cdot & \cdot & \cdot & \cdot \\ \cdot & \cdot & \cdot & \cdot & \cdot \\ \beta_{G1} & \beta_{G2} & \beta_{G3} & \cdots & 1 \end{bmatrix}
$$

together define a *diagonally recursive model*, for which OLS estimators remain unbiased if all the explanatory variables are exogenous variables or consistent where they also include lagged endogenous variables providing the disturbances in these equations are not autocorrelated. While it is often plausible to specify groups of equations for which the interrelationships between endogenous variables are restricted in this way, it is unfortunately not an approach which can be widely adopted even if it seems reasonable to believe that the values of economic variables are usually established by cause and

---

[2] Consistency requires that the sampling distribution of an estimator becomes concentrated on the population value of the parameter concerned as the sample size approaches infinity, which means that an estimator must be unbiased and its estimates must have zero dispersion in the limit of an infinite sample for the estimator to be a *consistent estimator*.

effect rather than by processes which result in their simultaneous determination. This is because, as noted earlier, the kind of data that are usually available in practice are not sufficiently disaggregated over time to allow sequences of events to be confined to separate observations.[1]

Although the disturbances of reduced form equations are linear combinations of structural form disturbances[2] and the explanatory variables of these equations may be all exogenous variables so that the OLS estimator of the equations is unbiased, unbiasedness is not maintained through linear transformations. However, consistency is maintained through linear transformations which means that a consistent estimator of structural parameters can be obtained in the case of any structural equations which can be uniquely derived from reduced forms equations. This last condition applies only if the equation is *just identified*, which is so if the number of parameter restrictions is exactly equal to $(G - 1)$. Any equation which has more than this number of parameter restrictions is said to be *overidentified* which, from what was noted earlier about identification in practice, can be seen to be the case which is most likely to be encountered in larger models. Thus this estimation procedure, known as *indirect least squares estimation*, is only of limited value in dealing with such models.

A simple alternative approach to consistent estimation which is applicable to overidentified equations is to use OLS estimated reduced form equations to obtain predictions of current values of endogenous variables which can then be used to replace observations on these variables where they appear as explanatory variables. As a result of this substitution of prediction for observation these variables are now also uncorrelated with disturbances at least asymptotically (i.e. as the sample size approaches infinity), so that (second-stage) OLS estimation of structural form equations yields consistent estimates. This procedure is known as *two-stage least squares estimation*. A second method of estimating an overidentified equation which is sometimes adopted, known as the *least variance ratio* (LVR) method (which is equivalent to the *limited information maximum-likelihood* (LIML) method), is based on the principle of finding a single synthetic endogenous variable ($\tilde{Y}$) which effectively replaces all the endogenous variables in a particular equation and which minimises the ratio of the sum of squared residuals from regressing $\tilde{Y}$ on those predetermined variables in the equation to the sum of squared residuals from regressing $\tilde{Y}$ on all the predetermined variables in the model.

Where the current disturbances of a model are correlated between equations then the asymptotic variances of estimates obtained from a single equation approach to the estimation of a simultaneous equation model, like two-stage least squares (2SLS), can be reduced by taking these correlations into account. This requires the use of a system estimation procedure in which the parameters of a model are estimated as a whole rather than for one equation at a time. The

[1] For further discussion of the simultaneity of economic variables see Wold (1954, 1956, 1964).

[2] See p. 178.

estimation procedure which is most commonly employed in practice in this case is an extension of the 2SLS procedure in which 2SLS estimates of each equation in turn are used to obtain residuals which are then used to estimate the elements of the variance–covariance matrix of the disturbances. This result can be substituted into the generalised least squares (GLS) estimator for the parameters of the model as a whole to estimate these in a final, third-stage, pass. The approach, known as *three-stage least squares estimation*, is therefore similar to the use made of the GLS estimator in the place of the OLS estimator where disturbances relating to a series of observations on the variables of a single equation are autocorrelated or heteroscedastic and where the next best alternative estimation procedure, i.e. OLS or 2SLS, is used to gain information on the variance–covariance matrix for the relevant set of disturbances.

Estimation of reduced form equations may present special problems in larger models because of the larger number of predetermined variables thereby usually involved so that serious multicollinearity is more likely while the number of degrees of freedom with which to estimate these equations may be drastically reduced, even if the number of observations is enough at all. One way of tackling this problem is to regress endogenous variables on leading principal components of predetermined variables. (See Johnston (1972) pp. 393–5, for a discussion of how these components might be selected.) An alternative approach has been suggested by Fisher (1965) in formulating means by which the Brookings model might be estimated. This procedure makes use of the near-recursive structure of the model to set it out in the form of a block-recursive system

$$B = \begin{bmatrix} B_{11} & 0 & \cdots & 0 \\ B_{21} & B_{22} & \cdots & 0 \\ \cdot & \cdot & \cdot & \cdot \\ \cdot & \cdot & \cdot & \cdot \\ \cdot & \cdot & \cdot & \cdot \\ B_{S1} & B_{S2} & \cdots & B_{SS} \end{bmatrix}$$

which, even though the structure of the model may not correspond to this pattern precisely, can be used as a guide in the choice of a restricted number of predetermined variables to be considered in the separate estimation of each block of equations. (Consistency can be shown to be retained even if not all the predetermined variables that should be used to estimate an equation are used.) These variables could include the exogenous variables of the sub-set of equations together with lagged endogenous variables from these equations, the explanatory value of which, since they may be highly serially correlated with the endogenous variables within the block, might be improved by regressing them on lagged exogenous variables and using predictions from these regressions to replace observations. Other variables from outside the block, including perhaps endogenous variables from higher blocks, if disturbances between blocks are assumed to be independent (or using predictions of these variables if they are not assumed to be independent), may be added to improve the fit of the estimated equation.

Asymptotic variance–covariance matrices can be derived for different consistent estimators so there arises the possibility of estimating their standard errors. For the 2SLS estimator the formula for this matrix is the same as the OLS formula for a single equation having replaced observations on any explanatory variables which are current endogenous variables by predictions obtained from OLS estimates of reduced form equations. This formula can be used with an estimate of the variance of the disturbances of an equation ($\hat{\sigma}_u^2$) to obtain estimated standard errors. As in the case of OLS estimation, an estimate of σ_u^2 is given by (1.13) where the residuals are obtained from the estimated equation using observations on any regressors which are endogenous variables in doing this, so that these residuals are *not* the residuals obtained from the second-stage OLS estimation of the equation.

Subject to the usual assumptions consistent estimators are asymptotically normal which would seem to suggest that estimates of their asymptotic variance–covariance matrices can be used to compute interval estimates of structural form parameters or to test the null hypothesis that the true value of a parameter is, say, β when the estimated value of this parameter has another value, $\hat{\beta}$. This is so, at least asymptotically, since the statistic $(\hat{\beta} - \beta)/\sqrt{\text{est. var } \hat{\beta}}$ is also asymptotically normal. (The same degrees of freedom can be considered to apply as in the case of a single equation.) However, the valid use, or the interpretation, of other statistics, like the Durbin–Watson test statistic and R^2, do not carry over without qualification to simultaneous equation models, although the lack of convenient alternatives means that they are used in applied work as though this were so.

Since the results briefly reviewed above only apply where the sample size approaches infinity, while in practice there is not often the opportunity of working with samples which are even approximately this large, it is necessary to ask what are the merits of alternative consistent estimators in the context of a small sample. Because of the difficulties of deriving theoretical answers to this question what evidence there is has been obtained mainly from Monte Carlo experimentation. This involves using models with known values for parameters and known distribution functions for disturbances to generate a series of artificial samples for fixed or randomly distributed values of exogenous variables and initial values of any lagged endogenous variables. The samples may then be used to obtain a set of parameter estimates for a particular estimator so that the properties of its sampling distribution can be established. In view of the empirical nature of this evidence it cannot be entirely free from ambiguity and yet subject to this qualification a number of generalisations can be made about the results obtained. Thus it seems evident that the OLS estimator usually exhibits the greatest bias, which seriously impairs its value in hypothesis testing, and yet it often has a small dispersion about the mean value of a set of estimates. (Despite its failings so far as biasedness is concerned, however, OLS estimation remains a convenient, if somewhat untrustworthy, means of testing individual equations where there is doubt about the pre-determined variables of a model, and, in the context of system methods of estimation, its structure.) Among consistent estimators no one estimation procedure can be regarded as being conclusively better than all others, but, as is to be expected, the system methods have lower variances than single equation methods while having much the same kind of performance so far as bias is concerned. The question as to which estimator should be used in practice is even more difficult to answer when matters are further complicated by the kind of problems mentioned in Chapter 1, for example, autocorrelated disturbances, multicollinearity and specification errors. Generally speaking, the 2SLS estimator performs as well as others and is often more robust in the face of these additional difficulties. This coupled with the relative ease with which it can be computed means that this procedure is relied on most often.

Despite the circumspection adopted in venturing to review the results of this work it remains necessary to emphasise that no one estimator is better than all others on all grounds under all circumstances and the research worker wishing to satisfy certain performance criteria, or suspecting that his data or model are characterised in some special way, must consult this experimental work for himself. (Ideally the suitability of an estimator should be established by at least limited tests of this kind for any models which do not correspond reasonably closely to those used in obtaining published results.) An excellent review of the literature on this subject is given by Johnston (1972), pp. 408–20, while the studies reported by Summers (1965) and Cragg (1967) are among the more comprehensive that have been undertaken.

Where the sample size is small it may be tempting to think that the conclusions reviewed above concerning hypothesis testing in the context of simultaneous equation systems can be extended to statistical inference based on the t-distribution as in the case of single equation models. Unfortunately, the ratio of a small sample estimate of a structural parameter to its estimated standard error is a statistic which does not have the t-distribution, although results from Monte Carlo studies suggest that reliable inferences may often be obtained by means of this statistic. Again, in the event of there being nothing better available this ratio, obtained using the consistent estimators referred to above, is commonly quoted in practice as a rough guide to statistical significance. As noted already, however, the OLS estimator is at a serious disadvantage in this particular respect compared with consistent estimators.

5.4 A COMPARATIVE REVIEW OF DIFFERENT MODELS: SOME INTRODUCTORY REMARKS

Even if only because of the multiplicity of different relationships to be included in any realistic macro-economic model, it would be impossible to provide a comprehensive comparison between even a small selection of these models in the space of a few pages. The form finally adopted for each one of these relationships can be expected to have its own separate justification in terms of what is theoretically plausible and what is found to be supported by empirical evidence, but even this view of a macro-economic model could not be regarded as a complete one since each model is something more than the sum of the individual equations of which it is composed. In particular it will have been designed to serve a particular set of objectives with the result that features like the selection of those variables for which an explanation is to be offered and the extent of disaggregation vary between models. An equation by equation comparison would therefore have to be constantly qualified by references to the way in which each equation ties in with the structure of the model as a whole and by reminders as to the overall objectives to be served by the model, while a concentration on the general structure of the model would tend to overlook the peculiarities of individual equations. For the purpose of this text, however, the drawbacks of the second approach are accepted in an attempt to provide a concise historical and comparative account of the development of the main structural features of the kind of comprehensive macro-economic models that have been built, notably by Klein and his associates, and also by others, following on the advances in theoretical and empirical analysis that are chiefly associated with Keynes and Tinbergen.

Apart from a preference for comprehensive models, in order to avoid *ad hoc* models which are designed to serve special theoretical and practical objectives, the models referred to below have been selected on the grounds that, with the exception of the historically interesting Klein III model, each one was originally designed with the intention that it should form the basis of a continuing research effort aimed at providing an empirically verified explanation of the observed time path of a set of macro-economic variables which in turn may be used as a means of providing conditional forecasts for these variables. Published studies of these models are, for the most part, readily available either in the form of the original research reports or in the form of later surveys and further developments.

The discussion avoids details concerning data problems, the theoretical justification of each equation of a model, the closeness of the fit of these equations to observation, the statistical significance of each and every variable, analyses of forecasting performance and related matters. Rather, attention is focused on the way in which each model hangs together as a whole and on the way in which the approach has been extended over time to offer a more comprehensive view of macro-economic systems. So far as the specification issue in particular is concerned, it is believed that this treatment is not unduly restrictive since the justifications offered for different equations have often tended to lag somewhat behind contemporary theory, even where they have been based on a generally accepted theory rather than more on intuition, or on simply what has proved to be satisfactory in empirical terms alone, and model-builders have generally been content to confine their innovations to matters relating to objectives and structure. Moreover, many of the ideas which are reflected in the specifications of individual equations have already been discussed over Chapters 2, 3 and 4 of this study.

Table 5.1. A tabular summary of seven

Economy and model. Reference Observation period and type of data	No. of stochastic (S) and other (O) equations. Estimation method	Dynamic and special features	Number and
			(I) Aggregate demand
1. United States, Klein III. Klein (1950) pp. 84–114. 1921/2–41, annual data	S 12 O 3 Total 15 OLS and LIML	Lags to $(t-2)$, cumulated investment and other stocks, time trends. Most behavioural equations in real terms, no explicit production fn., several non-linear equations, detailed housing sector	(6) Consumption. 4 components of net investment. Private sector output
2. United States, Klein-Goldberger II. Klein and Goldberger (1955). 1929–41 and 1946–52, annual data	S 15 O 5 Total 20 LIML	Lags to $(t-5)$, cumulated investment and corporate savings and other stocks, time trends. Use of Koyck distributed lag transform and dynamic adjustment mechanisms (as in Klein III). Imports endogenous, separate endogenous agric. sector. Most behavioural equations in real terms. Several non-linear equations	(3) Consumption. Gross private investment (inc. inventories). Imports of goods and services
3. Canada, Canadian Model IX. Brown (1970) pp. 379–86. 1926–41 and 1946–56, annual data	S 13 O 34 Total 47 2SLS	Lags to $(t-1)$, use of first differences in combination with levels of other variables and other usual dynamic features. Usual non-linearities apart from use of a variable operable only beyond some threshold level in 2 equations. Economy separated beyond usual sectors and markets into 3 industrial groups to allow for different technologies and marketing characteristics. Detailed treatment of income and employment	(11) Consumption. Gross investment in plant and equipment. Change in inventories. Imports plus related services. GDF (gross domestic flow of new and final goods) supply and demand. GDP. GNP Gross domestic sales. In value terms as well as volume: equilibrium GDF

of endogenous variables					*Total no. of (and list of more unusual) exogenous variables*
") Income, employment and resources	*(III) Prices and compensation rates*	*(IV) Money and finance*	*(V) Taxes and transfers*		
4) Private wage bill. Disposable income. Capital stock. Fraction of non-farm housing occupied	(3) Price index for total output. Non-farm rent index. Corporate bond yield	(2) Active balances. Idle balances	—		(13) Farm rent index. Aggregated gov't. revenues and corporate savings and transfers and gov't. interest payments. Non-farm housing units available
0) National income. Private wage bill. Non-wage, non-farm income. Farm income. Corporate profits. Corporate savings. Corporate surplus. Depreciation. Private employment. Capital stock	(5) GNP price index. Farm price index. Wage rate index. Yield on short-term commercial paper. Yield on corporate bonds	(2) Liquid assets held by (a) persons and (b) enterprises	—		(18) 5 taxation (less transfers) categories. Population. Index of hours worked per person p.a. 4 categories of employment. Price index for imports. Index of agricultural exports. Excess bank reserves as a fraction of total reserves
23) Total wage bill. 6 disposable income categories (in real and money terms: labour and non-wage incomes; in money terms only: two component parts of latter). 5 categories of profit. 4 categories of employment and 2 of unemployment. Average labour force participation rates. Average and standard hours of work. Capital and inventory stocks	(5) Price indices for GDP, GDF and NDP/NNP. Average hourly wage rate. Long-term interest rate	(3) Total public money holdings. Money held for (a) transactions and (b) savings purposes	(5) 4 tax categories (wages, 2 profits categories and indirect). Transfer payments to labour and non-profit incomes		(31) 2 depreciation allowances. Expenditure on tourist travel abroad. Population. 5 special employment categories. 3 price indices (inc. price index for equities). 2 wage rates. Cash reserves of commercial or money-creating banks. Gov't deposits in above banks. 5 categories transfer payments. Shift variable to allow for effects of past import controls in import function

Table 5.1. A tabular summary of sever

Economy and model. Reference Observation period and type of data	No. of stochastic (S) and other (O) equations. Estimation method	Dynamic and special features	Number and (I) Aggregate demand
4. Holland, Central Planning Bureau. de Wolff (1967) pp. 313–35. 1923–38 and 1949–60. Annual data expressed mostly as relative first differences: $[(X_t - X_{t-1})/X_{t-1}]100$	S 13 O 25 Total 38 Mostly LIML some 2SLS	Lags to $(t-2)$ and fractional lags used as well as changes in percentage changes. Several non-linear functions including an elaborate expression for capacity utilisation in terms of the unemployment rate. Exports, imports and 5 prices included as endogenous variables. Many components of aggregate demand expressed in both value and volume terms. Measure of severe weather used in determining the level of unemployment	(16) In value and volume terms: consumption; gross investment (excl. dwellings); exports; imports, total output; total output (less inventory changes and net invisibles). In value terms: last 2 variables reweighted by (a) intensities of labour demand and (b) import requirements. In volume terms: change in inventories; autonomous expenditure
5. United States, Research Seminar in Quantitative Economics, University of Michigan. Suits (1967) pp. 243–89.[1] 1952–64, annual data	S 21 O 32 Total 53 OLS	Lags to $(t-1)$ and one lead to $(t+1)$ Nearly all variables are expressed as first differences and nearly all equations are linear. Model specially developed for short-term forecast purposes. Detailed treatment of aggregate demand (especially consumption but plant and equipment investment figure obtained from survey of investment intentions. Elaborate taxation and social insurance section. No explicit production function. No explanations offered for exports, prices or financial sector	(19) Consumption: 3 categories of durables (cars, h'hold furniture and others); 4 categories of nondurables (food, clothing, petrol and oil, others); services excl. housing. Investment: housing starts and expenditures; 3 categories of inventories (farm, non-farm nondurables, and durables). 4 Import categories (total, finished materials and unfinished materials and food). Private GNP. Output of goods

[1] Another version of this model may be seen in Suits (1965)

macro-economic models (*cont.*)

	list of endogenous variables				Total no. of (and list of more unusual) exogenous variables
(II) Income, employment and resources	*(III) Prices and compensation rates*	*(IV) Money and finance*	*(V) Taxes and transfers*		
(9) Total and disposable private wage and non-labour income. Private sector employment. Level of and change in unemployment. Index of capacity utilisation. An adjusted ratio of dependent working population to population between 14 and 65	(9) Price indices for: total output, consumption, investment, exports and autonomous expenditure. Margin between import price and price of total output Average gross wage. Rate at which wage costs increase in excess of labour productivity. Gross profits per unit of output	(2) Time plus demand deposits. Balance of payments	(2) Indirect taxes less subsidies. Variation in the incidence of direct taxes on non-labour income		(21) 1 tax and 2 transfer categories. Short term rate of interest. Exchange rate. Volume and prices of competing exports. Net invisibles. Depreciation. Allowance for quantitative import restrictions (1932–7). Rate of import liberalisation (1945–55). Minimum temperature below 0°C
(17) Total private, manufacturing and other wage bills. Property and dividend incomes. Corporate profits. Gross depreciation. Disposable income. For durables production: value added, average weekly hours, productivity and employment. 4 other employment levels (non-durables, construction, and service industries, total). Unemployment	(3) Three wage-rate categories (durables, non-durables, and service industries)	—	(14) 4 categories of federal taxation (personal income, corporate profits, excise taxes and customs duties). 3 categories of state taxation (personal income, corporate income and sales). 5 payments to and 2 from social insurance funds		(43) Private investment in plant and equipment. 3 categories of imports. Exports. Wage bills, employment and wage rates (variously) in several industrial groupings. Farm income. Durable goods capacity index. Producers durable equipment. Civilian labour force. Private GNP deflator and 5 other price indices. Liquid assets of consumers. Change in mortgage lending. 5 tax and 4 transfer payments. Net new car registrations. Stock of unoccupied housing

Table 5.1. A tabular summary of seven

Economy and model. Reference. Observation period and type of data	No. of stochastic (S) and other (O) equations. Estimation method	Dynamic and special features	Number and
			(I) Aggregate demand
6. United States, Econometric and Forecasting Unit, Wharton School of Finance and Commerce, Univ. of Pennsylvania. Evans and Klein (1968) and Evans (1969) pp. 429–42. 1952(3)–64(2), quarterly data	S 44 O 22 Total 66 2SLS	Lags to $(t-9)$, use of first differences in combination with levels of other variables and other usual dynamic features. Usual non-linearities including log-linear production functions. Detailed treatment of aggregate demand, income and employment, and prices. Like Canadian and Michigan models, industrial sector is dis-aggregated to level of broad groupings. Capacity utilisation index obtained from computation of total possible output. Measures of anticipations used in short-term forecast versions of durables other than cars and 2 investment functions	(17) Consumption: cars, other durables, non-durables. Investment: plant and equipment for (a) manufacturing (b) regulated and mining and (c) commercial industries; non-farm housing; 2 categories of inventory changes. Imports: foods, materials and unfinished goods, and others. Exports. Max. and actual gross output from manufacturing. Latter only for non-manufacturing non-farm, non-rent sector. GNP

list of endogenous variables

(II) Income, employment and resources	(III) Prices and compensation rates	(IV) Money and finance	(V) Taxes and transfers	Total no. of (and list of more unusual) exogenous variables
(28) For (a) manufacturing, (b) non-manufacturing non-farm sectors: employment, hours worked per person p.a., and total wage bills. Capacity utilisation index. Unemployment rates (overall and males between 25 and 34). Corporate profits. Dividends. Non-farm unincorporated business income. Rent and net interest paid. Retained income (total and manufacturing corporations). Personal income (total and disposable). National income. Total and manufacturing sector labour forces. Capital stocks and depreciation for manufacturing, regulated and mining, and commercial sectors. Capital stock for non-manu' non-farm sector. Depreciation for housing construction	(14) Price indices for: GNP, consumption, cars, other consumer durables, non-durables and services, non-farm housing construction, business investment, exports, and output originating in (a) manufacturing and (b) non-manufacturing non-farm sectors. Wage-rates for (a) manufacturing and (b) non-manufacturing non-farm sectors. Short-term interest rate. Average yield on bonds	(1) Cash flow in manufacturing sector	(4) Personal, corporate income and indirect taxes. Transfer payments	(37) 8 variables relating to the agricultural sector: investment in plant and equipment, change in inventories, level of employment, index of prices received, etc. 6 dummy variables relating to periods of war, supply shortages, unfilled orders, strikes, etc. Almon weighted lag structure used in investment functions. Net free reserves as a fraction of total required reserves. Population plus 4 special employment categories. Price indices for world trade, imports, rents, gov't purchases. Index of world trade

(4) Other endogenous variables. Inventory valuation adjustment. Stock of (a) cars and (b) other durables. Unfilled orders

Table 5.1. A tabular summary of seven

Economy and model. Reference. Observation period [and type of data	No. of stochastic (S) and other (O) equations. Estimation method	Dynamic and special features	Number and	
			(I) Aggregate demand	
7. United States, Brookings Project. Duesenberry, Fromm, Klein and Kuh (eds) (1965). 1953 (3)–60, quarterly data	S 115 O 88 Total 203 Mainly LIML but some 2SLS and some OLS (for recursive block)	Lags to $(t-8)$ and other usual dynamic features. Many variables in the form of the product or quotient of two or more other variables. Many non-linear identities. Detailed treatment of the investment, construction, financial, public and agricultural sectors. In the first, full use is made of survey information by a distinction between intentions and realisation. (The edited preliminary version of the model includes an alternative, more conventional, set of equations for this sector.) The unedited version of the financial sector includes an attempt to explain holdings of six financial assets as a fraction of total wealth. Unusual endogenous variables include (a) demographic variables such as the no. of new marriages and (b) variables relating to the public sector, e.g. employment, wage rates and total wage bills.

Other detail is largely associated with the degree of sectoral disaggregation that is adopted. Much of the attention to detail throughout the model is, however, achieved by heavy reliance on autogressive 'explanations'. An input–output table is used to relate final demands to production totals | (46) 6 consumption categories plus 1 associated variable. 4 categories of investment (a) realisations and (b) intentions. 3 categories of residential construction + non-residential const. + 9 associated variables. 4 inventory changes. Exports. 2 categories of imports. 3 categories of government expenditure. 7 final demand categories. GNP.

(23) Aggregations relating to the totals and various components of: Consumption (6). Change in inventories of (a) manufacturing industries and (b) farm business inventory stock.

Gross business investment in plant and equipment. Govt. expenditures (7). Manufacturing gross product. GNP (5). Imports | |

list of endogenous variables

(II) Income, employment and resources	(III) Prices and compensation rates	(IV) Money and finance	(V) Taxes and transfer	Total no. of (and list of more unusual) exogenous variables
(50) 3 wage bill categories in the public sector. 7 categories of profits. Dividends. Retained earnings. 2 categories of interest income. Agricultural sector depreciation. 3 categories of depreciation (accounting prices); 7 categories of replacement costs. Gross and net farm income. Personal income. Disposable income. 9 employment levels and 1 trend. 2 total hours of employment p.a. 4 average hours worked per man per week. 4 labour force categories. Capital stock.	(40) 20 price indices. 9 'unreconciled' constructed deflators. Wage rates: 3 public sector, 6 private sector. Yield on commercial bank time deposits. Yield on gov't securities	(3) Private (a) demand and (b) time deposits of commercial Banks. Federal Reserve Banks' time deposits.	(15) 8 categories of taxation (incl. separate federal and state taxes). 5 transfer payments. 2 contributions to social insurance funds.	Over 200. Index of consumer attitudes and intentions to buy. Consumer credit extensions. World exports and unit value index of world exports. Various components of imports and exports. Conscription rate, no. of expected marriages, no. of expected households and various other demographic variables. Realised capital gains. Rent income of persons. Various components of public sector receipts, expenditures and transfer payments. Various price indices. Various explanatory variables used in the more specialised components of the model
(7) Aggregates: 2 wage bill totals. 2 labour force totals. 3 unemployment totals		(1) Aggregates: Holdings of currency plus time and demand deposits.	(8) Aggregates: 4 taxation totals. 2 transfer payments. 1 social insurance contribution. Federal govt. surplus or deficit.	such as the agric' sector (e.g. prod. of feed crops in the current year, inventory stock of cattle and pigs, etc.) and the financial sector (e.g. various categories of marketable gov't debt). Several binary variables.
(10) Other endogenous variables: Stock of (a) durables and (b) durables other than cars. Inventory valuation adjustment. Farm operation expenditures. User cost of capital. 2 categories of (a) net new orders and (b) unfilled orders. Number of marriages.				

The first two of the seven models discussed below are small enough to be reproduced in full and are therefore used as a means of illustrating the structure of a complete model. So far as the other models are concerned, reference is made only to certain sections of the models in pointing out particular areas of development. However, a broad review of all seven models is given in the tabulated summary in Table 5.1.[1] The order in which they are presented is largely chronological, that is it corresponds to the dates by which most of the work on the particular version of each model cited had been completed (which are considerably different from the publication dates of the references given for four of the models). An exception is made in considering the Brookings model last, however, in view of its marked dissimilarities from the other six models. It should also be noted that the particular edited version of the Brookings model dealt with here is the 'approximation' that was presented in the first complete report on this project. See Fromm and Klein (1965). Although it has been followed by a series of modifications,[2] it is believed that this version still serves as a particularly useful introduction to the project since it is expressly set out against the background of work done by specialists on the different components of the model while the main characteristics of the system, and the research strategy behind it, have remained essentially the same.

The layout adopted in the summary and the features of the models described are intended to provide a convenient guide to the comparative size and scope of the models. However, caution should be exercised in interpreting what is no more than limited description; in particular the summary can in no way be regarded as a substitute for an understanding of this work that is based on detailed reference to the models themselves. For example, one model may appear to have a wider scope than another judging from the number of endogenous variables, each of which requires an explanation. However, many of the additional 'explanations' may be largely based on simple autoregressions.

So far as size is concerned, the number of stochastic equations is a better guide than the total number of equations. This is because the number of definitions and accounting identities added to the stochastic equations can be somewhat arbitrary. Some non-stochastic relationships may simply express the aggregation of the sub-divisions of one variable (for example total consumption is the sum of expenditures on different categories of consumer goods and services) and an attempt has been made to eliminate these, even though their removal is subject to the same kind of arbitrariness that is involved in their original selection as part of a model. (There are so many examples of this particular kind of non-stochastic relationship in the case of the Brookings model, however, that a separate category of endogenous variable is adopted under the heading 'aggregations'.) Other definitions have, however, a more

---

[1] See also Nerlove (1966), for a similar review of 25 macro-economic models.

[2] See, for example, Fromm and Taubman's (1968), 'still preliminary', condensed, 177-equation version of the model that they use to examine how policy actions can be analysed using a large-scale model and a second volume of essays on the model edited by Duesenberry, Fromm, Klein and Kuh (1969), Chapter 11.

important role in 'closing the model' by providing an explanation of one variable once others have been accounted for elsewhere (such as profits as a residual component of aggregate income).

5.5 KLEIN III

Although circumscribed by the available data and by weaknesses which have been tackled in subsequent work, Klein's third model in his Cowles Commission study (1950), *Economic fluctuations in the United States, 1921–41* still provides an instructive introduction to the formulation of macro-economic models. It is also an early example of Klein's influential work in this area which has continued through to the present day. It may thus serve both as an illustration of what is involved in the specification of a simple macro-economic model and as an important contribution to an appreciation of the evolution of these models.

Described at the time as a 'large structural model', Klein III is, however, small by comparison with its modern counterparts and is reproduced in full over pp. 132–4.[1] It consists of twelve stochastic equations and four non-stochastic relationships in the form of identities and definitions which together cover not only five components of aggregate demand (i.e. consumption (C),[2] net investment in private producers' plant and equipment (I), gross construction expenditure on owner-occupied non-farm housing (D_1) and on rented non-farm housing (D_2) and the stock of inventories (H)) and two components of national income (the private sector wage bill (W_1) and non-farm rentals (R_1)), but also the price index for output as a whole (p), two factor compensation rates (a rent index (r) and the average corporate bond yield (i)) and two components of liquidity (demand deposits plus circulating currency (M_1^D) and time deposits (M_2^D)). The principal omissions in the scope of the model are, therefore, a neglect of foreign trade, the absence of an important item of income in the form of business profits and the losses involved in rolling all categories of government reserve and transfer payment, plus government i nterest payments and corporate savings, into a single exogenous variable (T).

The components of aggregate demand are reckoned in real terms using various sources to provide the different price deflators required. Price determination within the model is reluctantly restricted to the price level for output as a whole because of the lack of data needed to provide explanations of other prices. Given the three exogenous variables (i) depreciation on all housing (recalling that investment in business plant and equipment is already expressed net of depreciation), (ii) gross construction expenditure on farm housing, and

---

[1] The sample statistics δ^2/S^2 and $\bar{S}$ refer to the von Neumann ratio $(= d \cdot N/(N-1))$ which is a check on the seriousness of autocorrelated disturbances, and the root mean square of the residuals adjusted for degrees of freedom, see (1.13).

[2] Variables measured in terms of current prices are in bold-face type; all other variables are expressed in real terms.

(iii) the composite variable G (which includes government expenditure, net exports and other items of investment not dealt with elsewhere), the net national product ($Y + T$) can be determined. Disposable income (Y) is fixed, and can therefore be used to complete the circular flow with respect to consumption and expenditure on new owner-occupied housing, given the composite variable, T. Net private output, excluding housing services (X) less excise taxes (E) (both of which are expressed in money terms and are then deflated using an exogenously determined price index for capital goods), is used as an explanatory variable in the determination of the level of business investment in plant and equipment in the belief that net sales income, as a return on capital (K_{-1}), is an important influence on the decision to invest. Other versions of the same variable also appear in the explanations offered for the demand for inventories (5.11c) and (even more curiously) for the total wage bill of the private sector (5.11h).

KLEIN III

Demand for consumer goods

$$C = 11{\cdot}87 + 0{\cdot}73\,Y + 0{\cdot}04(t - 1931) + u_1'$$

$$\frac{\delta^2}{S^2} = 1{\cdot}20 \qquad \bar{S} = 1{\cdot}36 \tag{5.11a}$$

Demand for private producers' plant and equipment

$$I = 2{\cdot}59 + 0{\cdot}12 \left(\frac{pN - \text{E}}{q} \right) + 0{\cdot}04 \left(\frac{pN - \text{E}}{q} \right)_{-1} - 0{\cdot}10K_{-1} + u_2'$$

$$\frac{\delta^2}{S^2} = 1{\cdot}59 \qquad \bar{S} = 0{\cdot}17 \tag{b}$$

Demand for inventories

$$H = 1{\cdot}17 + 4{\cdot}60p + 0{\cdot}12(X - \Delta H) + 0{\cdot}50H_{-1} + u_3'$$

$$\frac{\delta^2}{S^2} = 2{\cdot}26 \qquad \bar{S} = 0{\cdot}55 \tag{c}$$

Demand for owner-occupied houses

$$D_1 = -9{\cdot}03 + 3{\cdot}74 \left(\frac{r}{q_1} \right) + 0{\cdot}02(Y + Y_{-1} + Y_{-2}) + 0{\cdot}0043\Delta F + u_4'$$

$$\frac{\delta^2}{S^2} = 2{\cdot}26 \qquad \bar{S} = 0{\cdot}21 \tag{d}$$

Demand for rented housing

$$D_2 = -2 \cdot 14 + 2 \cdot 81 r_{-1} + 0 \cdot 02(q_1)_{-1} - 0 \cdot 44(q_1)_{-2}$$
$$+ 0 \cdot 0016(\Delta F)_{-1} - 0 \cdot 18i + u'_5$$

$$\frac{\delta^2}{S^2} = 2 \cdot 07 \qquad \bar{S} = 0 \cdot 26 \qquad\qquad (e)$$

Proportion of non-farm housing units occupied at the end of the year

$$v = 178 \cdot 01 + 0 \cdot 29\,Y - 2 \cdot 62r + 1 \cdot 42(t - 1931) - 3 \cdot 76N^S + u'_6$$

$$\frac{\delta^2}{S^2} = 1 \cdot 52 \qquad \bar{S} = 0 \cdot 97 \qquad\qquad (f)$$

Rent adjustment

$$\Delta r = -2 \cdot 15 + 0 \cdot 02v_{-1} + 0 \cdot 00071\,Y + 0 \cdot 17\frac{1}{r_{-1}} + u'_7$$

$$\frac{\delta^2}{S^2} = 1 \cdot 04 \qquad \bar{S} = 0 \cdot 03 \qquad\qquad (g)$$

Demand for labour

$$\mathbf{W}_1 = 5 \cdot 04 + 0 \cdot 41(pX - \mathbf{E}) + 0 \cdot 17(pX - \mathbf{E})_{-1} + 0 \cdot 17(t - 1931) + u'_8$$

$$\frac{\delta^2}{S^2} = 1 \cdot 89 \qquad \bar{S} = 1 \cdot 00 \qquad\qquad (h)$$

Demand for active balances

$$\mathbf{M}_1^D = 8 \cdot 45 + 0 \cdot 24p(Y + T) + 0 \cdot 03p(Y + T)(t - 1931)$$
$$- 1 \cdot 43(t - 1931) + u'_9$$

$$\frac{\delta^2}{S^2} = 1 \cdot 33 \qquad \bar{S} = 1 \cdot 26 \qquad\qquad (i)$$

Demand for idle cash balances

$$\mathbf{M}_2^D = 15 \cdot 37 + 0 \cdot 28i - 1 \cdot 90i_{-1} + 0 \cdot 74(\mathbf{M}_2^D)_{-1} - 0 \cdot 18(t - 1931) + u'_{10}$$

$$\frac{\delta^2}{S^2} = 1 \cdot 49 \qquad \bar{S} = 0 \cdot 67 \qquad\qquad (j)$$

Interest rate adjustment

$$\Delta i = 2 \cdot 00 - 0 \cdot 17\mathbf{E}_R - 0 \cdot 37i_{-1} - 0 \cdot 0052(t - 1931) + u'_{11}$$

$$\frac{\delta^2}{S^2} = 1 \cdot 77 \qquad \bar{S} = 0 \cdot 47 \qquad\qquad (k)$$

Output adjustment

$$\Delta X = 2\cdot55 - 4\cdot46(u_3)_{-1} + 82\cdot76\Delta p + u'_{12}$$

$$\frac{\delta^2}{S^2} = 1\cdot83 \qquad \bar{S} = 2\cdot61 \tag{l}$$

Net national product identity

$$Y + T = I + \Delta H + C + D_1 + D_2 + D_3 - D'' + G \tag{m}$$

Stock of capital identity

$$\Delta K = I \tag{n}$$

Definition of private output excluding housing

$$X = \frac{p(Y + T) - \mathbf{W}_2 - \mathbf{R}_1 - \mathbf{R}_2}{p} \tag{o}$$

Definition of rental payments

$$\mathbf{R}_1 = 0\cdot278r \left(\frac{vN^S}{100} + \frac{v_{-1}N^S_{-1}}{100} \right) \frac{1}{2} \tag{p}$$

Endogenous variables:

$$C, Y, I, X, K, H, p, D_1, r, D_2, \mathbf{W}_1, i, v, \mathbf{M}^D_1, \mathbf{M}^D_2, \mathbf{R}_1.$$

Exogenous variables:

$$\mathbf{E}, t, q, q_1, \Delta F, N^S, T, \mathbf{E}_R, D_3, D'', G, \mathbf{W}_2, \mathbf{R}_2.$$

The special attention given to housing in the separate investment functions (5.11*d*) and (5.11*e*) is extended by explanations of the level of rents, the proportion of non-farm housing units occupied at the end of the year and total non-farm rentals. All of these functions can be seen to be integrated parts of the model since not only do they establish variables which are used elsewhere in the model as explanatory variables but they themselves use other endogenous variables as explanatory variables so that a group of endogenous variables are specified as being mutually determined. In contrast, the monetary and financial equations of the model are either segmentable or recursive. Equations (5.11*i*) and (5.11*j*) contribute nothing to the explanation of other variables and simply enlarge the range of output from the model once certain other variables have been mutually determined within the model. On the other hand, equation (5.11*k*) is simply an 'input channel' which can be estimated without bias using OLS formulae and which could be removed, leaving *i* an exogenous variable, without substantially changing any solution of the model used for the purposes of forecasting. Similarly, the private wage bill is determined in isolation from the rest of the model while, again in contrast to the attention given to housing, none of the component parts of the private wage bill are dealt with (these include labour productivity, the level of employment, the number of hours worked per person per unit period of time and the wage rate).

The rent and interest rate equations are adjustment mechanisms which account for movements in these two variables that are necessary to balance supply and demand in the housing and money markets. An adjustment of this kind is considered inappropriate for an economy as a whole; in this case output is reckoned as the adjustment variable rather than price (5.11*l*). The hypotheses here is that aggregate supply and demand balance but for a random disturbance, which may be taken as excessive or inadequate inventories relative to some desired level so that this variable can be regarded as being accounted for by the disturbance, u_3, in the equation for inventory demand (5.11*c*). The term Δp is added to show that price fluctuations also have a bearing on variations in output. The price index, p, is thereby established.

Although crude by present standards, Klein III can be seen as an important prototype for the models which have followed. The circular flow between expenditures and incomes is used as the basis of the simultaneous and mutual determination of a series of variables and although attention is focused on demand, using seven categories of aggregate demand, five of which are endogenously determined, total disposable income and the total wage bill of the private sector are explained by the model. Several other vital features are also recognised, albeit in an undeveloped form: a distinction is observed between variables expressed in real terms and in terms of current prices while the general price level is explained by the model even though it is overworked and other prices are taken as given; dynamic adjustment equations are used to determine the compensation rates for two factors even though the wage rate and other factors in the determination of the total wage bill of the private sector are ignored as are other items of income distribution (e.g. profits and dividends); other dynamic features include the appearance of lagged endogenous variables elsewhere in the model, including other endogenous variables expressed in terms of first differences, and time trends; the money market is considered even though it is poorly integrated with the rest of the model; and two variables are introduced to take account of the impact of government fiscal policy although they are insufficiently disaggregated for the model to be sensitive to the different instruments of this policy.

5.6 KLEIN–GOLDBERGER II

Among the more important differences between Klein III and the well-known Klein–Goldberger (1955) model of the United States' economy for the period 1929–52 are those which relate to the components of national income.[1] In addition to the determination of the total wage bill for the private sector (W_1), which is, incidentally, in this instance related to the *total* output of the

---

[1] As in the case of estimates of the previous model, δ^2/S^2 refers to estimates of the von Neumann ratio while figures in parentheses below each estimated parameter are estimated standard errors of these estimates.

private sector rather than total output less excise taxes as in Klein III, explanations are also provided for non-wage, non-farm income, P (as a residual in (5.12q)) and farm income, excluding government payments to farmers, A_1 (A_2 consists wholly of government payments to farmers); used separately (as in the consumption function) or in conjunction (as in the investment function and the household liquidity preference function), they are more useful than the rentals found in Klein III. A corporate savings function is also included using three explanatory variables: (i) net corporate income after corporate taxes have been paid, as a relevant measure of disposable income; (ii) lagged dividend payments, assuming a stable dividends policy; and (iii) accumulated corporate surpluses, which may serve as a reserve fund in the pursuit of stable dividends. Having covered these variables it is now possible to write a consumption function using three (endogenous) disposable income components (relating to wage, distributed non-wage, non-farm and farm incomes), which are regarded as separate explanatory variables in an attempt to cope with the high level of consumption experienced in the post-war years by recognising the possibility of different marginal propensities to consume associated with these different categories of income.[1] A gross income variable in the form of disposable non-wage, non-farm income ($P - T_P$) and disposable agricultural income ($A - T_A$) plus depreciation allowances (D), is retained as an explanatory variable in the investment function and the long-term rate of interest (found to be not statistically significant) and liquid assets held by enterprises are also included as explanatory variables. Imports (F_T) are added to the endogenous components of aggregate demand but expenditure on new housing construction is no longer separately accounted for.

KLEIN–GOLDBERGER II

A consumption function

$$C = -22\cdot26 + 0\cdot55(W_1 + W_2 - T_W) + 0\cdot41(P - T_P - S_P)$$
$$\quad (9\cdot66) \quad (0\cdot06) \qquad\qquad\qquad (0\cdot05)$$
$$+ 0\cdot34(A_1 + A_2 - T_A) + 0\cdot26C_{-1} + 0\cdot072(L_1)_{-1} + 0\cdot26N_P$$
$$\quad (0\cdot04) \qquad\qquad\quad (0\cdot075) \quad\quad (0\cdot025) \qquad\quad (0\cdot10) \qquad (5.12a)$$
$$\delta^2/S^2 = 1\cdot98$$

[1] The problem of accurately distinguishing the separate effects of each of these explanatory variables on consumption that is raised by multicollinearity is overcome by the use of cross-section data to obtain the ratios of the three marginal propensities to consume first. One of the parameters may then be obtained in isolation from the time-series data leaving the others to be determined by means of the cross-section information.

This approach presents its own problems however. For example, Christ (1956), p. 392, argues that labour incomes are less subject to erratic variation than farm and property incomes so that the consumption picture obtained for the last two categories of income in any given year is relatively poor. In particular, consumption levels tend to be recorded at too low a level for better remunerated farmers and property-income receivers in any given year, while this is less of a problem for the less well paid so that, overall, the marginal propensity to consume is underestimated and is too low relative to the estimated marginal propensity to consume for wage-earners.

An investment function

$$I = -16{\cdot}71 + 0{\cdot}78(P - T_P + A_1 + A_2 - T_A + D)_{-1} - 0{\cdot}073K_{-1}$$
$$(4{\cdot}74)\quad(0{\cdot}18)\phantom{(P - T_P + A_1 + A_2 - T_A + D)_{-1} - }(0{\cdot}067)$$

$$+0{\cdot}14(L_2)_{-1} \qquad\qquad\qquad (b)$$
$$(0{\cdot}11)$$

$$\delta^2/S^2 = 2{\cdot}08$$

A corporate savings function

$$S_P = -3{\cdot}53 + 0{\cdot}72(P_C - T_C) + 0{\cdot}076(P_C - T_C - S_P)_{-1} - 0{\cdot}028B_{-1}$$
$$(1{\cdot}02)\quad(0{\cdot}06)(0{\cdot}254)\phantom{(P_C - T_C - S_P)_{-1} - }(0{\cdot}019)$$

$$(c)$$

$$\delta^2/S^2 = 0{\cdot}99$$

A relationship between corporate savings and non-wage, non-farm income

$$P_C = -7{\cdot}60 + 0{\cdot}68P \qquad\qquad\qquad (d)$$
$$(0{\cdot}54)\quad(0{\cdot}02)$$

$$\delta^2/S^2 = 1{\cdot}28$$

A depreciation function

$$D = 7{\cdot}25 + 0{\cdot}10\,\frac{K + K_{-1}}{2} + 0{\cdot}044(Y + T + D - W_2) \qquad (e)$$
$$(0{\cdot}80)\quad(0{\cdot}01)\phantom{\frac{K + K_{-1}}{2} + }(0{\cdot}008)$$

$$\delta^2/S^2 = 0{\cdot}94$$

A demand for labour function

$$W_1 = -1{\cdot}40 + 0{\cdot}24(Y + T + D - W_2) + 0{\cdot}24(Y + T + D - W_2)_{-1}$$
$$(1{\cdot}46)\quad(0{\cdot}07)(0{\cdot}06)$$

$$+0{\cdot}29t \qquad\qquad\qquad\qquad (f)$$
$$(0{\cdot}125)$$

$$\delta^2/S^2 = 2{\cdot}45$$

A production function

$$(Y + T + D - W_2) = -26{\cdot}08 + 2{\cdot}17[h(N_W - N_G) + N_E + N_F]$$
$$(7{\cdot}27)\quad(0{\cdot}18)$$

$$+0{\cdot}16\,\frac{K + K_{-1}}{2} + 2{\cdot}05t \qquad (g)$$
$$(0{\cdot}05)\phantom{\frac{K + K_{-1}}{2} + }(0{\cdot}16)$$

$$\delta^2/S^2 = 1{\cdot}09$$

A labour market adjustment function

$$w - w_{-1} = 4.11 - 0.74(N - N_W - N_E - N_F) + 0.52(p_{-1} - p_{-2}) + 0.54t$$
$$\quad\quad\quad (4.85)\ (0.61) \quad\quad\quad\quad\quad\quad\quad\quad\quad (0.28) \quad\quad\quad\quad (0.24)$$

$$\delta^2/S^2 = 2.38 \tag{h}$$

An import function

$$F_1 = 0.32$$
$$\quad\ (0.49)$$

$$+ 0.0060(W_1 + W_2 - T_W + P - T_P + A_1 + A_2 - T_A)\frac{p}{p_I} + 0.81(F_I)_{-1}$$
$$(0.0084) \quad\quad\quad\quad\quad\quad\quad\quad\quad\quad\quad\quad\quad\quad\quad\quad\quad (0.21)$$

$$\tag{i}$$

$$\delta^2/S^2 = 2.33$$

An agricultural income function

$$A_1\frac{p}{p_A} = -0.36 + 0.054(W_1 + W_2 - T_W + P - T_P - S)_p\frac{p}{p_A}$$
$$\quad\quad\quad (2.12)\ (0.045)$$

$$- 0.007(W_1 + W_2 - T_W + P - T_P - S_P)_{-1}\frac{p_1}{(p_A)_{-1}} + 0.012(F_1)$$
$$(0.043) \quad\quad\quad\quad\quad\quad\quad\quad\quad\quad\quad\quad\quad\quad\quad (0.006)$$

$$\tag{j}$$

$$\delta^2/S^2 = 0.85$$

A relationship between agricultural and non-agricultural prices

$$p_A = -131.17 + 2.32p \tag{k}$$
$$\quad\quad (15.3)\quad (0.11)$$

$$\delta^2/S^2 = 0.74$$

A household liquidity preference function

$$L_1 = 0.14(W_1 + W_2 - T_W + P - T_P - S_P + A_1 + A_2 - T_A)$$
$$+ 76.03(i_L - 2.0)^{(0.03)}_{-0.84} \tag{l}$$
$$(15.31)$$

$$\delta^2/S^2 = 0.73 \text{ (for the logarithmic form of residuals)}$$

A business liquidity preference function

$$L_2 = -0.34 + 0.26(W_1) - 1.02(i_S) - 0.26(p - p_{-1}) + 0.61(L_2)_{-1}$$
$$\quad\ (0.99)\ (0.03)\quad\quad (0.19)\quad\quad (0.06)\quad\quad\quad\quad (0.06)$$

$$\tag{m}$$

$$\delta^2/S^2 = 1.72$$

A relationship between short and long-term interest notes

$$i_L = 2 \cdot 58 + 0 \cdot 44(i_S)_{-3} + 0 \cdot 26(i_S)_{-5} \qquad (n)$$
$$(0 \cdot 15) \quad (0 \cdot 10) \qquad\qquad (0 \cdot 09)$$

$$\delta^2/S^2 = 0 \cdot 84$$

A money market adjustment function

$$100 \frac{(i_S) - (i_S)_{-1}}{(i_S)_{-1}} = 11 \cdot 17 - 0 \cdot 67R \qquad (o)$$
$$(7 \cdot 81) \quad (0 \cdot 30)$$

$$\delta^2/S^2 = 1 \cdot 59$$

Identities and definitions

$$C + I + G + F_E - F_I = Y + T + D \qquad (p)$$

$$W_1 + W_2 + P + A_1 + A_2 = Y \qquad (q)$$

$$h \frac{w}{p}(N_W) = W_1 + W_2 \qquad (r)$$

$$K - K_{-1} = I - D \qquad (s)$$

$$B - B_{-1} = S_P \qquad (t)$$

Endogenous variables:

$p, C, W_1, P, S_P, A_1, L_2, I, D, i_L, K, L_2, P_C, B, Y, N_W, w, F_I, p_A, i_S.$

Exogenous variables:

$W_2, T_W, T_P, T_A, A_2, N_P, T_C, t, h, N_G, N_E, N_F, N, p_I, F_A, R, G, F_E, T.$

As part of an explicit treatment of supply considerations, a production function is included, which may be used to establish the total labour input of the private sector of the economy (in terms of man-hours) if private GNP, i.e. GNP, $(Y + T + D)$, less the public sector wage bill (W_2), isi already explained in the form of aggregate demand and the capital stock is also explained elsewhere in the model. Given the level of employment in the public sector (N_G), the number of non-farm entrepreneurs (N_E), the number of farm operators (N_F) and the numbers of hours worked per person per year (h) as exogenous variables, the number of wage-earners in the private sector (N_W) is determined. The labour market adjustment equation (5.12h) can now be used to establish the money wage rate (w) from the level of unemployment (the total labour force is added as an exogenous variable), the change in the general price level (lagged) and a time count which allows for an upward trend in money wages 'in an age of general inflation', Klein and Goldberger (1955), p. 18. Lastly, since the private sector real wage bill (W_1) is accounted for by (5.12f) in terms of the total output of the sector and a time trend, the general price level (p) is established by the identity (5.12r) that the total real wage bill is the product of the level of employment, the number of hours worked per person per year and the real wage rate. Thus in contrast to Klein III, use is made of the endogenous wage bill to determine the general price level while explanations are offered for the average money wage rate and the level of employment.[1]

Theoretical justifications are advanced for other functions including those relating to total depreciation charges, liquid assets held by persons (L_1), liquid assets held by enterprises (L_2) and movements in the short-term interest rate. The remaining equations, which establish corporate profits, an index of agricultural income and the long-term interest rate, are added in order to complete the model and are grounded largely on empirical evidence.

It will be seen that the money market equations are again not fully integrated into the structure of the model; although lagged terms in the liquid assets variables L_1 and L_2 variously appear in the consumption and investment functions, so contributing to the dynamic character of the model, these variables are determined by a segmentable sub-section. It may be noted that the reason given for the addition of the two liquidity preference functions is that they are necessary in order to obtain a more complete picture of economic fluctuations. More formally, final equations for these variables, which express each one in terms of its own past values and of the exogenous variables of the model, so defining its time path, can be obtained when the variables are included in the model as endogenous variables.

The different instruments of fiscal policy are represented in far greater detail than in Klein III; they include five categories of taxation (less transfers and subsidies in four instances), two categories of expenditure and the number of employees in the public sector, all of which are represented by exogenous variables. In forecasting the impact of a change in fiscal policy it is further recognised that government budgeting is done in money rather than real terms while taxation rates are fixed rather than levels of appropriations, which are also affected by other factors which are not directly under the control of government. Forecasts of government expenditures are, therefore, converted to real terms, by using the general price deflator, p, so increasing the non-linearity of the solution of the model used in forecasting. Net revenues are related to rates of taxation and relevant categories of income for each version of the model associated with a particular conditional forecast by means of functions fitted to hypothetical data on revenue and income which are based on an assumed tax structure and the amounts of taxes and transfers which would be associated with a few selected income levels. The parameters of these functions are then

---

[1] The possibility of further sectoral disaggregation in order to make such a model a more sensitive means of analysing economic policy has been discussed by Fox (1956) with special reference to the agricultural sector.

adjusted in making different assumptions about the tax structure in the prediction period.[1] The forecasts thereby obtained are expressed in terms of current prices and once again recourse is made to the general price index to obtain the required levels of taxation in real terms.

In contrast to these improvements in forecasting the impact of fiscal policy, the channels through which monetary policy may operate remain neglected. The only exogenous variable offered here is excess bank reserves as a fraction of total reserves (R) through which the effects of each instrument of monetary policy, like a change in bank rate, open-market operations and restrictions on the level of lending by the commercial banks, must be assessed in much the same way as government revenues and transfers are all rolled into the one variable, along with other factors, in Klein III.

Although the Klein–Goldberger model distinguishes between variables expressed in real and money terms, the accounting definitions are expressed in real terms when, strictly speaking, as Christ (1956) points out, these definitions apply to variables expressed in money terms. Ideally, both deflated and money values should be given for each variable, together with the relevant price index, as in two of the models discussed below. However, if the definitions are made to hold in real terms then either the general price index must be applied to all variables, which overlooks variations in relative prices, or each variable must be deflated by its own price index, as in the two models reviewed so far. The second approach presents difficulties so far as the components of income are concerned. If these difficulties are avoided simply by using the general price index as a deflator for these components strange effects may result. For example, in a relationship such as the consumption function, the consumption and GNP deflators used may well move relative to each other over the sample period. Christ shows that for the data used by Klein and Goldberger, their deflated personal savings, i.e. the differences between deflated consumption and disposable income, is too high at the beginning of the period and too low at the end – and is even negative in 1949 – because the GNP deflator rose by 8 per cent relative to the consumption deflator over the sample period, 1929–52.

5.7 CANADIAN MODEL IX

The model discussed in this section is one of a series produced over a seventeen-year period by a programme of research commissioned by the Government of Canada aimed at developing econometric models of the Canadian economy which would assist both in economic forecasting and in formulating economic policy. The history of this programme goes back as far as 1947 so that, although Canadian model IX was built in 1959, only four years after the publication of the Klein-Goldberger study, it is not surprising that it includes several important differences.

[1] For a given conditional forecast the functions are presented as 'auxiliary equations' which for the purpose of each forecast are effectively part of the model in the form of five definitions establishing that many more endogenous variables.

Referring first to those aspects of the model which are broadly the same as Klein–Goldberger, the principal point of similarity can be seen to be their scope, even though their structures are somewhat different (as is immediately evident from the different balance between the number of stochastic and non-stochastic relationships). Thus the same degree of disaggregation of the components of aggregate demand is adopted, apart from the addition of a function explaining changes in inventories separately from gross fixed capital formation in plant and equipment in the non-agricultural business sector (GI_{PM}^{na}), while more or less the same amount of attention is given to supply considerations, although the treatment of the market for labour is considerably expanded, in a way which is described below.

The money market is represented in the form of endogenous variables for money held for transactions and for savings purposes and the long-term interest rate. A measure of the liquid assets of households (L_h) is included as an exogenous variable and appears in two of the additional functions relating to the market for labour, i.e. functions determining the participation rate of the labour force and the standard number of hours worked per worker per annum. Again, however, the endogenous variables are not integrated with the rest of the model since none of them are used elsewhere in the model as explanatory variables, while only one is related to an endogenous variable established elsewhere in the model. So far as the demand for money in particular is concerned, the same device is used as in the Klein–Goldberger model to establish the ratio of the transactions demand for money to total income (in this instance in the form of the gross domestic flow of new final goods through the economy (GDF), i.e. GDP plus imports), in referring to a year in which this ratio is a minimum (m_0) when idle money balances are assumed to be zero. The total demand for money (M) is then

$$M = M_t + M_s \tag{5.13a}$$

$$M_t = m_0 GDF \cdot P^+ \tag{b}$$

$$M_s = 4{\cdot}2184 - 0{\cdot}9928i_l - 0{\cdot}0007995P_e + u_{12} \qquad \bar{R} = 0{\cdot}657, \tag{c}$$
$$\phantom{M_s = 4{\cdot}2184 - }(5{\cdot}3) \qquad\quad (0{\cdot}004) \qquad\qquad \delta^2/S^2 = 0{\cdot}991$$

where P^+ is a price deflator for GDF and P_e is a price index for equities (which was found to be statistically non-significant).[1]

Lastly among these points of similarity with the Klein–Goldberger model, it is noted that again rates of taxation, rather than revenues, are regarded as being exogenous. In this case four definitions relating amounts of taxation to different categories of income are explicitly included as part of the specification of the model although it is of course recognised that the parameters of these functions vary as tax rates and laws change from year to year. One transfer

---

[1] The numbers in parentheses below each regression coefficient are estimated t-ratios and the von Neumann ratio estimate (δ^2/S^2) is added as a test of the randomness of the residuals.

payment, from government to labour or non-profit incomes, is similarly included, expressed in this instance in terms of the level of unemployment (N_u). For 1958

$$Tr_w = 1.946 + 1.2458N_u. \tag{5.14}$$

In turning to the main differences between the Klein–Goldberger model and Canadian model IX reference is made first to the distinction drawn between the agricultural and non-agricultural business sectors of the economy. This is carried further in the later model so that the investment function, as well as a separate inventories function and the production function, together with variables relating to the labour market (e.g. the wage rate, hours worked per person and total labour demand in man-hours), are all restricted to the non-agricultural (n.a.) business sector. Secondly, greater attention is given to price determination within the model by having separate price deflators for $GDF(P^+)$ $GDP(P)$ and $NDP/NNP(P_N)$, i.e. net domestic or national product, where

$$NDP = GDP - D$$

and *NNP* is *NDP* adjusted by net interest, dividends and profits from abroad. The last price variable is used as a more appropriate deflator than P^+ or P for the various components of aggregate income, which in contrast to Klein–Goldberger's study are determined (as shown below) in money terms rather than directly in real terms. For long-term analysis, P^+ may be obtained either as a weighted arithmetic mean of the exogenous price levels of the component parts of *GDF* with weights equal to the relative *ex post* real expenditures on these components

$$GDF_m = P^+GDF = P_CC + P_CG + P_hGI_h + P_{PM}GI_{PM}$$
$$+P_H\Delta H + P_EE \tag{5.15a}$$

or, equivalently, as the weighted harmonic mean of the price indices $P_c, \ldots,$ P_E with weights equal to the relative *ex post* money expenditures on each of the components of *GDF*

$$P^+ = \frac{C_m + GI_m + \Delta H_m + G_m + E_m}{C_m/P_C + \ldots + E_m/P_E}. \tag{5.15b}$$

For short-term analysis, P^+ is obtained from

$$P^+ = a_0 + a_1P^+_{-1} + a_2\left[\frac{GDF^d - GDF^s}{GDF^s}\right]_{-1} \tag{5.16}$$

where

$$GDF^d = C^d + G^d + GI_h^d + GI_{PM}^d + \Delta H^{nad} + \Delta H^{ad} + E^d - R_2$$

and $GDF^s = GDF^{nas} + GDP^{as} + GDP_g^s + IM_{ps}^s + IM_{tr}$

some components of which are given by the model as endogenous variables (for example, consumption, non-agricultural (n.a.) investment in plant and equipment (subscript PM), non-agricultural changes in inventories, n.a. production, and imports of goods and services (subscript ps)) while the remainder are exogenous, including a residual error on the expenditure side of the national accounts, R_2. For medium- and long-term analysis GDF^d is set equal to GDF^s, which assumes that all inventory change in the system is equal to desired inventory change.

From the definition in money terms

$$GDF_m = GDP_m + IM_m,$$

P can be obtained from

$$P^+ . GDF = P . GDP + P_{IM} . IM \qquad (5.17)$$

Similarly P_N can be determined from P using P_{PM} as the deflator for expenditures on replacing fixed investment (D_m)

$$P_N = \frac{GDP_m - D_m}{(GDP_m/P) - (D_m/P_{PM})} = \frac{P . GDP - P_{PM}D}{GDP - D}. \qquad (5.18)$$

Again in contrast to the Klein–Goldberger model, profits are calculated as a residual component of GNP rather than directly through an appropriate stochastic equation,

$$\Pi = P . GDP - P_{PM}D - P_N T_{cr} - W^{\cdot} + CG_H - P_N R_1 \qquad (5.19)$$

where

Π = total profit earned in the economy by all sectors, private and public.
T_{cr} = indirect taxes less subsidies in real (r) terms.
$W^{\cdot}$ = total wage bill, as in the national accounts.
CG_H = capital gains arising from price changes on inventories held by firms = $\Delta P_H(H_{-1} + \frac{1}{2}\Delta H)$.
R_1 = residual error on the GNP, or income as opposed to expenditure, side of the national accounts.

The components of this total profits variable may then be obtained from various definitions

$$\Pi^* = \Pi + \Pi_{id} - \Pi_{di} \qquad (5.20a)$$

$$\Pi_p = f_1(\Pi^*) \qquad \Pi_c = f_2(\Pi) \qquad (b)$$

$$\Pi_{np} = \Pi^* - \Pi_p \qquad (c)$$

$$Y_{\pi p} = \Pi_p - Tr_{\pi p} + Tr_{c3} - T_{\pi p} \qquad (d)$$

$$Y_{\pi np} = \Pi_{np} + Tr_{\pi np} - Tr_{c1} - Tr_{c2} - Tr_{c3} - Tr_{\pi np} \qquad (e)$$

$$Y_{\pi} = Y_{\pi p} + Y_{\pi np} \qquad (f)$$

$$Y_{\pi r} = Y_{\pi}/P_N \qquad (g)$$

where

$\Pi^* = $ total profit in the economy on a GNP basis.

$\Pi_{id} - \Pi_{di} = $ (net) interest, dividends and profits paid to the domestic economy from abroad (exogenous).

$\Pi_p = $ non-wage income received by persons.

$\Pi_{np} = $ property-enterprise or non-wage income not paid to persons.

$\Pi_c = $ total profit of private sector corporations.

$Tr_{\pi p} = $ transfer payments from government to personal non-wage incomes.

$Tr_{c1} = $ charitable contributions of corporations.

$Tr_{c2} = $ bad debt losses of corporations to wage sector.

$Tr_{c3} = $ bad debt losses of corporations to non-corporate business sector.

$Tr_{\pi np} = $ transfer payments from government to non-wage or property-enterprise incomes not paid out to persons. (With the exception of Tr_w, see (5.14), all transfer payments are regarded as exogenous variables and include, in $Tr_{\pi p}$ and $Tr_{\pi np}$, interest on the public debt.)

$T_{\pi p}, T_{\pi np} = $ taxes on profit income and on wealth, paid by persons and not paid by persons, respectively.

$Y_{\pi p} = $ disposable non-labour or property-enterprise income of the personal sector or households, excluding CG_h.

$Y_{\pi np} = $ disposable non-wage income not paid out to persons.

$Y_\pi = $ total disposable non-wage income (which appears as an explanatory variable in real (r) terms in the consumption function).

Last among these points of special interest from Canadian Model IX, note is made of the large sub-section of the model which is devoted to the labour market. This consists of six stochastic and six non-stochastic equations which together account for twelve endogenous variable as follows:

Average labour force participation rate applicable to N_{14}

$$pr^{\cdot} = 0{\cdot}6129 - 0{\cdot}05338 \underset{(3{\cdot}3)}{\frac{w_{ph}^{na}}{P_C}} - 0{\cdot}001063 \underset{(1{\cdot}3)}{\frac{L_h^{\cdot}}{P_C}}^{-1} + u_2 \tag{5.21a}$$

$$\bar{R} = 0{\cdot}891,\ \delta^2/S^2 = 0{\cdot}769$$

Supply of standard hours of work

$$h_s^{na} = 3{\cdot}2804 - 0{\cdot}8302 \underset{(13{\cdot}7)}{\frac{w_{ph}^{na}}{P_C}} - 0{\cdot}007262 \underset{(2{\cdot}32)}{\frac{L_h^{\cdot}}{P_C}}^{-1} + u_3 \tag{b}$$

$$\bar{R} = 0{\cdot}990,\ \delta^2/S^2 = 0{\cdot}799$$

The number of business sector paid employees (N_p^{na}) and the average hours worked per person per annum (h^{na}); demand for labour in man-hours

$$N_p^{na}h^{na} = 0.1287 + 0.4110GDP^{na} + 0.07771GDP_{-1}^{na} - 6.0430\,w_{ph}^{na}$$
$$(11.9) \qquad\qquad (1.64) \qquad\qquad (12.6)$$

$$+ 6.1872P + u_4 \qquad \bar{R} = 0.999,\ \delta^2/S^2 = 2.03 \qquad\qquad (c)$$
$$(11.0)$$

$$h^{na} = 0.01075 - 0.08240\left(\frac{Nh_u^{na}}{N_l^{na}h_s^{na}}\right) + 0.9953\,h_s^{na} + u_5 \qquad\qquad (d)$$
$$(7.1) \qquad\qquad\qquad\qquad (14.2)$$

$$\bar{R} = 0.944,\ \delta^2/S^2 = 0.415$$

A production function

$$GDP^{na} = -6.4215 + 1.7373(N_p^{na} + N_{oa}^{na} + N_{np}^{na})h^{na} + 0.2024(K_{PM}^{na} + H_j^{na})$$
$$(12.9) \qquad\qquad\qquad\qquad\qquad (7.7)$$

$$+ 0.01055t + u_9 \qquad \bar{R} = 0.997,\ \delta^2/S^2 = 1.59 \qquad\qquad (e)$$
$$(5.0)$$

Average hourly earning of paid workers in the business sector[1]

$$w_{ph}^{na} = -0.005682 + 0.9552(w_{ph}^{na})_{-1} - 0.005367Nh_u^{na}$$
$$(35.2) \qquad\qquad\qquad (0.65)$$

$$+ 0.09602\left[c_u - 100\,\frac{N_u}{N_{lc}}\right]_{\text{zero}}^{+\text{ or }+} 0.004143t + u_{10} \qquad\qquad (f)$$
$$(3.7) \qquad\qquad\qquad\qquad\qquad (3.9)$$

$$\bar{R} = 0.999,\ \delta^2/S^2 = 2.14$$

$$N_{14}^{\cdot} = N_{14} - (N_{eY} + N_M) \qquad\qquad (g)$$
$$N_l = pr^{\cdot}\,N_{14}^{\cdot} + N_{eY} + N_M \qquad\qquad (h)$$
$$N_l^{na} = N_l - (N_M + N_g + N_e^a) \qquad\qquad (i)$$
$$N_{lc} = N_l - (N_{eY} + N_M) \qquad\qquad (j)$$
$$Nh_u^{na} = N_l^{na}h_s^{na} - N_e^{na}h^{na} \qquad\qquad (k)$$
$$N_u = N_l - (N_M + N_g + N_{oa} + N_{np} + N_p^a + N_p^{na}) \qquad\qquad (l)$$

[1] The fourth term on the right-hand side of this relationship (which also appears in the import function) represents an example of the use of a special kind of non-linearity to represent the effects of a capacity limit. The variables in the term include the percentage unemployment (c_u) when all cyclical unemployment has been eliminated, leaving only structural and frictional unemployment, and the ratio of the number unemployed to the civilian labour force, N_u/N_{lc}. The variable is only added once unemployment has been reduced to the critical or threshold rate c_u (set originally at 5 per cent and later changed to 3 per cent), which has the effect of producing a corner point in the short-run supply curve for labour with a higher slope once unemployment is reduced below c_u. This is a device introduced into the Canadian models by S. J. May of the Ottawa team to give effect to a belief that 'the wage rate is not equally sticky upward as it is downward, once the labour market has begun to get tight', Brown (1970), p. 379.

Other variables not previously mentioned are as follows:

Nh_u = number of unemployed man-hours in the private sector ($= N_l h_s - N_e h$).

N_l = total number of workers in the labour force ($= N_e + N_g + N_M + N_u$).

N_p, N_{oa}, N_{np} = paid employees, own-account worker-enterprisers, and un-paid family-workers in the business sector.

K_{PM} = stock of fixed capital in plant, construction, machinery and equipment owned by the business sector.

H_j = inventory stocks of the business sector averaged over the time period, sometimes approximated by mid-period value (e.g. June 30 value for annual data) or by averaging end of period values.

c_u, N_u, N_c: see footnote, p. 146. t = time count.

N_{14} = total resident and non-institutional population, 14 years old and over.

N_{eY} = number of workers in remote areas.

N_M = total military employment in the armed forces of the country.

N_g = total civilian employment in the government sector.

N_e = total number of workers employed in the business sector ($= N_p + N_{oa} + N_{np}$).

The addition of the last six definitions ($5.21g$–l) to those associated with matters concerning taxation and profits further illustrates how the number of non-stochastic equations has come to be increased beyond the number found in the Klein–Goldberger model without substantially changing the character of the model. The principal innovations rather relate to the explanations which are offered for the labour force participation rate ($pr^{\cdot}$), the hours worked per person in the form of a trend value of the supply of hours of work (referred to as the 'standard' hours of work, h_s) and the average hours actually worked per annum per worker in the business sector (h). The first two of these three variables are related to the same explanatory variables and refer to the supply of labour while the third refers to the demand for labour.

As a concluding point, it is interesting to see the balance between this sub-section and the rest of the model. Twelve endogenous variables ($pr^{\cdot}$, w_{ph}^{na}, h_s^{na}, N_p^{na}, h^{na}, GDP^{na}, Nh_u^{na}, N_l^{na}, N_u, N_{lc}, $N_{14}^{\cdot}$, N_l) are determined if P, K_{PM}^{na} and H_j^{na} are determined elsewhere in the model. The sub-section is not, however, segmentable and indeed the use made of these three endogenous variables is matched by the explanations offered for four variables which are used elsewhere to provide three explanatory variables. They are (i) the total wage bill ($W^{\cdot}$) which is used to determine both disposable wage income (Y_w) and (using the identities given above) disposable non-wage income (Y_π)

$$W^{\cdot} = w_{ph}^{na} h^{na} N_p^{na} + w_p^a N_p^a + w_g N_g + w_M N_M \tag{5.22}$$

$$Y_w = W^{\cdot} + Tr_w + Tr_{c1} + Tr_{c2} - T_w \tag{5.23}$$

$$Y_{wr} = Y_w / P_N, \tag{5.24}$$

(ii) the unemployment rate expressed as a proportion of the civilian labour force, Nu/N_{lc}, and (iii) the gross domestic product of the non-agricultural business sector, GDP^{na}, which appears as an explanatory variable in the function for GI_{PM}^{na}.

5.8 THE DUTCH FORECASTING AND POLICY MODEL

Like the Canadian authorities, the Dutch were amongst the first to make use of an econometric model of the national economy in economic forecasting and planning. Once again, therefore, the particular model referred to here is but one of a series which together form part of a considerable research effort, undertaken in this instance by the Netherlands Central Planning Bureau. It is also a model which bears all the characteristics of having been designed, tested and refined with the express objective that it should produce, in this case for the year ahead, both accurate forecasts of what might be anticipated from current trends and policies and a reliable, analytical and consistent estimate of the consequences to be expected of various changes in policy that might be adopted. This second aspect of the model's orientation is emphasised in the way in which certain endogenous variables are seen to be associated with the main targets for the economy while several of the exogenous variables represent the various means by which government may direct the economy towards these objectives. Each of the following goals of economic policy is, for example, closely identified with a particular endogenous variable:

(i) external equilibrium: the balance on current account ($\tilde{E}$);[1]
(ii) internal equilibrium: the rate of unemployment ($\tilde{w}$);
(iii) growth: the rate of increase of total output (v) and, so far as medium- and long-term matters are concerned, change in the level of investment (i) which excludes housing construction and the public sector; and
(iv) price stability: the rate of change in the price of consumer goods (p_c). The distribution of income is not dealt with explicitly but the share of wages in national income is at least obtained from the model.

Those instruments of policy which are considered to be almost completely under the control of government are confined to total government expenditure plus spending on new housing, which is largely controlled by public policy. These are represented by a single aggregate, autonomous expenditure (x). Levels of taxation relating to labour income (T_L') and non-labour income (T_Z')

---

[1] Capitals refer to variables expressed in terms of current prices while lower-case letters refer to variables expressed in real terms. Most variables throughout the model are expressed in relative first differences, i.e.

$$x_t = 100\Delta \tilde{x}_t/\tilde{x}_{t-1}$$

where the swung-dash signifies the absolute value of a variable. This transformation of the variables is adopted in order to reduce multicollinearity and to facilitate the estimation of time lags as well as to simplify the linking of post-war observations with those of the pre-war period by avoiding sharp changes in the absolute levels of the variables concerned.

and the level of indirect taxation (T'_K) are recognised as being not so precisely determined by the available levers of policy while a second group of variables which are even less firmly under the direct control of government are referred to as semi-instruments. The latter include the wage rate (l), prices of consumer goods (p_c) and a measure of liquidity (c^r), all of which may be influenced only to a limited extent by government regulation. For the purposes of assessing the impact of policy, the semi-instruments may be first left to be entirely determined by the model as endogenous variables. The effect of such changes in the variables as it may be believed can be brought about by government intervention may then be traced from a solution of the estimated model. (See Chapter 6, Section 6.2.)

As is to be expected given the short-term forecasting role of the model and the open nature of the Dutch economy, the model is essentially built around an explanation of effective demand. Five of the thirteen stochastic equations are concerned with various categories of demand: consumption (C), investment (I), inventories (N), exports (b) and imports (m). There is no production function but supply considerations are believed to be adequately accounted for, so far as the purposes of short-term analysis are concerned, by the introduction of four price functions and a capacity variable $(\Delta \tilde{w}_l)$ which is curvilinear in the rate of unemployment $(\tilde{w})$. For 1966, $\Delta \tilde{w}_l$ is defined to be

$$\Delta \tilde{w}_l = \begin{cases} 4 \cdot 34 \Delta \ln (\tilde{w} + 2) - 0 \cdot 20 \Delta \tilde{w} & (5.25a) \\ [4 \cdot 34/(\tilde{w}_{-1} + 2) - 0 \cdot 20] \Delta \tilde{w} & (5.25b) \end{cases}$$

where the second of these alternative expressions of (5.25) is a linear approximation of (5.25a) which may be used for small changes in $\tilde{w}$ and

$$\tilde{w} \equiv \Delta \tilde{w} + \tilde{w}_{-1}$$

$$\Delta \tilde{w} = -0 \cdot 52a + 0 \cdot 34 \frac{\Delta \tilde{P} - \Delta \tilde{a}_0}{(\tilde{P}_B)_{-1}} - 0 \cdot 03 \Delta \tilde{T}_c + \Pi \left[\frac{\tilde{P}}{\tilde{P}_B} \right]_{-1} - 9 \cdot 68 + \hat{u}$$

$$(5.26)$$

where a and a_0 are respectively the number of persons employed in the private and public sectors, P is the population between the working ages 14–65, P_B is the total working population, $\tilde{T}_c$, is a climatological variable in the form of the average minimum winter temperature below 0°C (sum of monthly averages) and Π is a factor which takes on the value 4·03 for the period 1923–38 and 4·66 for 1949–60. Since $\Delta \tilde{w}_1$ appears as an explanatory variable in six of the stochastic functions, i.e. the investment, export, import, employment and wage rate functions plus the function for export prices, the system is made sensitive to changes in the level of unemployment, particularly when unemployment is very low.

Although it is recognised that the availability of either capital or labour or basic materials may set a limit on the capacity to produce, capacity effects are expressed with reference to labour alone in view of the lack of reliable figures for capital stock, the openness of the Dutch economy (which means that short-ages of basic materials can be readily relieved by imports), and earlier empirical evidence which supports this view of the importance of labour. See Verdoorn and Post (1964), who also justify the choice of (5.25) as a non-linear transforma-tion of the rate of unemployment in order to represent the effects of changes in the availability of labour as the market for labour tightens. Variants of four different transformations are discussed. They are, expressed in terms of the original values of the unemployment variable $(\tilde{w})$ and its transform $(\tilde{y})$,

1. Hyperbolic (a) $\tilde{y} = \dfrac{\alpha\tilde{w}}{(\tilde{w} + \zeta)}$ 2. Semi-logarithmic $\tilde{y} = \alpha\, e^{-\beta/(w+\zeta)}$
(i.e. exponential)

(b) $\tilde{y} = \left[\dfrac{\alpha\tilde{w}}{\tilde{w} + \zeta}\right]^{\beta/\zeta}$ 3. Double-logarithmic $\tilde{y} = (\tilde{w} + \zeta)^{\beta}\, e^{-\alpha\beta\tilde{w}}$

Since the variables used throughout are relative first differences, $d\tilde{y}/\tilde{y}$ $(= d\ln\tilde{y})$, the relative first derivatives of these transforms are of interest. They are

$1(a).$ $\dfrac{\zeta\, d\tilde{w}}{\tilde{w}(\tilde{w} + \zeta)}$ 2. $\dfrac{\beta\, d\tilde{w}}{(\tilde{w} + \zeta)^2}$

$1(b).$ $\dfrac{\beta\, d\tilde{w}}{\tilde{w}(\tilde{w} + \zeta)}$ 3. $\beta\left[\dfrac{1}{(\tilde{w} + \zeta)} - \alpha\right]d\tilde{w}.$

The first of the hyperbolic functions is ruled out since both ζ and α are parameters chosen on *a priori* grounds so that the parameter of the transformed variable would also be fixed *a priori* in this case. The exponential version of the function avoids this difficulty but, like the semi-logarithmic transformation, it suffers from the disadvantage of having $\tilde{w}^2$ in the denominator of the deriva-tive so that the slope is extremely steep for low values of $\tilde{w}$ which means that extrapolation is a 'hazardous undertaking' as full employment is approached. The double-logarithmic transformation is therefore chosen[1] and interest centres on $\ln y = \beta\{\ln(\tilde{w} + \zeta) - \alpha\tilde{w}\}$, the derivative of which is the required relative derivative of $\tilde{y}$. The parameter β is estimated in each of the six functions in which the transform appears as an explanatory variable. The {} bracketed factor is the natural logarithm of the transform. The common or Briggsian (i.e. base 10) logarithm is denoted by $\tilde{w}_l$ so that on adding a scale factor of 10

[1] The alternative

$$\tilde{y}_t = \gamma\tilde{y}_{t-1}\, e^{\beta\tilde{w}}$$

so that

$$d\tilde{y}/\tilde{y} = \beta\tilde{w} + \ln\gamma,$$

is also reported to have been tried. However, this is not an improvement on the double logarithmic transformation and has the drawback of being awkward to use in a complete model.

and values for ζ and α which give the curvilinearity a reasonable *a priori* form,

$$\tilde{w}_t = 10 \log_{10}(\tilde{w} + 2) - 0.20\tilde{w} = 4.34 \ln(\tilde{w} + 2) - 0.20\tilde{w}$$

the first difference of which, i.e. (5.25a), gives the required relative first difference of the transform of $\tilde{w}$.[1]

A distinction is made between real and current price measures of total output, less inventory charges and net invisibles (v') and its four components[2] (consumption, investment, exports and autonomous expenditures) as well as for imports. One associated result of this is that six of the definitions of the model simply relate money values of the variables concerned to their real values. (A seventh definition of this kind is added for total output, v, using the same deflater, $p_{v'}$, as for v'.) With the exception of the price index for imports, the prices found in these definitions are determined within the model. The price indices of the four components of total output v' are determined by stochastic relationships, all of which include terms in (i) the rate at which wage costs increase in excess of labour productivity and (ii) import prices, and two of which include lagged terms in the dependent variable. The general price level, $p_{v'}$, is obtained as weighted average of the price indices for the components of v'.

Other stochastic equations determine the level of employment in the private sector of the economy and the average gross wage per worker per standard year of 300 days. The total wage bill of the private sector (L) is thereby established while disposable labour income (L^B), which appears as an explanatory variable in the consumption function (which is also expressed in money terms), is given by the definition, for 1966,

$$L^B = 0.87L + 0.87O'_L \tag{5.27}$$

where O'_L is a measure of income transfers relating to labour income. Non-labour income (Z) is obtained as a residual in the same way as in Canadian model IX and appears as an explanatory variable in both the consumption function (in the form of disposable income) and the investment function, which is also expressed in money terms so again the need for a deflater for income is avoided.

The last of the thirteen stochastic equations is a liquidity function covering time and demand deposits at the beginning of the year,

$$c^r = 1.97\tilde{E} + 1.12\tilde{E}_{-1} + 0.47V' - 8.84(r_k)_{-1} + 1.67N_{-2} + 0.38r_e$$
$$- 1.00(p_{v'})_{-1} - 2.46 \tag{5.28}$$

where r_k is a short-term rate of interest, N is inventory changes (expressed as a percentage of total output, V'), and r_e is the exchange rate, all of which are exogenous variables and the first two of which are less statistically significant

---

[1] The [] bracketed multiplier in (5.25b) is negative for $\tilde{w}_{-1} > 19.5$ but this figure is outside what is observed in reality, including the unemployment levels recorded in the 'thirties.

[2] Inventories and invisibles are reckoned only in money terms.

then the other explanatory variables. The lagged price variable ($p_{v'}$) serves as a deflator. The coefficient of 0·47 for V' is seen as an indication of the 'automatic half-way adaptation of available liquidities to total output', de Wolff (1967) p. 327.

Although c_r is the only endogenous variable for the money market in the Dutch model it is much more closely integrated with the rest of the model than in the other examples looked at so far, since it appears as an explanatory variable in no less than four other functions, i.e. in the consumption, investment, employment and consumer goods price index equations. In view of the strong positive associations between c_r and the external balance on current account and between c_r and the level of employment, which of course corresponds to a negative correlation with unemployment, these relationships act as a built-in stabiliser.

5.9 THE MICHIGAN RSQE MODEL

The model described in this section is a direct development of the work of Klein and Goldberger and was undertaken by the Research Seminar in Quantitative Economics of the University of Michigan with the express object of forecasting the behaviour of the United States economy for one year ahead. (The particular version of the model referred to here is one which was used in November 1965 to provide a forecast for 1966). The aims of this research effort are therefore essentially the same as those of the work of the Central Planning Bureau of the Netherlands examined in the preceding section, and like the Dutch model this is very much an example of a business-like model which has been subject to a continuous process of revision based on hard-won experience. Again the variables are expressed in terms of first differences, in the belief that the crucial test of forecasting lies in the ability to forecast change accurately, as much as in order to help reduce multicollinearity and serial correlation in the disturbances of the model. Unlike the Dutch model, however, the different relationships expressed between the variables are deliberately restricted to linear functions in order to simplify the work involved in obtaining an analytical solution of the model for the purposes of forecasting.

The most striking difference between the Michigan model and those reviewed so far is in the further disaggregation of the components of aggregate demand. Consumer expenditures are broken down into three categories of durable goods (cars, household furniture and other durables), four categories of non-durable goods (foods and beverages, clothing and shoes, petrol and oil and other non-durables) and two categories of services in the form of housing, which is an exogenous variable, and other services. Gross capital expenditure is dealt with under five heads: plant and equipment, housing construction (which involves a separate stochastic function for housing starts), farm inventories, non-farm, non-durable inventories and durable inventories. Imports are disaggregated into six categories: unfinished materials, food and beverages (except sugar which is treated separately as an exogenous variable because it is subject to an import quota), finished materials and two other kinds of imports, which are left as exogenous variables. In addition to those variables listed so far that have already been labelled as exogenous, business expenditures on plant and equipment is projected by a survey of investment intentions in preference to an estimated regression equation while expenditure on petrol and oil is expressed as an exact linear function of the number of cars in use. The remaining fifteen variables are explained by stochastic equations. All of the stochastic consumption functions, as well as the import function for finished materials, include disposable income as an explanatory variable and four of the functions, plus the import function for food and beverages, include a price variable, all of which are exogenous in contrast to the attention given to the explanation of prices in the Dutch model. Only three of the consumption functions have explanatory variables other than income and price: the 'other services' function includes a lagged term in the dependent variable, the household furniture function includes expenditures on new housing, while the car function, relating to expenditure on both new and net second-hand cars, is the most detailed of these functions

$$\Delta A = 0.1666\Delta(Y - X_u - X_1 - X_2) + 0.8090\Delta L_{-1} - 0.0542t\Delta L_{-1}$$
$$\quad (0.0960) \qquad\qquad\qquad (0.2623) \qquad\qquad (0.0179)$$

$$\quad -3.6985(NR - SC)_{-1} + 4.1285 \qquad R^2 = 0.82. \qquad (5.29)$$
$$\quad (1.1327)$$

The first of the explanatory variables in this function is disposable income, less unemployment benefits and other transfer payments (to the aged, dependent children, etc.) which are considered to be only weakly associated with the demand for cars. The second explanatory variable, L, is a measure of the liquid assets of consumers while $(NR - SC)_{-1}$ is new car registrations in the preceding year less scrapping. The last can be seen to be a stock item which, in keeping with the other variables of the model, is already effectively reckoned in difference terms. The interaction term $t\Delta L_{-1}$ allows for a decline in the influence of household liquidity on the demand for cars, i.e. the two terms in L_{-1} combine to give $(0.81-0.05t)\Delta L_{-1}$ in the above regression result so that ΔL_{-1} has a coefficient which is declining over time.

The three stochastic import functions are formulated on much the same lines as the consumption functions while the inventories functions include the usual explanatory variables such as lagged dependent variables and relevant measures of total sales. Housing starts are explained in terms of household formations, disposable income, the stock of unoccupied housing and an index of the supply of credit available for new housing. Housing starts, lagged and unlagged, appear in turn as the explanatory variables in the new housing expenditures equation.

There are several reasons for the further disaggregation of the components of aggregate demand found in the Michigan model. In the first place, this kind of detail is useful in itself in a forecasting model when many of those who use the forecasts may be more interested in disaggregated measures. Secondly, it helps reduce aggregation errors for the reasons discussed in Section 2 of this chapter. Thirdly, the use of a separate equation for the different components of an aggregate enables the explanatory variables in each equation to be confined to those which are especially relevant. This helps to keep up the degrees of freedom available in the estimation of each equation and perhaps also reduces the problem of multicollinearity. In the Michigan model, for example, nine equations are used for expenditure on consumer goods using twelve different explanatory variables. Thus for the observation period 1952–64, which was used in estimating the 1965 version of the model, the number of explanatory variables, together with the intercept, would equal the number of observations if they were included in a single consumption function. Lastly, the disaggregation enables the different functions to be more precisely specified using constraints which may, if appropriate, improve the fit of the equation to the data. These are points which are especially well illustrated in the demand function for cars. This is an item of expenditure which has a considerable impact on the rest of the economy and yet it is more volatile than expenditure on some consumer goods and is more closely related to special variants of even the obvious explanatory variables.

As in the Dutch model, there is no explicit restriction on output so far as capacity is concerned, nor even, unlike the Dutch model, any expression of the impact of demands in excess of capacity on prices, although the impact of a tight labour market on the money wage rate goes part of the way in explaining this process. A second important shortcoming is that the model offers no explanation of interest rates nor of any measure of liquidity. Even among the exogenous variables the only measure relating to the money market, apart from the special measure of credit used in the explanation of housing starts, is in the form of liquid assets held by households which, as noted already, appears in the consumption function for cars. This quantity includes cash, demand and savings deposits, savings and loan shares and government savings bonds, so that even in the case of the demand for cars, let alone the other variables of the model, the effects of monetary policy cannot be explored in detail.

The circular flow within the macro-economy is accounted for in the usual way by tracing the impact of aggregate demand on employment and thence various categories of income. The connection between a particular category of expenditure and a related total wage bill is followed through in more detail for durable goods production workers than for other categories of employment. In this case the links of the chain first include a value added (VA) function in which (i) expenditures on two categories of durable goods, i.e. cars and all other durables, (ii) inventories of durable goods, and (iii) producers' durable equipment (PDE) appear as explanatory variables. The average hours worked per man per week (h) and the value added per worker (π), are then explained by two regression equations

$$\Delta h = 0 \cdot 091 \Delta VA - 0 \cdot 549 h_{-1} + 22 \cdot 09 \qquad R^2 = 0 \cdot 87 \qquad (5.30)$$
$$\quad\;\; (0 \cdot 013) \qquad\quad (0 \cdot 130)$$

$$\Delta \pi = 0{\cdot}216 \Delta VA - 0{\cdot}536 C^d_{-1} + 0{\cdot}839\ \Delta \left[\frac{CED + PDE}{D} \right] + 55{\cdot}89 \quad (5.31)$$
$$(0{\cdot}146) \quad\ \ (0{\cdot}136)$$
$$R^2 = 0{\cdot}82$$

where C^d is a durable goods capacity index, CED is consumer expenditures on durable goods and D is total demand for durable equipment. The significance of the first explanatory variable in (5.30) is seen to reflect the tendency for more or less hours to be worked as output varies, at least until the change becomes more firmly established. Over longer periods of time, however, it is believed that firms adjust their work force to meet a standard 40 hour week per employee. This could be examined by writing

$$\Delta h = 0{\cdot}091 \Delta VA + 0{\cdot}549(40{\cdot}0 - h_{-1}) + 0{\cdot}13 \quad\quad (5.32)$$

to see how far changes in hours worked are related to past deviations from the standard working week.

A strong trend in productivity may be seen in the large intercept for the second equation (5.31). Productivity also rises when output (VA) is increasing but is slowed down as capacity limits (C^d) are approached. The ratio term is included to allow for changes in the output mix of durables since π is an average over the whole of the durable goods producing sector but higher productivity is found in output associated with expenditures on consumer durables (CED) and producers' durable equipment (PDE), with the result that π rises as these rise in proportion to the total demand for durables (D). Once VA, h and π are known then employment can be obtained from the definition

$$E = VA/h\pi.$$

Employment in other industrial sectors is given either as an exogenous variable or as a single stochastic function of a relevant category of expenditure and other appropriate variables. Given the labour force, unemployment can now be explained and this can be used with h, since the latter affects both the total number of hours and the rates of overtime pay, to obtain the weekly wage rate (w) in money terms, for those industries for which data on this quantity are available. The total wage bill for some sectors can now be written as the product Ew, while for others it is included as an exogenous variable. Total property income may therefore be established, in money terms, as a residual component of the privately produced part of the gross national product given, in addition to the total wage bill, a deflator for private GNP, depreciation (obtained from a simple time trend) and the level of indirect taxation.

The component parts of total property income are variously established. Farm property income is an exogenous variable but non-farm property income, in the form of corporate profits and an inventory valuation adjustment, is given as a residual. This leaves dividend income to be determined by a stochastic relationship in which lagged and unlagged terms in corporate profits net of corporate profits and income taxes appear as explanatory variables.

Three component parts of disposable income (i.e., those relating to wages, property income other than corporate profits, and dividends) can now be established given the relevant taxes and transfers while given a price deflator for disposable income, this variable is also available in real terms, Y, in which form it appears as an explanatory variable in many of the equations which together explain the endogenous components of aggregate demand. (A large number of different categories of taxation and transfer payments are included in the version of the model discussed here in order to facilitate the needs of a special study of the multiplier implications of changes in social insurance taxes and benefits. Thus 23 separate tax and transfer categories are included in the model, 16 of which are explained by definitions.)

5.10 THE WHARTON EFU MODEL

Like the Michigan model, the Wharton Econometric and Forecasting Unit's (EFU) quarterly model of the United States can be regarded as a development of the Klein–Goldberger study, although its direct antecedents are to be found in independent work on quarterly models of the United States economy by Klein (1964) and Evans (1966). Despite similarities in size and scope, the Wharton model closes a number of the gaps left in the Michigan model that were discussed above. In particular, there is an explicit treatment of supply conditions and of the impact of unit labour costs and capacity utilisation on prices. Manufacturing industry is placed in a key position in this respect since a price index for gross output originating in this section (p_m) is directly related to the ratio of the wage bill to output and an index of capacity utilisation for the sector. This is in contrast to (i) five price indices which are included as exogenous variables, (ii) six other price indices which are related through stochastic relationships to either the price index for manufactures or a price deflator for output as a whole, and (iii) a price index for the non-manufacturing non-farm sector, which is obtained as a residual once price levels for the other sectors and for the economy as a whole are known. The main explanatory variables of the p_m equation are obtained with reference to a log-linear production function which relates manufacturing output (X_m) to utilised labour and capital and an exogenous productivity trend. The estimated parameters of this function are used to obtain a figure for the total putput (X_m^c) which could be produced by the sector using the total labour force available to the sector and the total capital stock. The ratio X_m/X_m^c is taken as an index of capacity utilisation for the sector. The production function is also used to determine employment in the manufacturing sector since output is related elsewhere in the model to various relevant components of aggregate demand[1]

---

[1] These are purchases of consumer non-durables and services (C_{ns}) and durables (C_d), non-farm investment in plant and equipment (I_p), change in the stock of non-farm inventories (ΔI_t) and government purchases for national defence (G_d). (Numbers in parentheses refer to estimates of the standard error of each regression coefficient while d refers to the Durbin–Watson statistic. It is recognised that a value of $d < 1\cdot4$ indicates significant positive autocorrelation of the residuals so that the standard error and $\bar{R}^2$ estimates should be treated with caution for many of the equations.)

$$X_m = -2.40 + 0.2213C_{ns} + 1.133C_d + 0.526I_p + 0.397\Delta I_t$$
$$\quad\ \ (0.0442) \quad\ \ (0.206) \quad\ (0.203) \quad\ (0.124)$$

$$+ 0.385G_d \qquad \bar{R}^2 = 0.983, \qquad d = 0.63 \qquad (5.33)$$
$$(0.038)$$

while the capital stock of the sector is determined by past investment, adjusted for depreciation,

$$K_m = \sum_{i=0}^{60} (0.953)^i (I_{pm})_{-t} \qquad (5.34)$$

Explanations of an index of hours worked in manufacturing (h_m) and the wage rate are given by further regression results[1]

$$h_m = 0.797 + 0.00076X_m + 0.00126\Delta X_m + 0.1906)(Xm/X_m^c)$$
$$\quad\ (0.00021) \qquad (0.00044) \qquad\ (0.0423)$$

$$- 0.0126wr_m \qquad \bar{R}^2 = 0.711, d = 1.61 \qquad (5.35)$$
$$(0.0050)$$

$$wr_m - (wr^m)_{-4} = 0.050 + 0.1481(\tfrac{1}{4}) \sum_{i=1}^{4} (Un - U^*)_{-i} + 4.824(p_{c_{-1}} - p_{c_{-4}})$$
$$\qquad\qquad\qquad\ (0.0234) \quad\ \ i=1 \qquad\qquad\qquad (0.521)$$

$$-0.1946[wr_m)_{-4} - (wr_m)_{-8}] \quad \bar{R}^2 = 0.657, d = 1.03$$
$$(0.0705) \qquad\qquad\qquad\qquad\qquad\qquad (5.36)$$

to complete the explanation of the total manufacturing wage bill (W_m) which is the other half of the wage bill/output ratio.

The non-manufacturing, non-farm, non-rent private sector is similarly represented by a production function and equations for hours worked and the hourly wage rate. Again the production function effectively establishes the total employment offered since, in this instance, the sector's output is obtained as a residual component of aggregate demand given manufacturing output and output originating in housing (explicit and implicit payments), X_h, as endogenous variables[2]

---

[1] The first and second of the explanatory variables in (5.36) are lagged terms in (i) the spread between the overall unemployment rate (Un) and the rate for men aged between 25 and 34 (U^*), and (ii) changes in the consumer price level (p_c). The first of these terms is introduced as a means of linearising the observed non-linearity between changes in the wage rate (wr) and the rate of unemployment (Un), i.e. $\Delta wr/wr$ is greater the lower is Un because unemployment tends to decrease more and more slowly as excess demand for labour increases. To produce a linear relationship, use is made of the fact that while U^* is usually lower than Un, as a result of the preference of employers for younger, and yet settled, men, the gap widens as unemployment decreases.

[2] The two explanatory variables in the X_h function are a measure of the stock of housing (in the form of the sum of past investment expenditures less depreciation in real terms) and personal disposable income (Y).

$$X_h = -7 \cdot 30 + 0 \cdot 0093 \sum_{i=0}^{N} \left[I_h \left[-\frac{D_h}{p_h} \right] \right]_{-i} + 0 \cdot 1321 \, Y \qquad (5.37)$$
$$ (0 \cdot 0024) \qquad\qquad\qquad\qquad\quad (0 \cdot 0125)$$

$$\bar{R}^2 = 0 \cdot 0995, \ d = 0 \cdot 42$$

and gross output originating in the farm (X_f) and government (X_g) sectors as exogenous variables. As noted already, the price level for this sector (p_n) is also obtained as a residual,

$$p_n = (pX - (p_m X_m + p_h X_h + p_f X_f + p_g X_g))/X_n \qquad (5.38)$$

which avoids the problem of defining the full capacity of the sector on this score while the ratio X_m/X_m^c for the manufacturing sector is used as a proxy for capacity utilisation in the equation explaining hours worked.

Given such detailed attention to prices it is possible to write each component of aggregate demand in both real and money terms so defining the GNP (X) deflator as the ratio of the two aggregate demand summations, as in Canadian model IX (5.15). An implicit consumption deflator is obtained in the same way as the ratio of the sum of the component parts of consumption expenditures (on cars, other durables and non-durables and services) in real and money terms. The latter is then used as a deflator for disposable income, which is obtained in money terms from aggregate demand in the usual way. As in the Michigan model corporate profits are established as a residual in an identity which sets the sum of factor shares equal to aggregate demand.

Unlike the Michigan model, the Wharton model has much the same degree of disaggregation for expenditures on consumption as found in Canadian model IX, while explanations are offered for changes in two categories of inventories[1] and for investment in non-farm residential construction, I_h, as well as for three categories of investment in plant and equipment[2] rather than leaving this item to a survey of businessmen's intentions. However, despite this last difference, the value of survey information is tested in alternative specifications of functions explaining car purchases, purchases of other durables and investment in plant and equipment in (i) manufacturing and (ii) regulated and mining industries by additional variables such as an index of consumer attitudes or the results of a survey of investment intentions. Use is also made of anticipations in the residential construction function in the form of lagged housing starts. With the exception of the modified equation for expenditures on durables other than cars, these variables appear to be significantly associated with the respective dependent variables although the resulting

---

[1] These changes relate to the stock of (i) manufacturing, I_{tm}, and (ii) non-manufacturing, non-farm inventories, I_{tn}.

[2] These are investments in plant and equipment for (i) manufacturing, I_{pm}, (ii) regulated and mining, I_{pr}, and (iii) commercial and other industries, I_{pc}.

regressions are reported to have been of limited practical value because the prediction period is restricted to just one quarter ahead in most cases.[1]

Again in contrast to the Michigan model, only three categories of taxation and one transfer payment are covered in the Wharton model. All are treated as endogenous variables which are related to appropriate categories of income or, in the case of the aggregated transfer payments variable, the level of unemployment. Two of these relationships are represented by regressions and two by definitions. Significant time trends are found in the two regression equations (for indirect business taxes and transfers and for the transfer payments variable).

As in the case of the Dutch model, an explanation is offered for the level of exports. The specification of the (single) exports functions adopted in the two models differs in the attention given to the alternative demand for domestic production that is presented by the domestic market although both functions emphasise the importance of world trading conditions. So far as the second of these issues is concerned, in the case of the exports (b) function of the Dutch model the weighted total exports (b_c) of closely competing countries and the price difference between export prices (p_b) and prices of competing exports (p'_b) are included as explanatory variables

$$b = 1{\cdot}32b_c - 2{\cdot}60(p_b - p'_b)_{-1/3} + 4{\cdot}63\Delta\tilde{w}_{l-5/12} - 0{\cdot}47\Delta p_{v'} + 0{\cdot}22. \quad (5.39)$$

It will be recalled that the variables of the Dutch model are in terms of proportional changes so that regression coefficients are estimated elasticities. The relative sizes of the parameter estimates relating to the first two variables therefore indicate that Dutch exports are more sensitive to the more general measure of trading conditions that is available in the price variable than to the level of competing exports. In addition to these influences, switches from exports to the supply of the home market are also found to play an important role. This aspect is reflected by the capacity utilisation variable $\tilde{w}_l$ (increasing capacity shortages giving rise to negative values for $\tilde{w}_l$) and by increases in the rate of inflation as measured by changes in the change of the price level of total output $p_{v'}$. In contrast, the Wharton model's exports (F_e) equation is related exclusively, at least in direct terms, to external demand factors in the form of an index of world trade (X_{wt}), the price of world trade (p_{wt}) relative to the price level of exports (p_e) and the average level of exports over the past four quarters

$$F_e = -38{\cdot}88 + 0{\cdot}1665X_{wt} + 34{\cdot}33(p_{wt}/p_e)$$
$$ (0{\cdot}0128) \phantom{+ 34{\cdot}33(} (4{\cdot}78)$$

$$+ 0{\cdot}4663(\tfrac{1}{4})\sum_{i=1}^{4}(F_e)_{-i} \qquad \bar{R}^2 = 0{\cdot}976, d = 1{\cdot}26. \qquad (5.40)$$
$$(0{\cdot}0534)$$

[1] Other refinements adopted in the specification of these equations include the use of Almon (1965) weights in the investment function to account for lags between investment decisions and expenditures, and the use of binary variables in the car sales equation in order to quantify the effects of past supply shortages for cars and changes in regulations governing consumer credit terms.

So far as the monetary sector is concerned, explanations are offered for the short-term interest rate on four to six-month commercial paper (i_S), in terms of the (exogenous) discount rate (i_d) and net free reserves as a percentage of total required reserves (*FR*), and for the average yield on bonds (i_L), in terms of a geometrically weighted sum of present and past short-term rates

$$i_S = 0.42 + 0.994i_d - 0.0895(FR) \qquad \bar{R}^2 = 0.961, \, d = 1.02 \quad (5.41)$$
$$\quad\;\; (0.034) \quad (0.0118)$$

$$i_L = 0.21 + 0.086i_S + 0.889(i_L)_{-1} \qquad \bar{R}^2 = 0.972, \, d = 1.79. \quad (5.42)$$
$$\quad\;\; (0.028) \quad (0.037)$$

The second of these variables appears as an explanatory variable in the I_{pm} and I_{pr} (see footnote 2, page 158) investment functions while the difference in the two rates is used as an explanatory variable in the I_{pc} and I_h investment functions in order to represent non-price credit rationing (on the basis of an observed rise in short-term rates relative to long-term rates during booms and *vice versa* during recessions).

Although Klein and Evans report that this condensed monetary sector proved to be a satisfactory means of taking account of the effects of monetary policies (whether in the form of changes in the discount rate, reserve require-ments or open market operations) via i_d and *FR*, the sector is expanded in a later version of the model in order to provide more information on monetary variables. The development adopted is a modification of a condensed version of the extensive 19-equation model of United States financial markets con-tributed by F. de Leeuw to the Brookings model (see pp. 166–7). The latter covers bank reserves, currency, demand deposits, time deposits, United States securities, and two broad aggregates labelled 'savings and insurance' and 'private securities', but the smaller version of this structure consists of only six equations covering the public's demand for holdings of demand deposits and for holdings of time deposits, bank holdings of free reserves, changes in the yield on bank time deposits, the term structure of United States security rates and a reserves identity. Despite their differences, however, de Leeuw (1969) notes that both versions should be 'better regarded as a set of tentative empirical explorations than a test of a well developed theory (and) there is evidence . . . suggesting that there are symptoms and important influences on financial markets not reflected in the condensed model – or in the earlier one', p. 272. The advantages of the smaller system are noted as being the ease with which it can be understood and fitted into broader models and the convenience of treating the larger model as two models when only minor approximations are required to do this since the system almost separates into two groups of equations, the first dealing with bank reserves, deposits and interest rates and the second with other financial stocks and flows which are related to the interest rates and flows determined by the first group.

The adaptation of de Leeuw's condensed model used in the Wharton EFU model consists of six stochastic equations: a third endogenous interest rate variable, in the form of the average rate paid on time deposits by member banks (i_T), is added to equations for i_S and i_L while three components of the money stock are accounted for in the form of currency outside banks ($CURR$) and demand (DD) and time (TD) deposits at all commercial banks. Evans and Klein have reported 2SLS estimates of these equations, using 12 principal components, for the period 1954. 1–1966.4. Their results are shown below:

$$\frac{CURR}{pW} = -0.001303 + \underset{(0.0341)}{0.8924} \left(\frac{CURR}{pW}\right)_{-1} \underset{(0.000436)}{-0.000665 i_T}$$

$$\underset{(0.000098)}{- 0.000249 i_s} + \underset{(0.0053)}{0.0090} \left(\frac{SALES}{pW}\right) \tag{5.43a}$$

$$\bar{R}^2 = 0.997, \ d = 1.76.$$

$$\frac{DD}{pW} = 0.06016 + \underset{(0.0485)}{0.7581} \left(\frac{DD}{pW}\right)_{-1} \underset{(0.002212)}{-0.008787 i_T} - \underset{(0.000491)}{0.002414 i_s}$$

$$+ \underset{(0.0352)}{0.0431} \left(\frac{p_c Y}{pW}\right) \tag{b}$$

$$\bar{R}^2 = 0.996, \ d = 2.07.$$

$$\frac{TD}{pW} = 0.001818 + \underset{(0.0157)}{0.9765} \left(\frac{TD}{pW}\right)_{-1} + \underset{(0.000909)}{0.005068 i_T} - \underset{(0.000392)}{0.002125 i_s} \tag{c}$$

$$\bar{R}^2 = 0.998, \ d = 1.28.$$

$$i_T = 0.2628 + \underset{(0.0607)}{0.9284}(i_T)_{-1} - \underset{(0.5517)}{0.7037} \left(\frac{TD}{DD + TD}\right)_{-1} + \underset{(0.0603)}{0.1652 d_{RQ}}$$

$$+ \underset{(0.01237)}{0.03376}[0.65(1.0 - RR_D) + (1.0 - RR_T)]i_S \tag{d}$$

$$\bar{R}^2 = 0.990, \ d = 1.68.$$

$$i_S = 0.1306 + \underset{(0.1119)}{0.2113}(i_S)_{-1} + \underset{(0.1193)}{0.8541} \, i_d - \underset{(0.0202)}{0.1005} \left(\frac{RF}{DD + TD}\right)$$

$$- \underset{(0.4517)}{0.5725} \left(\frac{\Delta RF}{DD + TD}\right)_{-1} - \underset{(2.633)}{4.398} \left(\frac{DEF}{pW}\right) \tag{e}$$

$$\bar{R}^2 = 0.969, \ d = 1.54.$$

$$i_L = 0\cdot1592 + 0\cdot9378(i_L)_{-1} + 0\cdot2117\, i_S - 0\cdot1729(i_S)_{-1} \qquad (f)$$
$$(0\cdot0438)\phantom{(i_L)_{-1} +}(0\cdot0497)(0\cdot0497)$$

$$\bar{R}^2 = 0\cdot963,\ d = 1\cdot86.$$

Three identities, defining the endogenous variables GNP less inventory investment (*SALES*), the consolidated government deficit on a national income accounts basis (*DEF*), and a surrogate for total wealth (*W*), are added to complete the sub-system

$$SALES = pX - p_m(\Delta I_{im} + \Delta I_{in}) - p_f\Delta I_{if} \qquad (5.43g)$$

$$DEF = (T_p + T_c + T_b + SocSec) - (p_gG + T_r + NIP + SSTF) \quad (h)$$

$$W = 0\cdot11 \sum_{i=1}^{19} (0\cdot89)^i(X)_{-i}. \qquad (i)$$

Following the procedure used by de Leeuw all three money stock variables are expressed as proportions of wealth, which is measured in real terms by de Leeuw's weighted average of recent GNP (5.43i) except real GNP (X) is substituted for current price GNP (pX) in order to avoid having to combine price levels for different periods. The current price measure of this variable is then given by pW. (All other non-ratio variables are also in current price terms.)[1]

Each of the three components of the money stock is a function of relevant interest rates. The estimated parameters of these variables are all negative except i_T in the time deposits equations because apart from this exception they refer to returns from holding assets other than the variable explained. The first two of these three equations also include a transaction variable; many possible transaction variables are reported to have been tried in the time deposit equation but none was found to have a significant coefficient. All three equations are of the dynamic stock adjustment type and therefore include lagged terms in the dependent variable.[2] The fourth equation is noted as being peculiar to the structure of this sub-system. It can be regarded as a supply equation for time deposits or the distribution of total deposits between time and demand deposits, since in contrast to the demand equation (5.43c) in which

---

[1] Other variables used that have not been referred to earlier are as follows: a dummy variable to account for the operation of a particular regulation affecting i_T, which appears as a percentage (d_{RQ}); government purchases of goods and service (G) and a corresponding deflator (p_g); net interest paid by government (NIP); free reserves held by member banks (RF); the required reserve ratio on demand deposits of member banks, which is a fraction (RR_D); the required reserve ratio on time deposits of member banks, which is also a fraction (RR_T); social security contributions ($SocSec$); government payments of subsidies less surpluses plus transfer payments to foreigners ($SSTF$); indirect business taxes and business transfers (T_b); corporate income taxes (T_c); personal tax and non-tax payments (T_p); and, transfer payments (T_r).

[2] The extent to which the adoption of this autoregressive structure improves the fit of the equations to observation is indicated by the relative sizes of the estimated standard errors of the variables concerned.

the estimated coefficient of i_T is positive, the coefficient of $[TD/(DD + TD)]_{-1}$ is negative. The last term in (5.43d) shows the net marginal profit for commercial banks on loans which influences the rate that they can afford to pay to depositors.

The previous i_S equation (5.41) is modified to replace the ratio of free to required reserves by the ratio $RF/(DD + TD)$. Since the denominator of the latter is a function of economic activity the new equation introduces an interaction between the real and monetary sectors in contrast to the recursive form of the original equation.[1] The last variable is seen as a means of showing the effects on credit markets of government borrowing to finance a deficit as well as a means of linking Treasury policy and Central Bank policy.

The i_L equation remains a term structure equation relating long- and short-term rates. The lagged term in i_S is found to help in reducing a pattern found in the residuals for (5.42) which indicated a persistent discrepancy in the timing between movements of the two rates. The new relationship is noted as being equivalent to

$$i_L = a_0 \sum_{j=0}^{\infty} \lambda^j (i_S)_{-j} + a_1 \sum_{j=0}^{\infty} \lambda^j (i_S)_{-1-j}$$

or

$$i_L = a_0 i_S + (a_0 \lambda + a_1) \sum_{j=0}^{\infty} \lambda^j (i_S)_{-1-j}$$

in contrast to (5.42) which, as indicated earlier, is equivalent to

$$i_L = a \sum_{j=0}^{\infty} \lambda^j (i_S)_{-j}.$$

5.11 THE BROOKINGS MODEL

Any attempt to sketch a broad review of efforts that have been made to construct econometric models of macro-economic systems would be incomplete without at least some reference to the Brookings model. And yet the size and continuing development of this project must mean that only its principal features can be covered within the scope of this text together with some reference to a limited selection of other aspects of the study which are of special interest.[2]

---

[1] No improvements in the linkage between the monetary and real sectors are introduced via other equations, but the hope is expressed of expanding the monetary sector further, and improving the treatment of mortgage markets in residential construction and consumer credit in consumer expenditures, and including capital transactions in the balance of payments.

[2] An introduction to the 1965 'first approximation', 150–200 equation, version of the model, which includes selected references to its structure, estimated parameters, predictive capability and impact multipliers, can be seen in Fromm and Klein (1965) while a review of this same version of the model is also presented in Evans (1969) pp. 503–16. This is also the version referred to in the tabular summary given in Section 5.3, which with few exceptions is the same specification subsequently used by Fromm and Taubman (1968) and others (see Duesenberry, Fromm, Klein and Kuh (1969)) for various simulation studies.

The outstanding feature of the Brookings model is of course its size; even in the edited preliminary version of the model referred to in the tabular summary above, the number of equations is in excess of 200 and there are as many exogenous variables. Although increasing the size of an econometric model is not in itself a guarantee that the model will be improved in any way, and indeed there is much to be said for the kind of simplicity in model building that is based on restricting the objectives of the analysis to be served by any one model, it is perhaps unavoidable in tackling questions relating to the structure of an economy. One of the costs may be that other properties are sacrificed. There are, for example, considerable problems with a model of this size in organising the frequent re-estimations of parameters and modifications of specification that are necessary to make the best use of the latest information to improve the accuracy of short-term forecasts. The difficulties encountered in this direction, despite the declared hope that some improvement would be achieved on the forecasting performance of existing models, are evident enough when a critic could claim that even by 1969 the model had yet to be used to produce a single *ex ante* forecast.

A number of other distinctive features of the model itself and the way it has been developed inevitably relate to the scale of the study. In the first place this is a team effort: the equations were first formulated by nineteen experts variously contributing equations relating to their own fields of specialisation, while others were involved in the estimation, solution, simulation and subsequent revisions of the model. The principal features of the model associated with this increase in the size of the Brookings model over all others are as follows:

(i) Explanations are offered for several variables relating to the agricultural sector while the treatment of other sectors (e.g. the public, foreign trade, housing and financial sectors) is considerably expanded.

(ii) Further disaggregation is introduced by expanding the classification of the various industrial sectors for which levels of output, price levels, wage rates, levels of employment, hours worked, etc., are explained.

(iii) A series of price conversion and final demand equations are included to relate the price levels of the components of final demand to the price levels of outputs from various sectors of production and to relate industrial sector outputs to different categories of expenditure. On balance the increase in the size of the model is more the result of further subdivision of the elements of aggregate demand and supply rather than extensions of the scope of explanation to new areas such as is found in the agricultural and financial sectors of the model and in the attempt to offer explanations for variables like manufacturers' orders (both net new and unfilled orders) and the number of marriages. Altogether this second category of innovations introduces only about twenty equations or less than one-fifth of the increase of about 150 equations found in the preliminary version of the Brookings model on the Canadian and Michigan models.

Quite apart from the need for a team effort to cope with the tasks of editing, estimating and testing such a large model, one of the particular advantages of this kind of approach to work on an econometric model for an economy as a whole is that specialised skills can be brought to bear in the formulation of the different functional relationships required. Space here restricts discussion of the many valuable exploratory studies contributed to the specification of the Brookings model but brief reference is made to the treatment of investment in producers' capital equipment, of the financial and public sectors and of price and output aggregation. The specification of equations relating to the first of these fields is undertaken by D. W. Jorgenson and R. Eisner. Jorgenson's pioneering efforts in the development and empirical verification of a neo-classical theory of investment (see Chapter 2) are the basis of a separate treatment of investment anticipations in the 1965 write-up of the Brookings project. In view of this restriction on Jorgenson's task, that is that it should relate to investment anticipations rather than realisations, a further chapter follows, this time from Eisner, explaining the gap between the two. The postulated explanatory variables in this second set of equations include variously lagged terms for proportional changes in variables such as sales, profits and unfilled orders as well as lagged terms in the dependent variable. On the basis of the empirical results obtained it would appear that these equations have little to add to what is already covered in the explanations of investment anticipations. Several of the variables are not statistically significant in the functions for the different sectors covered in the model and the fit is largely dependent on the lagged terms in the dependent variable. Although it is admitted in the editing of the model that Jorgenson's equations could be used, with actual investments as dependent variables, to determine capital formation without using Eisner's realisation equations, the best equation estimates from both sets of equations are selected for use in the preliminary version of the complete model which is used in the 1965 study to examine the behaviour of the model over the observation period. However, a reminder of the problems that may be encountered in ensuring that equations based on more sophisticated theory are compatible with the kind of analysis that is possible with the other equations of a model which has to relate to wider issues is found in this edited version of the model where some 'plausible estimates of linear investment functions of a very ordinary type . . . (that) might be fairly reliable for simulation studies' are presented as an alternative set of relationships to those proposed by Jorgenson and Eisner. These simply relate realised investment to the relevant capital stock, a number of lagged terms in the gross output from the sector concerned and the average yield on government securities maturing or callable in ten years or more. No comparisons are presented between the alternative sets of equations but as Griliches (1968) observes 'it seems unlikely that it (i.e. the second set) could do as well, given the variety of insignficant and wrong sign coefficients in it', (1968) p. 233.[1]

---

[1] It might be noted that current terms in endogenous variables do not appear as explanatory variables in any of the investment functions, neither in those proposed by Jorgenson and Eisner nor in any of those of the alternative set. OLS estimators of these functions are therefore consistent and indeed these equations form the lowest order block of the block

With regard to the treatment of the financial sector, several portfolio balance equations are formulated by F. de Leeuw which relate levels of, or changes in, the holdings of an asset (as a fraction of a measure of wealth) to various interest rates, to appropriate measures of short-run constraints on adjustments between actual and desired holdings (such as funds readily available to financial institutions, business firms and households) and to lagged holdings of the asset (also expressed as a fraction of wealth). As noted already, the measure of wealth used is a 'permanent income' concept in the form of a weighted average of recent values of GNP. Once the holdings of demand deposits and time deposits have been established using this kind of behavioural relationship, the required reserves of the commercial banks are known from the definition that they are equal to the product of these quantities and the respective required reserve ratios for demand and time deposits. Required reserves can now be used to determine free reserves from the identity that the sum of required and free reserves must equal unborrowed reserves, which are included in the form of an exogenous variable. A behavioural equation relating free reserves to excess reserves, the short-term treasury bill rate and the discount rate may then be regarded as determining the second of these explanatory variables. The difference between long- and short-term interest rates is related to various terms, two of which respectively measure deviations in the long-term rate from two weighted averages of past values of this rate and others of which measure changes in the maturity structure of the public debt. The model also attempts to account for the yields on private securities and on commercial bank time deposits and holdings of various other financial assets.

Despite the comprehensiveness of this treatment of the financial sector it is perhaps less integrated with the rest of the model than might have been expected; although interest rates do appear as explanatory variables and liquid assets available to consumers appear in the functions for consumer services and elsewhere, the money supply has no direct impact on prices while price expectations are not used in the explanation of observed prices, interest rates and the demand for various assets. Griliches (1968) is therefore led to conclude that the link between the monetary and real sectors of the 1965 model is both 'tenuous and superficial'. In particular, 'there is no way for monetary policy to affect the economy directly, and its indirect effects, mainly via the impact of nominal interest rates on housing and investment, manifest themselves only after a very significant lag'. In reply Fromm and Klein (1968) report that 'in de Leeuw's preliminary presentation of the partially complete Federal

---

recursive structure of the model whereby sets of simultaneous equations feed into one another in a causal chain. (As pointed out in Section 5.3, this property of recursivity can be used to simplify the problem of estimating such a large model.) In contrast, the consumption functions are part of a large simultaneous block of the system since current terms in both prices and disposable income appear in these as explanatory variables. Inventory changes, orders, labour requirements and factor income formation also make up a large simultaneous block.

Reserve Board–Massachusetts Institute of Technology model that concentrates on this very issue (i.e. on the link between monetary and real sectors), he finds, de Leeuw and Gramlich (1968), that the Brookings model has almost as high a multiplier impact of unborrowed reserves on real output as does the new monetary model'.

Some idea of the extent of disaggregation involved in the proposals for dealing with the revenues and expenditures of the public sector at federal, state and local levels of government by A. Ando, E. C. Brown and E. W. Adams, can be judged from their specification and estimation of over thirty stochastic equations for taxes and transfers together with more than twenty others for expenditures. (This is an array which is reduced to a total of 20 stochastic equations, although twice as many definitions and identities are added to these, in the preliminary complete version of the model.) In the taxation equations an attempt to use explanatory variables which are as closely related to the actual tax base as the available data permit, leaving the task of relating these variables to those accounted for elsewhere by the model as a separate exercise. In the case of federal personal taxation, the movement of the effective average rate of tax is approximated by changes in the starting rate but elsewhere tax-rate indices are created which may be used to represent the effects of a rate change with varying degrees of precision. In contrast to these advances, however, the 'explanations' offered for expenditures on goods and services within the public sector appear less satisfactory. For example, two stochastic equations are used to determine the wage bill of the federal government; one of these relates the average wage rate per civilian employee of the federal government to the same variable for the economy as a whole, and the other gives the total wage bill as a log-linear function of the wage rate and the level of employment. It is admitted, however, that no satisfactory explanation of the last of these explanatory variables can be found with the result that this, the crucial variable, remains exogenous. Better luck is met in explaining the number of employees in education (in terms of the population between five and eighteen and the lagged dependent variable) and in this instance the total wage bill is determined simply from the product of the (endogenous) wage rate and the level of employment. A number of economic variables are reported to have been tried in attempts to explain federal government expenditures on various categories of new construction but none were found satisfactory. Resort is therefore made either to (i) relating these categories of expenditure to relevant budget proposals (in the case of new construction expenditures on military and industrial facilities as well as expenditures on all other goods and services not dealt with elsewhere), or (ii) leaving the variable exogenous where budgeting proves to be more erratic (i.e. for new construction works relating to conservation and development), or (iii) relating expenditure to the civilian population, the rate of unemployed and the lagged dependent variable (for the miscellaneous category of all other new construction). Of state and local government expenditures on new construction, three are explained with reference to a capital stock adjustment process (of varying degrees of refinement) while others (including purchases of all other goods and services) are related to variables such as size of population and new construction expenditures in either the private sector or the federal domain of the public sector.

The last of the special features employed in the formulation of the Brookings model referred to here concerns the reconciliation of the output and price variables used. This is the same problem that is encountered in other models in which both aggregate demand and production are broken down by sector, when, as is usually the case in view of the available data and the 'natural' groupings of different economic activities, this breakdown involves the consideration of different sectors on the expenditure side of the economy than on the income side. The scale of the problem is different in the case of the Brookings project, however, so that the solution adopted is formally set out in terms which are more generally applicable.

For n producing sectors and m final demand sectors, the n-component column vector of deliveries to final demand organised by sector of production, f_t, may be related to the m-component column vector of deliveries to final demand organised by sector of final demand, g_t,

$$h_n' f_t = h_m' g_t \tag{5.44}$$

where h_k denotes a k-component column vector of unit elements. Assuming that deliveries to final demand from sectors of production are distributed among sectors of final demand in a regular and systematic way, the two vectors f_t and g_t may also be connected by the stochastic relationships

$$f_t = Bg_t + u_t \tag{5.45}$$

where B is an $n \times m$ matrix of parameters. This is not so much a set of structural equations as a 'data-splicing' device linking various parts of the model with the result that OLS procedures may be used in the estimation of the array B using observations on f_t and g_t.

If the model is in gross-flow (as opposed to value-added) terms, then it is unlikely that data are available on f_t (i.e. deliveries to final demand from sectors of production) but rather on total output originating in each sector of production, x_t. In this case an $n \times n$ input–output matrix A may be used to obtain f_t.

$$x_t = Ax_t + f_t$$

so that
$$f_t = (I - A)X_t. \tag{5.46}$$

(For a value-added model, f_t is irrelevant and it is the components of x_t, i.e. production in value-added terms, that sum to the sum of the components of g_t, i.e. expenditures in value-added terms.)

Given the identity that total final demand must equal total production in money as well as real terms, the reconciliation between the components of final demand and of total output achieved in (5.44) may be extended to price variables

$$\mathbf{p}'_n \mathbf{f}_t = \mathbf{p}'_m \mathbf{g}_t \tag{5.47}$$

which on substituting predicted values of $\mathbf{f}_t$ gives

$$\mathbf{p}'_n \hat{\mathbf{B}} \mathbf{g}_t = \hat{\mathbf{p}}'_m \mathbf{g}_t$$

so that

$$\mathbf{p}'_m = \mathbf{p}'_n \hat{\mathbf{B}} \tag{5.48}$$

and prices relating to different categories of expenditure are expressed in terms of the prices of the components of output.

For a number of reasons, including the use of a constant input–output array **A** throughout the observation period, the predicted deflators for items of expenditure are found to be somewhat different from observed values. In view of there being no time available in which to improve the conversion weights, $\hat{\mathbf{B}}$, used in the 1965 project report, it was considered necessary to reconcile actual and predicted series by the use of empirical autoregressive relationships. Three different versions of such a relationship are reported to have been tried of which the following kind of result (for the deflator relating to expenditures on durable goods other than cars) was considered to be the most satisfactory

$$P_{CDEA} = 0\cdot12 + 0\cdot88 \hat{P}_{CDEA} + 0\cdot83(P_{CDEA} - \hat{P}_{CDEA})_{-1}$$
$$(0\cdot07)\quad(0\cdot07)\qquad\quad(0\cdot09)$$

$$S_e = 0\cdot015. \tag{5.49}$$

5.12 FURTHER READING

For an introduction to the practicalities of constructing an econometric model of a macro-economy the reader is referred to Christ's (1966) very simple illustrative seven-equation linear model of the United States for 1929–41 and 1946–59. The data are presented, together with definitions and sources, so that the author's OLS, 2SLS and LIML/LVR estimates and non-predictive and predictive tests of the model can be checked, and augmented at least within the limits of the information given. Recent texts by Evans (1969*b*) and Brown (1970) present answers to the specification problem with detailed reference to economic theory and the operation of economic institutions. Evans lays more emphasis on a review of empirical evidence at each stage, which is related in particular to results obtained from the Wharton EFU model. Brown builds an understanding of a macro-economy from micro-economic foundations drawing out at each stage specific equation hypotheses which are ready for econometric testing. This is a study which reflects a belief that careful specification is fundamental to econometric work since many alternative specifications may be found to fit more or less equally well when, as is usually so in practice, small samples have to be used.

Another model of the United States economy, developed primarily as a forecasting instrument for the United States Office of Business Economics, has been reported by Liebenberg, Hirsch and Popkin (1966). The characteristics of the model and the steps involved in its construction are first clearly explained with reference to a simplified version of the actual model. A particularly well-organised flow diagram of the main features of the model is used to illustrate how the specification adopted constitutes an interdependent system through the linkage between production and income and between wages and prices in particular as well as other closed paths or loops connecting series of endogenous variables.

Various models have been constructed for the United Kingdom economy of which three are referred to here. The earliest of these is the Klein, Ball, Hazelwood and Vandome (1961a) quarterly, 1948–56, 37-equation model. A special feature of this system is the detailed attention given to exports and imports in view of the open nature of the United Kingdom economy: the behaviour of three categories of imports are separately accounted for while exports are covered by seven endogenous variables which distinguish between three commodity categories and (for total exports in each case) four economic areas. A small 11-equation, annual, 2SLS-estimated model is also presented as a prelude to the main model which is estimated by the LIML/LVR procedure, the application of which is explained in detail. The sources and preparation of the data for both models are also set out in full together with tables of the data finally used. A modified version of the model for the period 1948–59 is reported elsewhere, see Klein, Ball, Hazelwood and Vandome (1961b), as is most of the evidence on the forecast performance of the model, see Ball, Hazelwood and Klein (1959) Hazelwood and Vandome (1961), and Vandome (1963). The model has been discussed in detail in two articles by Nerlove (1962, 1965), the first of which concentrates on statistical problems while the second deals more with economic aspects of the model in the light of the main characteristics of the British economy over the period. (The second article also adopts the same viewpoint to examine Tinbergen's (1951) 1870–1914 model of the United Kingdom economy which was designed for the purpose of analysing business cycles.)

A quarterly model of the United Kingdom economy has also been reported by Ball and Burns (1968). This is a short-term forecasting model wihch concentrates on expenditure behaviour although other equations are added to account for prices and the average wage level. A similarly orientated 17-equation model developed by the United Kingdom National Institute of Economic and Social Research (NISER) has been described by Surrey (1971). This is an example of how small a macro-economic model can be given restricted objectives and yet prove useful within the scope of these objectives. The smallness of the NISER model (which has no export or investment functions let alone any explicit treatment of supply constraints) is essentially a reflection of the advantage seen in the ease with which a small system can be kept up to date. (Other econometric studies of the short-run behaviour of the United

Kingdom economy are reported in a series of conference papers edited by Hilton and Heathfield (1970).)

The kind of simplification adopted in the NISER model has been carried even further in the work of Friend and Jones (1964) and Friend and Taubman (1964) in the belief that there is 'little evidence that otherwise important niceties, such as production functions, demand-for-labour equations, labour market adjustment equations, interest rate and price equations, disaggregated consumption functions, or perhaps even distributive share and financial variables, add significantly to short-term predictions of GNP and its major components', Friend and Jones (1964) p. 279. They therefore propose a five-equation model (which accounts for changes in consumption, residential construction, plant and equipment expenditures, non-farm inventory investment, and GNP) the forecast performance of which is reviewed in Chapter 6. A much more comprehensive short-term forecasting model of the French economy has been presented by Evans (1969a). Emphasis is again given to the demand side in view of the purpose of the model; special attention is given to unfilled vacancies and unfilled orders in view of the influence of these variables on the level of aggregate demand.

Long-term models of the Japanese economy have been published by Klein and Shinkai (1963) and Ueno (1963). Both models rely on an observation period which is divided into two parts after removing the years 1937–51/2. Structural shifts between the two periods are allowed for by binary variables in the Klein–Shinkai model; no other structural shifts are assumed to have taken place which is a hypothesis subsequently tested by Blumenthal (1965) together with the predictive performance of this model. Special attention is given to the structure of the economy in both models; in the Klein–Shinkai model, for example, the importance of the balance between the agricultural sector and the rest of the economy is taken into account by separate production functions, a relationship between food imports and domestic agricultural production, and an equation for the shift of labour between the two sectors. Further similations of the development of the Japanese economy using a modified version of Ueno's model have been reported by Ueno and Kinoshita (1968). A quarterly model of the Japanese economy for the post-war period 1952–59 has been published by Ichimura, Klein, Koizumi, Sato and Shinkai (1964).

The kind of econometric model of a macro-economy that is required in dealing with a developing economy has been discussed by Klein (1965). A macro-economic model with a difference can also be seen in the efforts of Officer (1968) to account for exchange rate behaviour by means of a model of the Canadian economy which relates only those variables which have a bearing on this objective. Four econometric models of the United States economy which have been used to study the effects of various of fiscal and monetary policies are noted on p. 221.

Details of the different estimation procedures mentioned in Section 5.3 can be seen in the texts referred to in Chapter 1, Section 1.4. Further references on aggregation can be obtained from Ijiri's (1971) survey of this subject. Analysis of the relative merits of using an aggregate equation rather than a set of disaggregated relationships to explain aggregate data has been presented by Grunfeld and Griliches (1960). The special problems posed by aggregation in respect of the production function have been analysed in detail by Fisher (1969). As noted in Chapter 3, Section 3.6, this work raises serious doubts concerning the existence of aggregate production functions, even though other relationships between aggregates may be more plausible.

5.13 REFERENCES

Almon, S. (1965), 'The Distributed Lag Between Capital Appropriations and Expenditures', *Econometrica*, vol. 33, 178–96. (Reprinted in Zellner (1968).

Ball, R. J. and Burns, T. (1968), 'An Econometric Approach to Short-run Analysis of the United Kingdom Economy, 1955–1966', *Operational Research Quarterly*, vol. 19, 225–56.

Ball, R. J., Hazelwood, A. and Klein, L. R. (1959), 'Econometric Forecasts for 1959', *Oxford University Institute of Statistics Bulletin*, vol. 21, 3–16.

Blumenthal, T. (1965), 'A Test of the Klein–Shinkai Econometric Model of Japan', *International Economic Review*, vol. 6, 211–28.

Brown, T. M. (1970), *Specification and Uses of Econometric Models* (London: Macmillan).

Christ, C. F. (1956), 'Aggregate Econometric Models', *American Economic Review*, vol. 46, 385–408.

Christ, C. F. (1966), *Econometric Models and Methods* (New York: John Wiley).

Cragg, J. G. (1967), 'On the Relative Small Sample Properties of Several Structural Equation Estimators', *Econometrica*, vol. 35, 89–110.

de Leeuw, F. (1969), 'A Condensed Model of Financial Behaviour', in Duesenberry *et al.* (1969).

de Leeuw, F. and Gramlich, E. (1968), 'The Federal Reserve – MIT Econometric Model', *Federal Reserve Bulletin*, vol. 54, 11–40.

de Wolff, P. (1967), 'Macroeconomic Forecasting', in Wold *et al.* (1967).

Duesenberry, J. S., Fromm, G., Klein, L. R. and Kuh, E. (eds) (1965), *The Brookings Quarterly Econometric Model of the United States Economy* (Chicago: Rand McNally).

Duesenberry, J. S., Fromm, G., Klein, L. R. and Kuh, E. (eds) (1969), *The Brookings Model: Some Further Results* (Chicago: Rand McNally).

Evans, M. K. (1966), 'Multiplier Analysis of a Postwar Quarterly U.S. Model and a Comparison with Several Other Models', *Review of Economic Studies*, vol. 33, 337–60.

Evans, M. K. (1969a), *An Econometric Model of the French Economy* (Paris: OECD).

Evans, M. K. (1969b), *Macroeconomic Activity* (New York: Harper & Row).

Evans, M. K. and Klein, L. R. (1968), *The Wharton Econometric Forecasting Model*, 2nd ed. (Philadelphia: Wharton School of Finance and Commerce, University of Pennsylvania).

Fisher, F. M. (1965), 'Dynamic Structure and Estimation in Economy-Wide Econometric Models', in Duesenberry *et al.* (1965).

Fisher, F. M. (1969), 'The Existence of Aggregate Production Functions', *Econometrica*, vol. 37, 553–77.

Fox, K. A. (1956), 'Econometric Models of the United States', *Journal of Political Economy*, vol. 44, 128–42.

Friend, I. and Jones, R. (1964), 'Short-Run Forecasting Models Incorporating Anticipatory Data', in *Models of Income Determination*, Studies in Income and Wealth, No. 28 (Princeton, N.J.: Princeton University Press for NBER).

Friend, I. and Taubman, P. (1964), 'A Short-Term Forecasting Model', *Review of Economics and Statistics*, vol. 46, 229–36.

Fromm, G. and Klein, L. R. (1965), 'The Complete Model: A First Approximation' in Duesenberry *et al.* (1965).

Fromm, G. and Klein, L. R. (1968), '"The Brookings Model Volume: A Review Article": A Comment', *Review of Economics and Statistics*, vol. 50, 235–40.

Fromm, G. and Taubman, P. (1968), *Policy Simulations with an Econometric Model* (Washington and Amsterdam: The Brookings Institute and North-Holland).

Griliches, Z. (1968), 'The Brookings Model Volume: A Review Article', *Review of Economics and Statistics*, vol. 50, 215–34.

Grunfeld, Y. and Griliches, Z. (1960), 'Is Aggregation Necessarily Bad?', *Review of Economics and Statistics*, vol. 42, 1–13.

Hart, P. E., Mills, G. and Whitaker, J. K. (eds) (1964), *Econometric Analysis for National Income Planning* (London: Butterworths).

Hazelwood, A. and Vandome, P. (1961), 'A Post Mortem on Econometric Forecasts for 1959', *Oxford University Institute of Statistics Bulletin*, no. 123 67–81.

Hilton, K. and Heathfield, D. F. (eds) (1970), *The Econometric Study of the United Kingdom* (London: Macmillan).

Ichimura, S., Klein, L. R., Koizumi, S., Sato, K. and Shinkai, Y. (1964), 'A Quarterly Econometric Model of Japan 1952–59', *Osaka Economic Papers*, vol. 12, 19–44.

Ijiri, Y. (1971), 'Fundamental Queries in Aggregation Theory', *Journal of the American Statistical Association*, vol. 66, 766–82.

Johnston, J. (1972), *Econometric Methods* 2nd ed. (New York: McGraw Hill).

Klein, L. R. (1950), *Economic Fluctuations in the United States, 1921–1941* (New York: John Wiley).

Klein, L. R. (1964), 'A Postwar Quarterly Model: Description and Application', in *Models of Economic Determination*, Studies in Income and Wealth, no. 28 (Princeton: Princeton University Press for NBER).

Klein, L. R. (1965), 'What Kind of Macroeconometric Model for Developing Economies?' *Econometric Annual of the Indian Economic Journal*, vol. 13, 313–24. Reprinted in Zellner (1968).

Klein, L. R., Ball, R. L., Hazelwood, A. and Vandome, P. (1961a), *An Econometric Model of the United Kingdom* (Oxford: Basil Blackwell).

Klein, L. R., Ball, R. L., Hazelwood, A. and Vandome, P. (1961b), 'Re-estimation of the Econometric Model of the United Kingdom and Forecasts for 1961', *Oxford University Institute of Statistics Bulletin*, vol. 23, 49–66.

Klein, L. R. and Goldberger, A. S. (1955), *An Econometric Model of the United States, 1929–1952* (Amsterdam: North-Holland).

Klein, L. R. and Shinkai, Y. (1963), 'An Econometric Model of Japan, 1930–59', *International Economic Review*, vol. 4, 1–28.

Liebenberg, M., Hirsch, A. A. and Popkin, P. (1966), 'A Quarterly Econometric Model of the United States', *Survey of Current Business*, vol. 46, no. 5, 13–39.

Nerlove, M. (1962), 'A Quarterly Econometric Model for the United Kingdom: A Review Article', *American Economic Review*, vol. 52, 154–76.

Nerlove, M. (1965), 'Two Models of the British Economy: A Fragment of a Critical Survey', *International Economic Review*, vol. 6, 127–81.

Nerlove, M. (1965), 'A Tabular Survey of Macro-Econometric Models', *International Economic Review*, vol. 7, 127–75.

Officer, L. H. (1968), *An Econometric Model of Canada under the Fluctuating Exchange Rate* (Cambridge, Mass.: Harvard University Press).

Orcutt, G. H. (1962), 'Microanalytic Models of the United States Economy: Need and Development', *American Economic Review*, vol. 52, 229–40.

Orcutt, G. H. (1967), 'Microeconomic Analysis for Prediction of National Accounts', in Wold *et al.* (1967).

Suits, D. B. (1962), 'Forecasting and Analysis with an Econometric Model', *American Economic Review*, vol. 52, 104–32. Reprinted in Zellner (1968).

Suits, D. B. (1967), 'Applied Econometric Forecasting and Policy Analysis', in Wold *et al.* (1967).

Summers, R. (1965), 'A Capital Intensive Approach to the Small Sample Properties of Various Simultaneous Equation Estimators', *Econometrica*, vol. 33, 1–41.

Surrey, M. J. C. (1971), *The Analysis and Forecasting of the British Economy* (Cambridge: Cambridge University Press for the National Institute of Economic and Social Research, Occasional Paper 25).

Theil, H. (1954), *Linear Aggregation of Economic Relations* (Amsterdam: North-Holland).

Tinbergen, J. (1951), *Business Cycles in the United Kingdom, 1870–1914* (Amsterdam: North-Holland).

Ueno, H. (1963), 'A Long-Term Model of the Japanese Economy, 1920–1958', *International Economic Review*, vol. 4, 171–93.

Ueno, H. and Kinoshita, S. (1968), 'A Simulation Experiment for Growth with a Long-Term Model of Japan', *International Economic Review*, vol. 9, 14–48.

Vandome, P. (1963), 'Econometric Forecasting for the United Kingdom', *Oxford University Institute of Statistics Bulletin*, vol. 25, 239–81.

Verdoorn, P. J. and Post, J. J. (1964), 'Capacity and Short-Term Multipliers', in Hart, Mills and Whitaker (1964).

Wold, H. (1954), 'Causality and Econometrics', *Econometrica*, vol. 22, 162–77.

Wold, H. (1956), 'Causal Inference from Observational Data: A Review of Ends and Means', *Journal of the Royal Statistical Society* (Series A), vol. 119, 28–61.

Wold, H. (ed) (1964), *Econometric Model Building. Essays on the Causal Chain Approach* (Amsterdam: North-Holland).

Wold, H., Orcutt, G. H., Robinson, E. A., Suits, D. B. and de Wolff, P. (1967), *Forecasting on a Scientific Basis* (Lisbon: Proceedings of an International Summer Institute sponsored by the NATO Science Committee and the Gulbenkian Foundation).

Zellner, A. (1968), *Readings in Economic Statistics and Econometrics* (Boston: Little, Brown).

6. Macro-economic Models II: The Preparation and Analysis of Forecasts

6.1 INTRODUCTION

In this chapter attention is turned to the use of estimated models, and estimated macro-economic systems in particular, for the purposes of various kinds of prediction. Together with the need to test hypotheses about the way in which economic variables are related, the generation of predictions constitutes a prime objective of applied econometric analysis. In view of the obvious practical value of the end-product, interest centres especially on what may perhaps be regarded as the only kind of predicting, namely, forecasting the future, which is, however, usually referred to as *ex ante* forecasting in order to distinguish it from other kinds of forecasting needed in the analysis of forecast error. Predictions of the future obtained from an econometric model can be expected to be subject to error on a number of counts. These include the use of estimated equations (the reliability of which is decreased by various violations of the assumptions of the classical linear regression model that may persist in estimating the model), the stochastic nature of the model used which means that the variable to be forecast is itself a random variable, errors in the specification of the estimated model that is finally adopted, the use of predicted or estimated values of predetermined variables, and shifts in the structure of the relationships used between the observation period and the forecast period.

The difficulty of tracing the sources of error in an *ex ante* forecast given this array of alternatives can be reduced somewhat from reference to other kinds of forecasts. In particular, the accuracy with which a model 'forecasts' observed past values of certain variables is likely to prove instructive. This is known as *ex post* forecasting, which may take one of a number of forms in order to avoid the effects of one or more of the different sources of error listed above. One possibility is to use actual values of predetermined variables to obtain predicted values of endogenous variables within the observation period used in estimating the model. An assessment of the accuracy of this kind of forecast can serve as an indication as to how well a simultaneous system succeeds as a whole in accounting for the behaviour of a group of endogenous variables when errors in predicting one variable can contribute to errors in predicting others. This may be contrasted with tests on the relevance of individual regressors and of the specification of individual equations. Secondly, *ex post* forecasts may be extended beyond the observation period, to either preceding or succeeding intervals of time, which allows the effects of structural changes between an observation and a forecast period to be felt. Thirdly, a distinction may be made in the treatment of exogenous and lagged endogenous variables within the category of predetermined variable and known values used only for the first and for initial values of the second in preparing a series of forecasts in which subsequent values of lagged endogenous variables yielded by the model itself are used rather than actual values. This is what would have to be done in practice in preparing a series of *ex ante* forecasts over time and *ex post* forecasts of this kind will help to give some indication whether the dynamic properties of a model are such that it is suitable for this purpose. The use of a model to obtain a series of forecasts through time in which only the values of exogenous variables and initial values of lagged endogenous variables are introduced from outside is often referred to as a *dynamic simulation* of the behaviour of the economic system represented by the model, or simply *simulation* of the system since a one period simulation, or a succession of these (using observed values of lagged endogenous variables), remains what is otherwise considered to be 'a forecast'. Thus this third kind of *ex post* prediction is often referred to as an *ex post simulation forecast*.

Up to now it has been implicitly assumed that the object of forecasting is to obtain some idea of what the values of certain economic variables will actually be in the future. However, it is also interesting to consider what the future might be if some exogenous variables were to have values other than those which they are perhaps expected to have in the future. In particular, since some exogenous variables may be subject to control, a model which has proven value in forecasting might be used to predict the effects of different economic policies. These predictions may be usefully summarised in the form of the effects of a unit change in the value of a given exogenous variable on various endogenous variables. Each of these results measures a particular *multiplier*, a familiar concept in economic analysis which is of special value in the design of policy. Furthermore, comparison of estimated multipliers with those obtained from other models or those suggested *a priori* may prove to be another means of detecting inadequacies or anomalies in the specification and estimation of a model.

Lastly among these introductory remarks it is noted that to use an estimated model in forecasting is to act as though estimated regression coefficients were true regression coefficients and as though econometric models were deterministic. So far as the first of these deficiencies is concerned, it is theoretically possible to obtain an estimate of the standard error of a forecast so that a prediction can be presented in the form of a 'confidence interval' which reflects the necessity of having to use estimated rather than true regression coefficients. A distinction should therefore be made between point and interval forecasts. Secondly, with regard to the stochastic nature of econometric models, it is also possible to introduce non-random disturbances into point forecasts based, for example, on the behaviour of the residuals of estimated equations, so that a distinction should be drawn too between forecasts and simulations which are *stochastic* and those which are *non-stochastic*.

6.2 FORECASTING AND THE ANALYSIS OF FORECAST PERFORMANCE

Predictions of the endogenous variables of linear model can be obtained simply enough in principle from the reduced form solution of the model in which each endogenous variable is expressed as a function of predetermined variables alone, as illustrated already in Section 4.4 of Chapter 4 for a two-equation model. This is a result which can be conveniently generalised with the use of matrix algebra. Thus a stochastic income-determination model consisting of a single aggregate consumption function and the usual macro-economic accounting identity between, in this case, income (Y) and expenditures on consumer (C) and other (I) goods

$$C_t = \alpha + \beta Y_t + \gamma C_{t-1} + u_t \tag{6.1a}$$

$$Y_t = C_t + I_t \tag{6.1b}$$

can also be written

$$\begin{bmatrix} 1 & -\beta \\ -1 & 1 \end{bmatrix}\begin{bmatrix} C_t \\ Y_t \end{bmatrix} + \begin{bmatrix} -\alpha & 0 & -\gamma \\ 0 & -1 & 0 \end{bmatrix}\begin{bmatrix} 1 \\ I_t \\ C_{t-1} \end{bmatrix} = \begin{bmatrix} u_t \\ 0 \end{bmatrix} \tag{6.2}$$

or more concisely

$$\mathbf{B}\mathbf{Y}_t + \mathbf{\Gamma}\mathbf{Z}_t = \mathbf{u}_t \tag{6.3}$$

where the matrices **B** and **Γ** represent the parameters of the endogenous and predetermined variables in the two equations and the vectors **Y**, $\mathbf{Z}_t$ and $\mathbf{u}_t$ represent the values of the endogenous,[1] predetermined and disturbance variables in period t (the intercept-forming variable being included in $\mathbf{Z}_t$). The reduced form of (6.1) is

$$C_t = [1/(1 - \beta)][\alpha + \beta I_t + \gamma C_{t-1}] + u_t/(1 - \beta) \tag{6.4a}$$

$$Y_t = [1/(1 - \beta)][\alpha + I_t + \gamma C_{t-1}] + u_t/(1 - \beta), \tag{6.4b}$$

which can also be expressed in matrix notation

$$\mathbf{Y}_t = \mathbf{\Pi}\mathbf{Z}_t + \mathbf{B}^{-1}\mathbf{u}_t \tag{6.5a}$$

where

$$\mathbf{\Pi} = \frac{1}{(1 - \beta)}\begin{bmatrix} \alpha & \beta & \gamma \\ \alpha & 1 & \gamma \end{bmatrix} \text{ and } \mathbf{B}^{-1} = \frac{1}{(1 - \beta)}\begin{bmatrix} 1 & \beta \\ 1 & 1 \end{bmatrix}.$$

---

[1] The vector $\mathbf{Y}_t$, representing values of *both* endogenous variables in period t, should not be confused with the scaler Y_t which in this particular example represents the value of the income variable in period t.

The same result can be obtained from (6.3) in general terms

$$Y_t = -\mathbf{B}^{-1}\mathbf{\Gamma}Z_t + \mathbf{B}^{-1}\mathbf{u}_t \qquad (6.5b)$$

where

$$\mathbf{\Pi} = -\mathbf{B}^{-1}\mathbf{\Gamma}.$$

Thus for an estimated simultaneous equation system

$$\hat{\mathbf{B}}Y_t + \hat{\mathbf{\Gamma}}Z_t = \hat{\mathbf{u}}_t \qquad (6.6)$$

in which $\hat{\mathbf{u}}_t$ is a vector of residuals, so that

$$\hat{\mathbf{B}}\hat{Y}_t + \hat{\mathbf{\Gamma}}Z_t = 0, \qquad (6.7)$$

non-stochastic predictions can be obtained from the solution

$$\hat{Y}_t = -\hat{\mathbf{B}}^{-1}\hat{\mathbf{\Gamma}}Z_t \qquad (6.8)$$

given the array Z_t, i.e. values of the predetermined variables of the model in the forecast interval t.[1] Where the model is non-linear, however, things are not this simple;[2] an algebraic solution of such a model is usually both difficult to obtain and tricky to interpret. One way of tackling this problem is to linearise any non-linear equations so that this alternative statement of the model can be solved in the same way as (6.7). To see how this is done reference is made first to the single-equation, two-variable, non-linear model

$$f(Y, Z) = 0, \qquad (6.9)$$

the total differential of which is

$$df = (\partial f/\partial Y)dY + (\partial f/\partial Z)dZ = 0$$

so that

$$dY = -(\partial f/\partial Y)^{-1}(\partial f/\partial Z)dZ \qquad (6.10)$$

[1] In the case of a linear model two different versions of the estimated reduced form equations may be used for forecasting: the solution of the estimated structural form equations, i.e. the solution implied by (6.8), and the estimated equations obtained from direct OLS estimation of the parameters of the array $\mathbf{\Pi}$ in (6.5a). For those equations of the model which are exactly identified these two results are identical but a difference emerges for any overidentified equations since only the solved structural form equations take account of those parameter restrictions imposed on the specification of the model which render these equations overidentified. A comparison of the accuracy of the two forecasts over the observation period may therefore conveniently serve as an indication of the validity of any overidentifying *a priori* restrictions that are adopted.

It should also be noted that the OLS estimated version of the reduced form equations may be useful where it is difficult to be sure about the structure of a simultaneous equation system and yet plausible arguments can be advanced for the inclusion of certain variables in the model and for considering some of these an endogenous and the others as exogenous.

[2] Unless the non-linearity of the equations of the model is such that they are effectively linear for any particular time period on substituting known values for predetermined values.

which is the reduced form of (6.9), showing how Y may be expected to change as a result of a change in Z just as the solution of a system of linear equations

$$\mathbf{Y}_t = \mathbf{\Pi}\mathbf{Z}_t$$

indicates

$$\hat{\mathbf{Y}}_t = \mathbf{\Pi}\dot{\mathbf{Z}}_t$$

where the arrays $\mathbf{Y}_t$ and $\dot{\mathbf{Z}}_t$ refer to changes in the endogenous and predetermined variables of the system between the intervals $(t - 1)$ and t, e.g. $\mathbf{Y}_{it} = (Y_{it} - Y_{i,t-1})$. The symbol π could be used to represent the ratio of partial derivatives $-(\partial f/\partial Z)/(\partial f/\partial Y)$ so that (6.10) becomes

$$dY = \pi dZ \tag{6.11}$$

but, unlike the array $\mathbf{\Pi}$, π is a function of Y and Z. However, this ratio is a constant for given values of the variables, Y_0, Z_0, so a linearised version of (6.11) can be written

$$dY = \pi_0 dZ \tag{6.12}$$

where

$$\pi_0 = -(\partial f/\partial Z)/(\partial f/\partial Y) \Bigg|_{\substack{Y = Y_0 \\ Z = Z_0}}.$$

The same procedure may be applied to a system of equations

$$f_i(Y_1, \ldots, Y_G, Z_1, \ldots, Z_K) = 0, \quad i = 1, \ldots, G, \tag{6.13}$$

which may include both linear and non-linear equations, to obtain

$$df_i = \sum_{g=1}^{G} (\partial f_i/\partial Y_g) dY_g + \sum_{k=1}^{K} (\partial f_i/\partial Z_k) dZ_k = 0, \quad i = 1, \ldots, G, \tag{6.14}$$

which can be evaluated at the point, $Y_{10}, \ldots, Y_{G0}, Z_{10}, \ldots, Z_{K0}$ to yield a set of linearised equations

$$\mathbf{B}_0 dY = -\mathbf{\Gamma}_0 dZ \tag{6.15}$$

where $\mathbf{B}_0$ and $\mathbf{\Gamma}_0$ are $G \times G$ and $G \times K$ matrices, the elements of which are evaluations of the partial derivatives

$$(\partial f_i/\partial Y_g) \Bigg|_{\substack{\mathbf{Y} = \mathbf{Y}_0 \\ \mathbf{Z} = \mathbf{Z}_0}} \quad \text{and} \quad (\partial f_i/\partial Z_k) \Bigg|_{\substack{\mathbf{Y} = \mathbf{Y}_0 \\ \mathbf{Z} = \mathbf{Z}_0}}$$

The solution of (6.15) is

$$dY = -\mathbf{B}_0^{-1}\mathbf{\Gamma}_0 dZ \equiv \mathbf{\Pi}_0 dZ \tag{6.15}$$

so that for changes effected between the intervals of time $t - 1$ and t the result is

$$\hat{\mathbf{Y}} = \mathbf{\Pi}_0\dot{\mathbf{Z}}. \tag{6.17}$$

The drawback of this approach is that (6.17) is, strictly speaking, valid only for small changes about the particular set of values, Y_0, Z_0, which in practice would be Y_{t-1}, Z_{t-1} or perhaps the sample means of the Y_g and Z_k recorded over the observation period. Other solutions are available, however, which can be used to obtain the numerical value of any endogenous variable associated with a particular set of values of the predetermined variables to any given level of accuracy. One such solution is Newton's method of solving a system of non-linear simultaneous equations. Again reference can be made to the general system of equations (6.13) each of the non-linear equations of which can be expanded in a Taylor's series about an initial set of trial values of the endogenous variables, $Y_{1t}^{(0)}, \ldots, Y_{Gt}^{(0)}$, which could be simply taken as their last known values plus, perhaps, any shifts which it seems reasonable to expect have occurred subsequently,

$$f_i \simeq f_i(Y_{1t}^{(0)}, \ldots, Y_{Gt}^{(0)}, Z_{1t}, \ldots, Z_{Kt})$$

$$+ \sum_{g=1}^{G}(\partial f_i/\partial Y_g)\bigg|_{\substack{Y = Y_t^{(0)} \\ Z = Z_t}} (Y_{gt} - Y_{gt}^{(0)}) = 0 \qquad (6.18)$$

where the predetermined variables Z_k are set at their values for the forecast period t so that the first term on the right-hand side is a constant and so too are the evaluated partial derivatives

$$(\partial f_i/\partial Y_g)\bigg|_{\substack{Y = Y_t^{(0)} \\ Z = Z_t}}.$$

As before the latter can be regarded as the elements of a matrix B_0, which is now written $B^{(0)}$ for notational purposes which will be evident below. The result is, therefore, a system of linear equations

$$B_t^{(0)}Y_t = \beta_t^{(0)}, \qquad (6.19)$$

where $\beta_t^{(0)}$ is a vector of constant terms,

$$-f_i(Y_{1t}^{(0)}, \ldots, Y_{Gt}^{(0)}, Z_{1t}, \ldots, Z_{Kt}) + \sum_{g=1}^{G}(\partial f_i/\partial Y_g)\bigg|_{\substack{Y = Y_t^{(0)} \\ Z = Z_t}} Y_{gt}^{(0)}$$

from which estimates of Y_{gt} can be obtained

$$\hat{Y}_t = (B_t^{(0)})^{-1}\beta_t^{(0)}. \qquad (6.20)$$

If (6.13) is expanded in a Taylor's series about the last known values of the Y_g, say Y_{t-1}, and the Y_g change only slowly over time then this initial approximation of the solution vector may be close to the estimate given by (6.20), in which case this estimate may be counted a reasonably accurate solution of the non-linear system even though it is obtained after having substituted any non-linear equations by linear approximations. In general this will not be so but the $\hat{Y}_t$ can then be used as at least a better approximation of the solution than the Y_{t-1} so that (6.13) can be expanded in a Taylor's series about the $\hat{Y}_t$, which are now regarded as simply first-round estimates of the solution, $Y_t^{(1)} = \hat{Y}_t$.

Thus

$$f_i \simeq f_i(Y_{1t}^{(1)}, \ldots, Y_{Gt}^{(1)}, Z_{1t}, \ldots, Z_{Kt})$$

$$+ \sum_{g=1}^{G} \partial f_i / \partial Y_g \left|_{\substack{Y = Y_t^{(1)} \\ Z = Z_t}} (Y_{gt} - Y_{gt}^{(1)}) = 0 \qquad (6.21)$$

from which

$$Y_t^{(2)} = (B_t^{(1)})^{-1} \beta_t^{(1)}. \qquad (6.22)$$

The result is an iterative procedure

$$Y_t^{(r)} = (B_t^{(r-1)})^{-1} \beta_t^{(r-1)} \qquad (6.23)$$

which can be continued to achieve any given level of accuracy ε for any required prediction, say Y_{gt},

$$(Y_{gt}^{(r)} - Y_{gt}^{(r-1)}) / Y_{gt}^{(r-1)} \leqslant \varepsilon. \qquad (6.24)$$

An adaptation of this approach has been used to find the solution of both the Wharton EFU model and the Brookings model. In each case the model is first laid out in blocks, beginning with one which is recursive, that is one which includes only those equations which either relate a single endogenous variable Y_g to predetermined variables alone or which contain current terms in other endogenous variables as explanatory variables only if these variables are not themselves explained by Y_g or by any variable that is explained by Y_g, whether directly or indirectly. If this is so the solution of this block can be found in a stepwise single-equation procedure beginning with equations which include predetermined variables alone as explanatory variables.

In the case of the solution procedures adopted for both the Wharton EFU model and the Brookings model those equations relating to mutually determined endogenous variables are divided into two blocks, one of which is called the 'real' or 'quantity' block and the other which is called the 'price' block. The first of these includes those relationships dealing with the expenditure components of GNP and with production. The price block includes the remaining equations which relate to mutually determined variables, while a fourth block needs to be added in the form of a final recursive block if any endogenous variables remain which depend entirely on predetermined variables or endogenous variables established by the first three blocks without themselves appearing as explanatory variables in these three blocks.

The real block is solved given the values of those endogenous variables computed from the recursive block and any predetermined variables plus initial approximations for those variables which are explained in the price block. These first estimates of the values of the variables of the real block can now be used in the price block to obtain a first estimate of the solution of the price block which in turn can be substituted back into the real block and so on until the solution remains unchanged between iterations to any required level of accuracy.

Evans and Klein report (1968) that convergence for the Wharton EFU model was achieved in six to ten iterations. They also note that if each equation is treated as a block itself the number of iterations increased by a factor between two and three but that the increase in the number of blocks produces a considerable saving in computer time so that a change was made to this alternative method of organising the solution procedure.

An alternative, less involved, iterative approach to the solution of a nonlinear equation system, known as the Gauss–Seidel method of solution, proceeds by solving the equations of the model in sequence within each iteration without resort to linear approximations. The method can be illustrated with reference to a three-equation system

$$\begin{aligned}
Y_{1t} &= f_1(Y_{2t},\ Y_{3t},\ Z_{1t},\ .\ .\ .,Z_{Kt}) \\
Y_{2t} &= f_2(Y_{1t},\ Y_{3t},\ Z_{1t},\ .\ .\ .,Z_{Kt}) \\
Y_{3t} &= f_3(Y_{1t},\ Y_{2t},\ Z_{1t},\ .\ .\ .,Z_{Kt}.
\end{aligned} \tag{6.25}$$

As before the values of the predetermined variables in the forecast interval t are all assumed to be known while initial trial values, $Y_{it}^{(0)}$, of the endogenous variables are also required. Given this much the first equation can be solved

$$Y_{1t}^{(1)} = f_1(Y_{2t}^{(0)},\ Y_{3t}^{(0)},\ Z_{1t},\ .\ .\ .,Z_{Kt}) \tag{6.26a}$$

Once this first-round estimate of Y_{1t} is known it is used immediately, i.e. still within the first iteration of the solution procedure, in solving the other equations of the model

$$Y_{2t}^{(1)} = f_2(Y_{1t}^{(1)},\ Y_{3t}^{(0)},\ Z_{1t},\ .\ .\ .,Z_{Kt}), \tag{6.26b}$$

while the same use is made of each solution in turn so that

$$Y_{3t}^{(1)} = f_3(Y_{1t}^{(1)},\ Y_{2t}^{(1)},\ Z_{1t},\ .\ .\ .,Z_{Kt}). \tag{6.26c}$$

The second iteration can now be effected, using $Y_{1t}^{(1)}$ and $Y_{3t}^{(1)}$ to evaluate $Y_{1t}^{(2)}$ to begin with, and so on until the solution converges to some required level of accuracy, as specified in (6.24).

Whether this procedure or algorithm indeed leads to convergence, and the speed with which convergence is achieved if it does, depends on a number of factors. One way in which convergence can be assisted is by adjusting the values of the Y_{it} obtained at any stage within a particular iteration before using these values as inputs to obtain other values of the Y_{it}. This adjustment takes the form of a weighted average of the value of the solution for any variable and the value of the variable used as an input prior to this latest evaluation.

The adjusted solution for Y_{it} at the rth iteration is then

$$Y_{it}^{(r)} = p f_i(Y_{1t}^{(r)}, \ldots, Y_{i-1,t}^{(r)}, Y_{i+1,t}^{(r-1)}, \ldots, Y_{Gt}^{(r-1)}, Z_{1t}, \ldots, Z_{Kt})$$
$$+ (1 - p) Y_{it}^{(r-1)} \qquad (6.27)$$

rather than simply

$$f_i(Y_{1t}^{(r)}, \ldots, Y_{i-1,t}^{(r)}, Y_{i+1,t}^{(r-)}, \ldots, Y_{Gt}^{(r-1)}, Z_{1t}, \ldots, Z_{Kt}).$$

The magnitude of p influences both the path of the Y_{it} through successive iterations to convergence or divergence and the speed of convergence in the case of the former. Values in the range $0 < p \leq 2$ may be tried.

Convergence is also affected by the normalisation adopted in the specification of the equations of the model, i.e. the choice made in deciding which variables should appear on the left-hand side with unit coefficients, and by the order in which the Y_{it} are evaluated within each iteration. While admitting that there are no simple rules in deciding what should be done in this respect, Klein and Evans (1969) p. 32, claim that 'if one traces the main lines of economic causation through a model and then normalises and orders equations to reproduce this pattern of causation, it is likely that a convergent algorithm will result'.

So far in this section attention has been confined to the solution of an estimated model assuming that the values of predetermined variables for some future period t are known. Getting this information, however, presents problems in practice. This is especially so in the case of the values of exogenous variables since these values are themselves forecasts. The way in which these predictions are obtained depends to a large extent on the kind of variable involved. Some of the variables may be demographic, and associated, quantities, such as the size of the labour force, the numbers eligible for various pensions, etc., which can be predicted reasonably accurately on the basis of observed trends. However, the prediction of other exogenous variables may present more serious difficulties. For example, a forecast of the level of exports, or of an explanatory variable appearing in an export function such as a world trade price index, requires an understanding of production, marketing and demand conditions influencing world trade, information on anticipated changes in these conditions and an assessment of the impact that these changes may have on the most recent figure for the variable concerned.

Other exogenous variables may be more or less subject to government policy. Differences in the ease with which different variables within this category may be predicted have already been touched on in the discussion of the Dutch forecasting and policy model. Public sector expenditures may, for example, be considered to be entirely at the discretion of government and yet even here unforeseeable events may upset the most carefully prepared budgets while these budgets may themselves be subject to amendment in the course of their preparation and may not be published much before, if at all, the year to which they relate. Other variables which can also be used as means by which government policy is put into effect but which are less amenable to precise control include levels of taxation and of liquid assets of various kinds and the levels and rates of change of various categories of prices and incomes.[1]

Where no changes in government policy have been announced, forecasts are usually made subject to the assumption that no changes will in fact be made. What constitutes a 'no-change' policy may, however, be far from clear when considering what may follow, and the duration of, policies which are usually of a short-term nature such as a wage freeze or credit restrictions. Furthermore, it may be that a no-change assumption indicates consequences that are likely to be considered undesirable. The reaction to this dilemma depends to some extent on whether the forecast is intended for publication as an official view of what the future holds in which case it takes on some of the character of a plan.

Although the problems of forecasting exogenous variables are usually more formidable, this is not to say that obtaining information on lagged variables some time during the period $(t-1)$, which is the latest that a forecast is usually made in practice for any period t, does not present its own snags. Observations on these variables only become available at the earliest during period t and even then they are usually subject to subsequent revision. Thus this information may also take the form of a forecast, which can be obtained from the model itself given estimates of the exogenous variables for period $(t-1)$, or it may be based on a splicing of the latest figures for some fraction of the interval $(t-1)$ and a forecast for the outstanding, as yet unrecorded, fraction. One source of assistance in forecasting the immediate past lies in the availability of various economic indicators that have an early publication date. Relationships between such variables and national accounting series may even be expressed in the form of regression equations as illustrated by Surrey (1971) pp. 85–7, in his review of procedures used by the United Kingdom National Institute of Economic and Social Research in preparing quarterly forecasts from a macro-economic model. Examples include relationships between total output and an index of industrial production, between consumers' expenditures (other than on cars and motor cycles) and an index of the volume of total retail sales, and between expenditures on cars and motor cycles and new registrations of these two categories of vehicle.

Various appraisals have been made of the reliability of different sources of early information on conditions relating to either a forecast period or the period(s) which immediately precede it. Three studies undertaken by Stekler (1967a), (1968), (1967b) are briefly reported here. They include examinations of the value of United States federal government budgets as forecasts of

---

[1] Forecasting government expenditures and other exogenous variables may be the subject of separate studies. See, for example, Brown and Taubman's (1962) inquiry into the value of forecasting U.S. federal government purchases of goods and services on the basis of previous budget recommendations using Koyck and Pascal distributed lag schemes to represent the pattern of the past stream of these recommendations. Models of this kind may be subject to frequent revision and the forecasts derived from them may be combined with varying weights with information from other sources before arriving at a final figure so that it may be considered more appropriate that they should be left outside the scope of the specification of the main body of the model to which they relate.

186 An Introduction to Applied Econometric Analysis

actual expenditures, the extent to which various monthly series are a sound advance guide to economic trends and quarterly figures (and in particular the balance between accuracy and reporting speed for certain series), and how well advance and provisional United States national income accounts data estimate final figures. The results obtained from all three studies are essentially in accord in showing these various kinds of predictive information to be, for the most part, sufficiently accurate to be useful and to improve in accuracy where they are subject to subsequent revision. Speedier reporting, using, for example, sampling, is shown to lead to increasing inaccuracy the earlier the date of release of the indicators looked at and yet has little cost in terms of *turning point error*, that is incorrect prediction of the direction of change of a particular variable. However, so far as national accounts estimates are concerned it is found that a large percentage of revisions made between the publication of advance and provisional data are unsuccessful so that there appears to be little to be gained 'in interpreting economic changes' by waiting for this later information.[1]

Even when the values to be given to predetermined variables have been decided it should be appreciated that *ex ante* forecasting in practice requires the exercise of further discretion. In particular it may be evident either that a certain situation is likely to obtain in the forecast period that it has not been possible to observe in the past or that the model has failed to forecast accurately for one reason or another over the recent past. In this case some adjustment is necessary without the support of past experience, or at least past experience which is entirely relevant or which is sufficient to allow the model to be accurately re-estimated. Examples of the kind of changes that may be involved include the possibility of a strike in a key industry, the use of new policies to control the economy, and the operation of new factors which appear to invalidate behavioural relationships observed in the past. Influences of this kind can be allowed for by simply adjusting forecasts that would otherwise be obtained, which amounts to adjustments of the intercepts of the relevant equations of a model, but where the forecasting exercise involves simulating behaviour over several periods, adjustments to other parameters may be appropriate and new variables may be called for.

Deciding on the kind of untested adjustment hypothesis that is required in these circumstances and on the magnitudes of the parameters to be used is another matter, of course. Inevitably the answer is a matter for judgement taking into account, as in the case of predicting the values of exogenous variables, the latest information available in the form of various economic

---

[1] The different demands for information on predetermined variables in forecasting in practice can be gauged from reference to three of the models looked at in Chapter 5. Thus, for example, the Dutch forecasting and policy model and the Michigan RSQE model are annual models having as a principal objective the provision of forecasts for year t as early as possible during year $(t - 1)$, subject to revisions thereafter as more reliable information becomes available. In contrast the Wharton EFU model is a quarterly model which has been used to forecast up to eight quarters ahead at quarterly intervals.

indicators, surveys of attitudes and of expectations, and expert technical opinion together with anything relevant that can be gleaned from the observation period. An example of what might be done in the last resort in respect of a unique event has been offered by Suits (1967). The problem cited concerns the size of the intercept adjustment to be made in anticipating the effect of the introduction of a new type of car on sales of cars. In this case the displacement was set equal to the maximum shift in the function that could be expected as measured by the largest residual of a fit of the demand for cars function of the (Michigan RSQE) model, although in the event the observed shift proved to be only half this amount.

Use of two other kinds of adjustment has been reported by Liebenberg, Hirsch and Popkin (1966) in preparing quarterly forecasts of the United States economy from a model developed for the United States Office of Business Economics (OBE). They note that most of the equations of the model showed serial correlation of residuals indicating either imperfections in specification or autocorrelated errors of measurement in the data. In order to minimise forecasting errors resulting from this serial correlation they adjust the intercepts of those equations thus affected in such a way that the computed value of the dependent variable in the last quarter preceding the forecast quarter coincides with either the value observed in that quarter or an average of the last four quarters 'depending on whether the serial correlation is deemed to be strong or moderate'. The same kind of correction, 'if *a priori* economic explanation can be adduced for the existence and continuation of this non-random character (of the residuals)', has been reported by Klein (1971) pp. 49–50, in using the Wharton EFU model for prediction. Secondly, in applying the OBE model beyond the observation period, Liebenberg, Hirsch and Popkin report that 'it is also appropriate to examine residuals in equations containing a trend to see if there has been a shift in the trend'. Where a drift in the residuals over the 'recent period' prior to the forecast interval is evident they adopt a trend correction.

The use of simultaneous equation models and the possibility of errors in the variables used in preparing *ex ante* forecasts or a series of *ex post* simulation forecasts very much complicates the application of statistical inference in judging the seriousness of forecast error. This being so a less precise procedure is usually adopted in practice based on comparisons of how close forecasts from two or more sources approximate reality. However, it is perhaps instructive to give some attention to the first approach before discussing the second in order to explore the balance between the theoretical and practical attractions of the two.

As noted in Chapter 1, Section 1.2, an estimate of the simple regression model

$$Y_t = \alpha + \beta X_t + u_t \tag{6.28}$$

can be used to obtain a forecast of the value of the dependent variable for a given value, X_0, of the independent variable

$$\hat{Y}_0 = \hat{\alpha} + \hat{\beta} X_0 \tag{6.29}$$

which may differ from observation, Y_0, even if (6.28) is valid in the observation and forecast periods, both because of the use of an estimated regression line in making this forecast and because of the disturbance, u_0, of the forecast period which means that Y_0 is also a random variable. Subject to the usual assumptions, the variance of the statistic $\hat{Y}_0$ can be shown to be given by

$$\text{var}\,(Y_0) = \sigma_u^2 \left[\frac{1}{N} + \frac{(X_0 - \bar{X})^2}{\Sigma x_i^2} \right] \tag{6.30}$$

which has a certain intuitive appeal, i.e. the variance of the predictor (6.29) is smaller the smaller the variance of the disturbances (σ_u^2), the larger the sample (N) on which this forecast is based, the greater the spread of observations on X in the sample (Σx_i^2, where $x_i = (X_i - \bar{X})$), and the smaller the separation between X_0 and the same mean $\bar{X}$. This is a result which can be used, again subject to the usual assumptions, to express a prediction as a probability statement, rather than a point forecast, in the form of a *confidence interval* for the mean population or true value of Y corresponding to X_0: from reference to tabulated values of the t distribution for a given probability $100(1 - \varepsilon)$ and $(N - K)$ degrees of freedom,

$$\hat{Y}_0 - t_{\varepsilon/2,(N-K)}\,\hat{\sigma}_u \sqrt{\frac{1}{N} + \frac{(X_0 - \bar{X})^2}{\Sigma x^2}} \leqslant Y_0 \leqslant \hat{Y}_0$$

$$+ t_{\varepsilon/2,(N-K)}\,\hat{\sigma}_u \sqrt{\frac{1}{N} + \frac{(X_0 - \bar{X})^2}{\Sigma x^2}}. \tag{6.31}$$

The variance of Y_0 is σ_u^2 if the disturbances remain homoscedastic. If the disturbances are also serially independent, the variances of $\hat{\alpha}$ and $\hat{\beta}$, and thereby $\hat{Y}_0$, are independent of the variance of Y_0 so that

$$\text{var}\,(\hat{Y}_0 - Y_0) = \sigma_u^2 \left[1 + \frac{1}{N} + \frac{(X_0 - \bar{X})^2}{\Sigma x_i^2} \right]. \tag{6.32]}$$

The hypothesis that the true forecast error is zero can now be tested in the usual way by comparing the ratio $(\hat{Y}_0 - Y_0)/\sqrt{\text{var}\,(\hat{Y}_0 - Y_0)}$ with tabulated values of the t distribution. This is effectively a test of the hypothesis that there is no difference between $\hat{Y}_0$ and Y_0 that cannot be accounted for by the stochastic model (6.28) and the use of estimates of the parameters of this model.

In this procedure two sources of forecast error have been taken account of and two others have been assumed away (in assuming that the classical normal linear regression model applies and that X_0 is an observation and is not itself a forecast) to enable a test to be made of the hypothesis that the structure of the model is unchanged between sample and forecast. The same procedures can be applied to *ex post* forecasts obtained from an estimated simultaneous equation system to examine whether shortcomings in the forecast performance of the system given actual values for predetermined variables appear to be the result of sampling or a change in the relationships between the variables of the model. It will be recalled that for the linear model (6.7) predictions can be obtained from the derived estimated reduced form equations (6.8). Just as var $(\hat{Y}_0)$ for the single equation model (6.28) can be shown to be a weighted sum of the variances and covariances of least squares estimators of α and β, so also the variances and covariances of a set of predictions $\mathbf{Y}_t$ can be derived from the variances and covariances of the reduced form parameter estimates $\hat{\mathbf{\Pi}}$. As noted in Chapter 5, Section 5.3, asymptotic variances and covariances of consistent estimators of $\mathbf{B}$ and $\mathbf{\Gamma}$ can be obtained so that it may be expected that these can be used to obtain the asymptotic variance–covariance matrix array for the consistent estimators of $\mathbf{\Pi}$ given by $\hat{\mathbf{\Pi}} = -\hat{\mathbf{B}}^{-1}\hat{\mathbf{\Gamma}}$. Goldberger, Nagar and Odeh (1961) have derived a formula both for this[1] and for the asymptotic variance–covariance matrix of forecast errors for predictions obtained from $\hat{\mathbf{\Pi}}$ while Hymans (1968) has developed confidence intervals for these predictions. Goldberger, Nagar and Odeh illustrate the use of their results with reference to 2SLS estimates of Klein's Model I (1950) and a set of *ex post* forecasts outside the period used to estimate the model. For all of the eight variables predicted, the forecast errors are shown to be less than their estimated asymptotic standard errors (which may be considered an achievement given the size of the model and the particular observation (1921–41) and forecast (1947) periods adopted).[2]

Despite the value of this approach to the analysis of forecast error it is not one which is commonly employed in practice because of the weight of computations involved and the limitations imposed by reference to the reduced form of a model which cannot be conveniently expressed in the case of non-linear systems. There also remains the problem, as noted earlier, of coping with the variability of predetermined variables in analysing the errors of *ex ante* forecasts or *ex post* simulation forecasts. One way around these difficulties is to use a Monte Carlo approach (see Klein (1971) pp. 35–8). To begin with a series of (S) artificial samples relating to the observation period can be created from the sequential solutions of an estimated model using, say, actual observations on exogenous variables and initial values for endogenous variables and adding random disturbances, with appropriate variances and covariances, to structural form equations. The model can now be re-estimated for each of these samples and for each of the resulting estimates a set of forecasts can be obtained for a given forecast period, a set of values of exogenous variables, initial values for lagged endogenous variables and a fresh set of random disturbances. The result is S artificial forecast series for each forecast variable (i) and each reference prediction obtained from the actual sample so that for

---

[1] These results are also reviewed by Goldberger (1964), pp. 369–71, and Johnston (1972) pp. 400–3.
[2] These results are also reviewed by Goldberger (1964), pp. 365–8 and 371–3 while a discussion of the asymptotic variance–covariance matrix of forecast errors and of the confidence intervals relating to forecasts from OLS estimates of reduced form equations can be seen in Johnston's (1972) text, pp. 404–7.

period j of the forecast period an estimate of the forecast variance is given by

$$\text{est var } \hat{Y}_{ij} = [\sum_{s=1}^{S} (\hat{Y}_{(s)ij} - \hat{Y}_{ij})^2]/S \qquad (6.33)$$

the square root of which is of course an estimate of the standard error of the forecast.

Although this result is a general one in that it can cope with all sources of forecast error for all kinds of model it also clearly requires the organisation of a considerable computational effort. In practice, therefore, most researchers

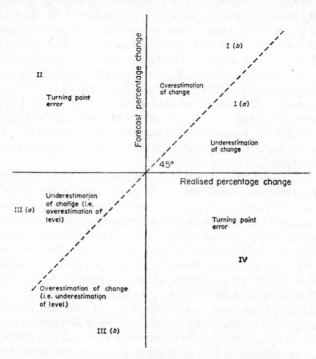

Figure 6.1. A graphical scheme of comparison between forecast and realised
changes

are content to confine their assessments of forecast performance to the size of the difference between prediction and realisation even though this is a complementary rather than an alternative procedure. One particularly illuminating approach to this kind of comparison takes the form of a plot of forecast percentage change against realised percentage change. Such a graph may be presented for a series of forecasts for any one variable or for a series of variables over a single forecast period. The result may be divided into six sectors labelled as in Figure 6.1. Where forecast and observation coincide then a point is recorded somewhere along the 45° line bisecting the first and third quadrants. Points in the second and fourth quadrants correspond to particularly serious forecast errors since in this case there has been a turning point error. Less serious errors, in the form of over- or underestimates of change, are found in the first and third quadrants away from the 45° line. The diagram also offers insight into other matters of interest since (i) a comparison of points scattered in quadrants I and IV with those in II and III gives some idea of the relative performance of the model in forecasting upward and downward shifts in the level of a variable, (ii) a comparison of points according to distance from the origin gives some idea of the model's ability to cope with small and large changes and (iii) distances between the horizontal axis and the 45° line through sectors I and III correspond to the forecast errors involved in using a simple naïve model in the form of a 'no-change' extrapolation which may be compared graphically with the forecast error of other models which are also indicated by the vertical separation between points graphed in Figure 6.1 and the 45° line.

Various other methods of weighing forecasts against realisations offer the advantage of compressing the comparison into a single measure at the cost of losing the subleties of the above analysis. The size of a single forecast error for a single variable may, for example, be measured by the (unitless) standardised forecast error (SFE)

$$\text{SFE} = (\hat{y}'_t - y'_t) \Big/ \sqrt{\frac{\Sigma_N(y'_i)^2}{N}} \qquad (6.34)$$

where the forecast $\hat{y}'_t$ and actual observation y'_t refer to proportional change in the variable Y between the intervals $t-1$ and t,[1] i.e.

$$\hat{y}'_t = \widehat{\Delta Y_t}/Y_{t-1}, \quad y'_t = \Delta Y_t/Y_{t-1}$$

and where $\Sigma_N(y'_i)^2$ is the sum of the squares of N observed in Y for $N+1$ successive intervals of an observation period,

$$y'_i = (Y_i - Y_{i-1})/Y_{i-1}.$$

The deflation of the forecast error by the root mean square of observed changes in the variable concerned is important if this error is to be used to compare the success achieved in forecasting variables which display different degrees of stability.

The principle of the SFE may be extended, in the form of the root mean square standardised forecast error (RMS–SFE), to obtain a measure of the

---

[1] In the case of a model which predicts change rather than level, $\widehat{\Delta Y_t}$ is obtained directly. If this is not so, $\widehat{\Delta Y_t}$, like ΔY_t, can be obtained with reference to definition

$$\widehat{\Delta Y_t} = \hat{Y}_t - Y_{t-1}, \Delta Y_t = Y_t - Y_{t-1}$$

so that the forecast error $(\hat{y}'_t - y_t')$ remains equal to $(\hat{Y}_t - Y_t)/Y_{t-1}$.

forecast error for (i) a group of R variables rather than a single variable as in (6.34)

$$\text{RMS–SFE}_R = \sqrt{\frac{\sum_R \text{SFE}_r^2}{R}} \qquad (6.35)$$

or (ii) a series of P forecasts relating to a single variable or (iii) a series of forecasts relating to a group of variables[1]

$$\text{RMS–SFE}_{P.R} = \sqrt{\frac{\sum_P \sum_R \text{SFE}_{p,r}^2}{PR}}. \qquad (6.36)$$

This measure takes the form of a comparison of a set of forecast errors with past year to year changes in the variable(s) concerned. Thus if the errors incurred in a series of predictions exceed, on average, this past observed variability then the RMS–SFE exceeds one and *vice versa*. Although it is clear that the measure has no upper bound it has at least a lower limit since if all predictions exactly correspond to what is in fact realised then the RMS–SFE must be zero.

The measure may be compared with two versions of an alternative *inequality coefficient* proposed by Theil (1958, 1966). The earlier version of this coefficient takes the form

$$U_{58} = \frac{\sqrt{\sum_R (P_i - A_i)^2 / R}}{\sqrt{\sum_R P_i^2 / R} + \sqrt{\sum_R A_i^2 / R}} \qquad (6.39)$$

where predictions, P_i, and actual observations, A_i, refer to predicted and actual changes. In this measure, therefore, the denominator includes, for the prediction period, both realised and predicted changes. The result is a coefficient which is confined, except in the trivial case where all the P's and A's are zero (when it is indeterminate), to the interval between zero, indicating perfect prediction, and unity, indicating 'maximum inequality' which occurs either if one of the variables is identically zero, so that zero predictions have been

---

[1] One advantage of using the RMS–SFE for a series of forecasts is that it avoids underestimating the sum forecast error as a result of positive errors being offset by negative errors. On the other hand if it is useful to have a measure which is able to distinguish a predominantly negative set of errors from a predominantly positive set then the arithmetic mean of a series of forecast errors (MFE) may be used

$$\text{MFE} = \sum_R (\hat{y}_r' - y_r') / R = \bar{\hat{y}}' - \bar{y}'. \qquad (6.37)$$

It is interesting to note that the mean square of a series of forecast errors relating to a single variable, i.e. $\sum_R (y_t' - y_t')^2 / R$, can be shown to break down into the square of (6.37) plus other terms including the standard deviations of the $\hat{y}_t'$ and y_t', $S\hat{y}_t'$ and Sy_t', and their correlation coefficient, r,

$$(\sum_R (\hat{y}_t' - y_t')^2) / R = (\bar{\hat{y}}' - \bar{y}')^2 + (S\hat{y}_t' - Sy_t')^2 + 2(1 - r) Sy_t' S\hat{y}_t' \qquad (6.38)$$

which variously account for errors relating to central tendency, variance and covariance.

made of non-zero actual changes or *vice versa*, or if there is negative proportionality, that is if

$$rP_i + sA_i = 0 \tag{6.40}$$

for all i where neither of the non-negative parameters r and s are zero.

Theil's later alternative definition of his inequality coefficient restricts the denominator to the root mean square of realised changes,

$$U_{66} = \sqrt{\sum_R (P_i - A_i)^2 / \sum_R A_i^2}, \tag{6.41}$$

which is the same as (6.35) if predicted and realised changes are expressed as relative differences and if the denominators in the two formulae relate to the prediction period. The change is argued with reference to the concept of the failure of a forecast and to the value of having the coefficient uniquely determined by the root mean square of prediction errors (since data on realisations are common to all forecasts of a variable over a given period of time) which is not so if other terms are introduced which also depend on the forecasts made. One loss, however, is that, like (6.35), (6.41) has no upper limit.

The above methods of analysis may be used to compare the forecasting performance of two or more models. In particular they are often found useful in judging whether or not forecasts obtained from one model are at least an improvement on those obtained from a naïve model, which for this purpose may take the form of an extrapolation based solely on past observations of the variable to be forecast. They include the simplest 'no-change' prediction, $Y_t = Y_{t-1}$, the forecast that $\Delta Y_t = \Delta Y_{t-1}$ and a stochastic version of the latter

$$\Delta Y_t = \rho \Delta Y_{t-1} + u_t. \tag{6.42}$$

It may be that where conditions in the forecast period are similar to those prevailing in the observation period, such naïve models could perform as well, if not better, than models which attempt to offer an explanation for the behaviour of one or more variables. Even where this is so, however, the possibility of analysing the consequences of change which is available in the second class of models, and which is missing altogether in simple autoregressive structures, is a valuable extension of the properties of an estimated model. This is a quality which adds interest in the reliability of information on the relationship between change and its effects to interest in the accuracy of the kind of prediction that has been discussed in this section.

6.3 MULTIPLIER ANALYSIS AND THE PROPERTIES OF DYNAMIC MODELS

One of the principal objectives in building econometric models of macroeconomic systems is to assess the influence of fiscal and monetary policies on the behaviour of certain variables over time. The foundations of this analysis are to be found in the notion of a multiplier which may be used, for example, to relate changes in autonomous government expenditure (G) to changes in income (Y) for the very simplest macro-economic model

$$C = \alpha + \beta Y \tag{6.43a}$$
$$Y = C + I + G. \tag{6.43b}$$

The reduced form of this model for Y is

$$Y = (\alpha + \beta Y) + I + G = (\alpha + I + G)/(1 - \beta) \tag{6.44}$$

so that the income multiplier effect of shifts in the level of G can be seen to be the parameter of this variable in (6.44), that is the reciprocal of the marginal propensity to save

$$\partial Y/\partial G = 1/(1 - \beta). \tag{6.45}$$

This analysis applies equally well to any static linear stochastic model

$$\mathbf{BY}_t + \mathbf{\Gamma Z}_t = \mathbf{u}_t \tag{6.46}$$

where $\mathbf{Y}_t$ is a vector of endogenous variables which relate to period t only and where $\mathbf{Z}_t$ refers to a set of exogenous variables, which may include both current and lagged terms in any one variable. The parameters of the exact part of the reduced form of the model, $-\mathbf{B}^{-1}\mathbf{\Gamma}$, then measure changes in the levels of endogenous variables that are effected by unit changes in the exogenous variables.

The analysis can also be extended to examine the behaviour of the endogenous variables through time when using a model which expresses a dynamic rather than a static theory, that is one which offers an explanation for changes in the endogenous variables over time even when the structure of the system adopted and the external forces acting on it are not subject to change. Thus any set of equations which includes lagged endogenous variables expresses a dynamic theory since changes in certain exogenous variables will have effects outside the time period in which they occur even though the change may take the form of an impulse. Delayed repercussions of this kind could be explored by tracing movements in the endogenous variables through successive time periods starting from some point at which the system is in equilibrium. For example, Y_t in the exact dynamic model

$$C_t = \alpha + \beta Y_{t-1} \tag{6.47a}$$
$$Y_t = C_t + I_t + G_t \tag{6.47b}$$

remains the same from one interval to the next if I_t and G_t remain fixed. However, if G rises to $(G_{t-1} + \Delta G)$ just for the period t and subsequently returns to its previous level, G_{t-1}, then the level of income in period (t) can be seen to be $(Y_{t-1} + \Delta G)$ and in subsequent periods $(t + T)$ it is $(Y_{t-1} + \beta^T \Delta G)$,

$$Y_{t-1} = Y_{t-2}$$
$$Y_{t-1} = \alpha + \beta Y_{t-2} + I_{t-1} + G_{t-1} \tag{6.48}$$

$$Y_t = \alpha + \beta Y_{t-1} + I_{t-1} + G_{t-1} + \Delta G$$
$$= Y_{t-1} + \Delta G$$
$$Y_{t+1} = \alpha + \beta Y_t + I_{t-1} + G_{t-1}$$
$$= \alpha + \beta(Y_{t-1} + \Delta G) + I_{t-1} + G_{t-1}$$
$$= Y_{t-1} + \beta \Delta G$$
$$Y_{t+2} = Y_{t-1} + \beta^2 \Delta G$$

.
.
.

$$Y_{t+T} = Y_{t-1} + \beta^T \Delta G \tag{6.49}$$

so that the total additional income generated by G is

$$\sum_T \Delta Y = \Delta G(1 + \beta + \beta^2 + \ldots + \beta^T) = \Delta G(1 - \beta^{T+1})/(1 - \beta) \tag{6.50}$$

and the model can be said to have a stable equilibrium position, in this case Y_{t-1}, which is approached through time, providing the marginal propensity to consume, β, is a fraction.[1] In addition it can be seen that the reduced form equation for Y_t, expressed in terms of the interval $(t - 1)$, is now (6.48). Thus the first-round effect of a change in G_t has a multiplier of 1. The same result is given by (6.50) on setting $T = 0$, while this expression also shows the cumulative income multiplier for subsequent intervals of time.

These conclusions relate to the particular first-order difference equation

$$Y_t = \alpha + \beta Y_{t-1}. \tag{6.51}$$

The solution of which may similarly be obtained by induction

$$Y_1 = \alpha + \beta Y_0$$
$$Y_2 = \alpha + \beta Y_1 = \alpha(1 + \beta) + \beta^2 Y_0$$

.
.
.

$$Y_T = \alpha(1 + \beta + \beta^2 + \ldots + \beta^{T-1}) + \beta^T Y_0$$
$$= \alpha(1 - \beta^T)/(1 - \beta) + \beta^T Y_0$$
$$= \beta^T[Y_0 - \alpha/(1 - \beta)] + \alpha/(1 - \beta). \tag{6.52}$$

[1] Similarly, if the increase in G_t over period t had been sustained over subsequent periods then it can be shown that income would have eventually reached a new level

$$\lim_{T \to \infty} Y_{t+T} = Y_{t-1} + \frac{\Delta G}{1 - \beta}. \tag{6.54}$$

This is the same result as is expressed in (6.45) since (6.47) becomes (6.43) on imposing the initial equilibrium condition $Y_t = Y_{t-1}$.

For the purposes of economic analysis, only positive values of β need be considered but for a negative fractional β, Y_{t+T} exhibits damped oscillations about the equilibrium point, Y_{t-1} where ΔG is not sustained or about the time path connecting Y_{t-1} and $Y_{t-1} + \Delta G/(1 - \beta)$ where it is sustained. For negative non-fractional β, the time path of Y_{t+T} is oscillatory and explosive.

This is the solution to the difference equation (6.51) in the sense that it shows the value of Y_t at any point in time without having to refer to past values of Y_t other than to some initial or boundary value, Y_0,[1] while at the same time satisfying the condition set out in (6.51). The same answer applies to the solution of (6.47) for Y_t on substituting $(\alpha + I_t + G_t)$ for α in (6.52). The result may be written

$$Y_t = \beta^T(Y_0 - Y_\varepsilon) + Y_\varepsilon \qquad (6.53)$$

where Y_ε is given by the equilibrium condition, $Y_t = Y_{t-1} = Y_\varepsilon$. In the case of the solution of (6.47) for Y_t, Y_ε corresponds to the reduced form solution (6.44) of the model (6.43) since (6.47) is the same as (6.43) given a long enough period in which the sum $(G_t + I_t)$ is sustained at a constant level so that an equilibrium income level, $Y_t = Y_{t-1} = Y_\varepsilon$, emerges, providing the system is stable. For any shock, ΔG, to the system which causes an initial displacement in Y_t from Y_ε

$$\Delta G = Y_0 - Y_\varepsilon$$

in time interval $t = 0$, (6.53) describes in the same way as (6.52) the time path followed by Y_t back to Y_ε, providing matters are not complicated by superimposing the effects of other, subsequent shocks.

This analysis may be extended to the general linear dynamic model

$$\mathbf{BY}_t + \mathbf{\Gamma X}_t + \mathbf{\Delta}_1 \mathbf{Y}_{t-1} + \ldots + \mathbf{\Delta}_s \mathbf{Y}_{t-s} = \mathbf{u}_t \qquad (6.55)$$

in which both lagged endogenous and (either current or lagged) exogenous variables appear as explanatory variables. The reduced form of this system of equations is

$$\mathbf{Y}_t = -\mathbf{B}^{-1}\mathbf{\Gamma X}_t - \mathbf{B}^{-1}\mathbf{\Delta}_1 \mathbf{Y}_{t-1} \ldots - \mathbf{B}^{-1}\mathbf{\Delta}_s \mathbf{Y}_{t-s} + \mathbf{B}^{-1}\mathbf{u}_t \qquad (6.56)$$

so that the same marginal relationship between the endogenous and exogenous variables applies as in the case of the static model (6.3)

$$\frac{\partial \mathbf{Y}_t}{\partial \mathbf{X}_t} = -\mathbf{B}^{-1}\mathbf{\Gamma}. \qquad (6.57)$$

However, since the sub-set of reduced form parameters $-\mathbf{B}^{-1}\mathbf{\Gamma}$ now relates only to the first-round effects of changes in the exogenous variables, they are more appropriately referred to as *impact multipliers*. Just as in the case of the above simple dynamic model (6.47), the dynamic character of the specification of model (6.55) means that the consequences of a shift in one of the exogenous variables may spill over into other time periods so that these impact multipliers are an incomplete view of the relationship between change and effect for such a model. Again as in the case of the above example, although the behaviour of the $\mathbf{Y}_t$ through time following on the impact of some shock like ΔG could be traced by successive substitutions, it is sometimes more

---

[1] This can be readily computed from any one known value for Y_t on substituting the value into (6.52) together with the interval count t to which it relates.

convenient (that is in the case of simple linear systems) and certainly always more enlightening, to do this by first solving the model in such a way as to relate each endogenous variable to its own lagged terms, exogenous variables and disturbances alone, and then seeking the solutions of the linear difference equations thus obtained. These equations are known as the *final form* of the model. The exact part of one such equation might be written

$$a_0 Y_t + a_1 Y_{t-1} + \ldots + a_s Y_{t-s} = f(t). \tag{6.58}$$

This is a generalisation of (6.51) in the form of a linear difference equation of order s. The solution to (6.58) may be appropriately sought in equally generalised terms in the form of the sum of its two components, namely the *complementary function* and the *particular integral* or *particular solution*. The first of these may be written

$$Y_t = A_1 \lambda_1^t + A_2 \lambda_2^t + \ldots + A_s \lambda_s^t \tag{6.59}$$

where the parameters $\lambda_1, \ldots, \lambda_s$ are the roots[1] of the polynominal equation, known as the *auxiliary equation*, which is obtained from (6.58) on substituting λ^{s-i} for Y_{t-i}, and setting $f(t) = 0$,

$$a_0 \lambda^s + a_1 \lambda^{s-1} + \ldots + a_s = 0. \tag{6.60}$$

For (6.51) the auxiliary equation is therefore

$$\lambda - \beta = 0 \tag{6.61}$$

so that the complementary function is

$$Y_t = A_1 \beta^t. \tag{6.62}$$

Where a difference equation contains current and lagged terms in Y_t alone, i.e. $f(t) = 0$, then the complementary function is itself a complete solution to the equation. Where this is not so there remains the problem of finding the particular integral of the solution. It may be that $f(t)$ is a constant (c), perhaps in the form of a series of exogenous variables $\mathbf{X}_t$ which are assumed fixed so that their influence on the $\mathbf{Y}_t$ remains unchanged through time. In this case the particular integral has the form[2]

$$Y_t = kt^i \text{ where } 0 \le i \le s \tag{6.63}$$

---

[1] For two coincident roots, $\lambda_1 = \lambda_2$, the first two terms in (6.59) become $(A_1 + A_2 t_1)\lambda_1^t$ while for three coincident roots, $\lambda_1 = \lambda_2 = \lambda_3$, the first three terms in (6.59) become $(A_1 + A_1 t + A_3 t^2)\lambda_1^t$, and so on.

[2] Where a final form difference equation includes a linear time trend so that $f(t) = c + bt$ then the particular integral takes the form

$$Y_t = \frac{b(a_1 + 2a_1 + \ldots + sa_s)}{(a_0 + a_1 + \ldots + a_s)^2} + \frac{c + bt}{(a_0 + a_1 + \ldots + a_s)} \tag{6.66}$$

and for an exponential time trend $f(t) = cb^t$ it has the form

$$Y_t = \frac{cb^s b^t}{(a_0 b^s + a_1 b^{s-1} + \ldots + a_s)}. \tag{6.67}$$

Any particular solution of (6.58) will serve and one may be found on substituting (6.63) into (6.58) for trial values of i. If

$$a_0 + a_1 + \ldots + a_j \neq 0$$

$i = 0$ will do so that

$$(a_0 + a_1 + \ldots + a_s)k = c.$$

The complete solution of (6.58) may then be written

$$Y_t = A_1\lambda_1^t + A_2\lambda_2^t + \ldots + A_s\lambda_s^t + c/(a_0 + a_1 + \ldots + a_s). \quad (6.64)$$

For (6.51) the result is the same as that obtained earlier

$$Y_t = A_1\beta^t + \alpha/(1 - \beta) \quad (6.65)$$

when the constant A_1 may be replaced by

$$Y_0 - \frac{\alpha}{(1 - \beta)}$$

on substituting the initial condition $Y_t = Y_0$ at $t = 0$. For a difference equation of order s, s known values for Y_t are required in order to fix the s arbitrary constants, $A_1, A_2, \ldots, A_s$ of the complementary function.

The interpretation of (6.64) may proceed along much the same, although more elaborate, lines as the interpretation of the solution (6.52) of the simple first-order linear difference equation (6.51). Again the stability of the time-path of the variable Y_t depends on the size of the parameters, $\lambda_1, \lambda_2, \ldots, \lambda_s$, and in this case only where they are *all* fractional is the solution, and thus the model to which it relates, stable. If this condition is met then Y_t remains in the equilibrium position[1]

$$Y_\varepsilon = c/(a_0 + a_1 + \ldots + a_s) \quad (6.68)$$

unless displaced by some shock in the form of movement in the external forces acting on the system. So long as movement in these forces is not sustained, then Y_ε is regained given enough time. Where the λ_i are not thus restricted the system is unstable and successive values of Y_t move further and further away from Y_ε once Y_t is displaced from the equilibrium position. The disturbed Y_t time-path is also oscillatory if any of the λ_i are negative while the total effect of the component terms of the complementary function on Y_t depends on whether these terms reinforce or weaken each other: they act in opposition when the A_i are of different sign and also when some terms are explosive ($|\lambda_i| > 1$) but others are damped ($|\lambda_i| < 1$).

If a system is stable, its *equilibrium* or *long-run multipliers* can be obtained from the equilibrium condition

$$\mathbf{Y}_t = \mathbf{Y}_{t-1} = \ldots = \mathbf{Y}_{t-s} = \mathbf{Y}_\varepsilon$$

[1] Or Y_t remains 'on trend' for the cases referred to in footnote 2, p. 197.

when the exact part of (6.55) becomes

$$(B + \Delta_1 + \ldots + \Delta_s)Y_\varepsilon + \Gamma X_\varepsilon = 0$$

and
$$\partial Y_\varepsilon / \partial X_\varepsilon = - \Gamma(B + \Delta_1 + \ldots + \Delta_s)^{-1}. \tag{6.69}$$

These show the expected shifts in the endogenous variables, given enough time, for sustained unit changes in each of the exogenous variables. The intermediate effects of such changes can be most conveniently obtained in practice for all but the smallest linear models by a computerised sequential solution of an estimated system of equations along the lines used in solving the first-order linear difference equation (6.51). In the case of a model in which the predetermined variables include endogenous variables which are lagged by no more than one period, the exact part of the reduced form of the model may be written

$$Y_t = - B^{-1}\Gamma X_t - B^{-1}\Delta_1 Y_{t-1} \equiv \Phi_0 X_t + \Phi_1 Y_{t-1}. \tag{6.70}$$

The Y_t for successive intervals of time, assuming the X_t remain constant, are then

$$Y_{t+1} = \Phi_0 X_t + \Phi_1 Y_t = \Phi_0 X_t(I + \Phi_1) + \Phi_1^2 Y_{t-1}$$
$$Y_{t+2} = \Phi_0 X_t + \Phi_1[\Phi_0 X_t(I + \Phi_1) + \Phi_1^2 Y_{t-1}]$$
$$= \Phi_0 X_0(I + \Phi_1 + \Phi_1^2) + \Phi_1^3 Y_{t-1}$$

$$\cdot$$
$$\cdot$$
$$\cdot$$

$$Y_{t+T} = \Phi_0 X_t(I + \Phi_1 + \Phi_1^2 + \ldots + \Phi_1^T) + \Phi_1^{T+1} Y_{t-1}. \tag{6.71}$$

Dynamic multipliers associated with sustained shifts in the X_t may therefore be written

$$\frac{\partial Y_{t+T}}{\partial X_t} = \Phi_0(I + \Phi_1 + \Phi_1^2 + \ldots + \Phi_1^T). \tag{6.72}$$

For model (6.55), which contains endogenous variables lagged back as far as period $(t - s)$, dynamic multipliers for period $(t + 1)$ may be similarly obtained from the exact part of the reduced form of the model

$$Y_t = - B^{-1}\Gamma X_t - B^{-1}\Delta_1 Y_{t-1} - B^{-1}\Delta_2 Y_{t-2} - \ldots - B^{-1}\Delta_s Y_{t-s}$$
$$\equiv \Phi_0 X_t + \Phi_1 Y_{t-1} + \Phi_2 Y_{t-2} + \ldots + \Phi_s Y_{t-s} \tag{6.73}$$
$$Y_{t+1} = \Phi_0 X_t + \Phi_1(\Phi_0 X_t + \Phi_1 X_{t-1} + \ldots + \Phi_s Y_{t-s})$$
$$+ \Phi_2(\Phi_0 X_t + \Phi_1 Y_{t-2} + \ldots + \Phi_s Y_{t-s-1})$$
$$+ \ldots + \Phi_s(\Phi_0 X_t + \Phi_1 Y_{t-s} + \ldots + \Phi_s Y_{t-2s+1})$$

so that

$$\frac{\partial Y_{t+1}}{\partial X_t} = \Phi_0(I + \Phi_1 + \Phi_2 + \ldots + \Phi_s). \tag{6.74}$$

In general it can be shown that

$$\frac{\partial \mathbf{Y}_{t+T}}{\partial \mathbf{X}_t} = \mathbf{\Phi}_0[\mathbf{I} + \sum_{i=1}^{s} \mathbf{\Phi}_i + (\sum_{t=1}^{s} \mathbf{\Phi}_i)^2 + \ldots + (\sum_{i=1}^{s} \mathbf{\Phi}_i)^T]. \qquad (6.75)$$

Where a change in the $\mathbf{X}_t$ takes the form of an impulse rather than a sustained shift, then these results may be amended to yield *impulse multipliers* on disregarding those terms which account for the effects of sustaining a change in the $\mathbf{X}_t$ into periods $(t + 1)$, $(t + 2)$, etc., to period T. Thus (6.75) becomes

$$\frac{\partial \mathbf{Y}_{t+T}}{\partial \mathbf{X}_t} = \mathbf{\Phi}_0(\sum_{i=1}^{s} \mathbf{\Phi}_i)^T. \qquad (6.76)$$

In the above analysis details of the λ_i, which dictate the behaviour of the endogenous variables through time once a system is disturbed, are sacrificed in favour of procedures which are more easily handled computationally.[1] Furthermore, although the algebraic expressions apply only to linear and to linearised non-linear models, the principle of tracing the time-paths of a set of endogenous variables for an estimated model by successive substitution is one which has wider application. In particular it can be used as the basis of a computerised analysis of non-linear models and of the behaviour of the $\mathbf{Y}_t$ using either linear or non-linear systems when the exogenous variables are subject to irregular change or when random disturbances are added, as in the case of Monte Carlo studies.

As a first step in this kind of analysis the behaviour of those endogenous variables which are of interest might be established for some 'standard' or 'control' behaviour of the exogenous variables, which could take the form of holding all these variables at some fixed level. Alternatively, and more realistically if the model is being used to help in the design of policy, some of the exogenous variables may be assumed to follow trends observed in the past while others, which may be more or less regarded as instruments of government policy, may be assigned values which reflect past, or otherwise 'accepted', policy. Realistic values for lagged endogenous variables can then be added and the current values of the endogenous variables computed. Further values for the endogenous variables may be computed for as far into the future as projections for the exogenous variables allow. The cyclical behaviour of these time-series projections might be of interest while the stability of the system can be tested by long-run projections keeping the exogenous variables constant

---

[1] However, the results obtained may be readily seen to be directly related to those obtained earlier for model (6.47) for which it will be recalled the time path for Y_i is given by

$$Y_{t+T} = \beta^T\left(Y_t - \frac{\alpha + I_t + G_t}{(1 - \beta)}\right) + \frac{\alpha + I_t + G_t}{(1 - \beta)}$$

where the system is initially in equilibrium, $Y_t = Y_\varepsilon = (\alpha + I_t + G_t)/(1 - \beta)$. If G_t becomes $G_{t-1} + \Delta G$ in period t but thereafter returns to G_{t-1} then Y_{t+T} is $\beta^T \Delta G + Y_\varepsilon$ so that the impulse multiplier is β^T. If the change is sustained then the results of the change must be added on for subsequent time periods, to give $\Delta G(\beta^{T-1} + \beta^{T-2} + \ldots + 1)$.

after once adding an impulse to each one in turn. Next the effects of the kind of changes in the exogenous variables which correspond to possible changes in government policy may be examined. These changes may be either temporary or sustained shifts in the levels or the trends of the variables and the effects may be assessed either in the form of graphs for certain endogenous variables for the 'control' and 'changed' sequences of the exogenous variables, or in the form of impact and dynamic multipliers which may be set out in tables for the variables, the changes and the period to which they relate.

6.4 FORECASTING AND FORECAST PERFORMANCE IN PRACTICE

As noted already forecasts can be readily obtained from an estimated linear system using (6.8) given the inverse matrix $\hat{B}^{-1}$ and a set of values, Z_t, for the predetermined variables of the system. The reader can see what is involved in this in practice for himself by referring to information published by Suits (1962) on the $\hat{B}^{-1}$ matrix and the column vector $\hat{\Gamma}Z_t$ of that version of the University of Michigan RSQE model that was used to obtain *ex ante* forecasts for the United States economy for 1962.[1]

The way in which the same approach can be used to obtain forecasts from a non-linear system once the non-linear equations of the model have been linearised has been demonstrated by Goldberger (1959) with reference to the Klein–Goldberger model. Thus for an estimate of the production function $(5.10g)$[2]

$$f = Q - W_2 + 26{\cdot}08 - 2{\cdot}17[h(N_W - N_G) + N_E]$$
$$- 0{\cdot}08(K + K_{-1}) - 2{\cdot}05t = 0 \quad (6.77)$$

the total differential is

$$f = \dot{Q} - \dot{W}_2 - 2{\cdot}17[h\dot{N}_W + N_W\dot{h} - h\dot{N}_G - N_G\dot{h} + \dot{N}_E]$$
$$- 0{\cdot}08(\dot{K} + \dot{K}_{-1}) - 2{\cdot}05t = 0 \quad (6.78)$$

---

[1] It will be seen that only an attenuated $\hat{B}^{-1}$ matrix is presented in Suits' article showing rows relating to 18 endogenous variables, which for the sake of convenience in printing have been transposed so as to appear as columns. The $\hat{B}^{-1}$ matrix also relates only to those equations which together constitute a non-recursive block; three equations forming a recursive sub-section or block have therefore been removed before solving and the endogenous variables concerned have been added to the predetermined variables, known values of which are entered in the vector $\hat{\Gamma}Z_t$. In addition the tax and transfer equations of the model have been run together to show totals only rather than separate amounts relating to federal, state and local government. The latter can be readily obtained from the model's structural equations given forecasts of the remaining endogenous variables.

The format of this information, for the 1965 version of the model and for just two endogenous variables and unspecified values of the parameters and variables of the vector $\hat{\Gamma}Z_t$, can also be seen in Table 6.5 below.

[2] The symbol Q is used in (6.77) to represent GNP $(= Y + T + D)$ and N_E represents both non-farm (N_E) and farm (N_F) entrepreneurs.

which Goldberger linearises by setting the variables, h, N_W and N_G equal to sample means for the period 1929–41 and 1946–52, to obtain, on separating endogenous and predetermined variables

$$\dot{Q} - 2{\cdot}274\dot{N}_W - 0{\cdot}08\dot{K} = W_2 + 74{\cdot}78h - 2{\cdot}274\dot{N}_G + 2{\cdot}17\dot{N}_E$$
$$+ 0{\cdot}08\dot{K}_{-1} + 2{\cdot}05\dot{t}. \qquad (6.79)$$

Alternatively, h, N_W and N_G could be substituted by their last known values if this seems more appropriate, as would generally be the case if the result were to be used for *ex ante* forecasting (in contrast to the analysis of *ex post* forecasts over the observation period undertaken by Goldberger). The other non-linear equations of the model can be similarly re-formulated in this way and the resulting linearised model solved,

$$\dot{Y} = \hat{\Pi}_0 \dot{Z}$$

The $\hat{\Pi}_0$ matrix obtained by Goldberger (1959) can be seen in his study, pp. 25–9.

Intermediate steps in the application of the two other methods of solving a non-linear model looked at in Section 6.2 cannot be so conveniently set out since these methods are geared to getting a numerical result specific to a given set of values for predetermined variables. However, those who have some knowledge of computer programming should be able to follow a program published by Surrey (1971) that applies the relatively uncomplicated Gauss–Seidel method of solution to a macro-economic model developed by the United Kingdom National Institute of Economic and Social Research. Klein and Evans (1969) have also discussed the use of this procedure to compute multipliers relating to a quarterly model of the United States economy.

In Goldberger's study the matrix $\hat{\Pi}_0$ is used to obtain *ex post* forecasts of year to year changes through the observation period using actual changes for both exogenous and lagged endogenous variables. Ideally, of course, the matrix should be re-computed for the situation, Y_0, Z_0, found in each base year, $t - 1$, and even then the solution is, strictly speaking, valid for only small changes about the point Y_0, Z_0. Just how severe a restriction this is on the results obtained depends on how far the model used departs from linearity and on the size of the year to year changes and the range of change over the period as a whole that are encountered in practice. From comparison of the elements of $\hat{\Pi}_0$ for 1930, 1951, 1953[1] and averages for the sample period Goldberger concludes, p. 138, that 'at least for the range of economic variation displayed over the 1929–52 sample period . . . a linearisation at sample period means does not substantially violate the estimated structure of the K–G model'.[2] However, despite these assurances in this particular instance,

[1] These years are reported to represent the extremes observed over the period 1929–41, 1946–52 in that in 1930 most variables were at, or close to, their sample period minima and *vice versa* for either 1951 or 1953.

[2] In contrast Ball and Burns (1968) report that in preparing forecasts from a quarterly model of the U.K. 18 months linearising around mid-values was about the maximum spread that could be used with 'any safety'.

the accuracy of solution offered by the alternative procedures referred to above means that they are greatly to be preferred and have in practice superseded the approximation adopted by Goldberger.

So far as the forecast changes themselves are concerned an important deficiency is evident from an examination of the model's ability to cope with turning points. Thus considerable inertia is indicated by the low number of correctly forecast turning points: 1 out of 4 for GNP, 2 out of 9 for investment, 1 out of 6 for the price level and 1 out of 4 for the wage rate. This, Goldberger feels it is reasonable to infer, indicates that the structural lags specified in the model are, in general, too long while the investment function is considered to be especially at fault in this respect in the specification of the profit-investment lag, and the lag of inventory accumulation in particular.

Close associations between forecast errors for GNP and errors in forecasting investment, on the one hand, and between errors in forecasting prices and in forecasting wages, on the other, in contrast to a weak association between success in forecasting GNP and success in forecasting prices, is taken as evidence that the real and monetary sectors of the model are 'effectively disjoint'.

Table 6.1. Changes in U.S. GNP: Michigan RSQE model *ex ante* forecast and actual changes. (Billions of 1954 dollars)

Year	Forecast	Observation	Error
1953	13·0	15·0	−2·0
1954	−4·5	−5·9	1·4
1955	4·4	29·6	−25·2
1956	9·0	8·2	0·8
1957	9·1	7·7	1·4
1958	−2·9	−7·3	4·4
1959	9·0	27·3	−18·3
1960	8·5	11·3	−2·8
1961	7·4	7·8	−0·4
1962	27·5	27·1	0·4
1963	14·1	15·9	−0·8
1964	23·9	24·1	−0·2
1965	15·8	30·8	−15·0

Source: Suits (1967), p. 275.

While, as noted earlier, this kind of analysis of *ex post* forecast errors over the observation period can throw some light on the value of an econometric model as a whole in forecasting, several sources of error are precluded. At the other extreme, a far severer test lies in an examination of how well the model predicts *ex ante*. The record of the Michigan RSQE model in this respect can be traced as far back as 1953 and figures for forecast and realised changes in GNP in particular for the thirteen years 1953–65 are given in Table 6.1. The comparison thereby expressed can be illustrated in Figure 6.2 in the manner of Figure 6.1 even though this information is not given in terms of *relative* first differences. It can be seen that although no turning point errors are made the *ex ante* forecast performance of the model is severely tested by the succession of booms and recessions through this period. It is evident that the model coped successfully with most of the observed changes between one year and the next, including those experienced in 1954, 1956, 1960, 1962, 1963 and 1964, but failed to predict the full measure of the upswings of 1955 and 1959 and the downswing of 1958 as well as the continuing increase in the rate of expansion in 1965.

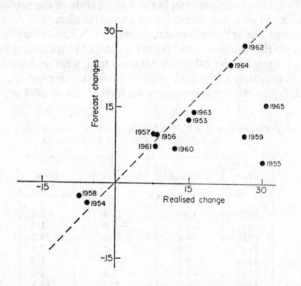

Figure 6.2. Changes in U.S. GNP: Michigan RSQE model *ex ante* forecasts and actual changes. (Billions of 1954 dollars.)

The overall performance of the model can also be gauged from a figure of 0·276 for Theil's bounded U_{58} coefficient for this period as compared to 0·521 for the naïve model $GNP_t - GNP_{t-1} = GNP_{t-1} - GNP_{t-2}$ (using a figure of $2·0 billion for the observed change in GNP for 1952) and 1 for a zero-change 'prediction'. The corresponding values using the alternative, U_{66}, form of this coefficient are 0·479, 1·081 and infinity.

The need to evaluate the *ex ante* forecast performance of a model with reference to as long a forecast series as possible, in order to reduce the possibility of being misled by unrepresentative results, and the value of a closer examination of the forecast performance of a model like the Michigan RSQE model by referring to predictions of the components of GNP has been demonstrated by Stekler (1966) for *ex ante* and *ex post* forecast and actual[1] changes for a single year, 1962. His results are given in Table 6.2. They show that *ex post* predictions of the components of GNP obtained from the model all exceed both the *ex ante* forecasts for this year and the actual changes which occurred.

Table 6.2. Changes in U.S. GNP and components for 1962: Michigan RSQE model *ex ante* and *ex post* forecasts and actual changes. (Billions of 1954 dollars)

	Ex ante forecast	*Ex post forecast*	*Actual*
Gross national product	27·5	35·0	28·5
Consumption			
Automobiles	4·5	5·0	3·1
Other durables	1·9	2·8	1·3
Non-durables	5·3	6·5	4·8
Services[1]	5·5	6·2	5·6
Gross private investment			
Plant and equipment	1·3[3]	3·0[3]	3·0[3]
Residential construction	0·1	1·9[3]	1·9[3]
Inventory investment	3·0	4·8	3·5
Exports	0·0[3]	1·7[3]	1·7[3]
Imports	1·9	2·2	2·0
Government expenditure on goods and services[2]	7·8[3]	5·5[3]	5·5[3]
Disposable income	n.a.	17·7	14·8

Source: Stekler (1966) p. 1247.

[1] Includes imputed services. [2] Does not include imputed expenditures.
[3] Estimated exogenously.

In contrast, *ex ante* forecasts of imports and two categories of investment underestimate actual changes. The overall effect is that the *ex ante* forecast of the change in GNP is considerably more accurate than the *ex post* forecast even though the latter is free of errors in the values of predetermined variables. There is evidence to suggest therefore that the accuracy of the *ex ante* forecast of the shift in GNP is somewhat fortuitous and obscures what appears to be a structural change which otherwise results in an overestimation of this shift.

[1] Since information on 'actual' values is subject to revision, Stekler notes that the actual values used in his study, including the values of predetermined variables used in computing *ex post* forecasts, are those available in 1964. This contrasts with the 'actual' changes given in Table 6.1 which are estimates recorded soon after the end of the forecast year so that they are as close as possible in definition and economic context to the data on which the forecast was based. It should also be noted that since the model's forecasts relate only to private sector GNP exclusive of imputed services, some adjustments were necessary to achieve comparability between forecast and actual changes on this score.

Some light on one, apparently important, fault in the model in this respect is available from a comparison of *ex post* predictions of changes in consumption and in disposable income. These are $20·5 billion and $17·7 billion which Stekler concludes would seem to suggest that other factors associated with consumption, such as liquid assets which appear in all four consumption equations of the 1962 version of the model, have been given too much weight. Further evidence on this is presented in the form of a comparison of actual changes with changes predicted by the structural equations of the model using actual values for all explanatory variables. The four consumption functions continue to overestimate actual change but forecasts of inventory investment and imports now slightly underestimate actual change. (It is interesting to note further that of the consumption functions of the 1965 version of the model referred to in Chapter 5, Section 5.9, only the automobile equation (5.29) continued to include liquid assets as an explanatory variable. None of the consumption functions of the 1963 version this variable although it reappeared in several of these functions in the 1964 version.)

Stekler (1968) has also undertaken a comparison of the published *ex post* forecast records of six macro-economic models. For four of these models sufficient data were available to be able to compute Theil's inequality coefficient, in this case in the form of U_{58}, for predictions obtained from the models and from the naïve model $Y_t - Y_{t-1} = Y_{t-1} - Y_{t-2}$. The results are shown in Table 6.3. The difficulties involved in comparing the forecast performance of different models are evident enough in the terms in which this comparison is offered. In particular, the measures of U_{58}, based on published forecasts, do not relate to the same variable or period of time nor even to the same kind of *ex post* forecast.[1] However, to some extent these limitations on direct comparisons are overcome by the standardisation adopted in U_{58} and by the use of the common yardstick available in the form of a naïve model, although the latter is only a crude test and it may be that different naïve models are more appropriate standards of comparison for different forecast periods and different variables.[2]

---

[1] Stekler (1969) has attempted elsewhere to tackle these problems of comparability by refitting different models to identical time periods and then using these new estimates to obtain *ex post* forecasts for a common prediction period. As he admits himself, however, even this approach is subject to its limitations. The models referred to were developed at different points in time and indeed some were based on experience gained in work done on earlier models which are also included in the study. The model specifications and fitted results looked at are therefore not necessarily those which the authors concerned would have adopted given the availability of new insights subsequently achieved by others together with, in several instances, new data series. There is also the possibility of structural changes between one observation period and another which too may call for revisions to the specification of a model. So far as this last point is concerned, tests on estimated parameters for the (two) observation periods adopted and for the original observation periods of the various studies indicated that the structures of only two out of nine equations appeared to remain unchanged between the new and old observation periods.

[2] It is interesting to note in this respect the different values of U_{58} recorded in Table 6.3 for the different forecast periods and variables.

Table 6.3. Theil's U_{58} coefficient for *ex post* projections obtained from four econometric models and the naïve model

$$Y_t - Y_{t-1} = Y_{t-1} - Y_{t-2}$$

Model	No. of equations	Observation period	Forecast variable	Forecast period	U_{58} coefficient	
					Model	Naïve prediction
Klein (1964)	34	1948(1)–1958(4)	GNP[1] (constant prices)	1953(1)–54(4) and 1957(1)–58(4)	0·54	0·63
OBE M. Liebenberg et al. (1966)	36	1953(1) 1964(4)	GNP[2]	1953(1)–1964(4)	Annual Constant prices 0·07 Current prices 0·05 Quarterly: Constant prices 0·27 Current prices 0·22	0·48 0·32 0·40 0·31
					0·15	0·38
Fromm (1962)	15	1953(1)–1960(4)	Disposable income[3] (current prices)	1953(1)–1960(4)		
Friend and Taubman (1964)	5	1953(1)–1960(4)	GNP (constant prices)	1960(4)/61(1)–1963(2)/(3)	0·11	0·21

Source: H. O. Stekler (1968).

[1] Simulation result using actual values for exogenous variables only apart from initial values of lagged endogenous variables.

[2] Adjusted forecasts obtained by adding forecast errors of the preceding period(s) to the constant terms of the relevant structural equations wherever serial correlation was believed to be present (see p. 187).

[3] Computed as a residual from actual GNP using estimates of all other components of GNP apart from actual values for government subsidies, wage accruals and a statistical discrepancy.

Subject to these caveats the performance of the first model appears to be the least satisfactory and indeed the model of the Office of Business Economics (OBE) of the United States Commerce Department referred to in the same table is a development of Klein's model which it was hoped would improve on the latter's poor performance in this respect. Although it is difficult to assess the success achieved unequivocally because of differences in the ways in which the two sets of forecasts were prepared, some improvement may be judged to have been made. The other two models can also be seen to have done better than the naïve model, even without the benefit of this kind of adjustment. The record of Friend and Taubman's model is particularly interesting since this is a macro-economic model which has been kept highly aggregative in order to examine the possibility of forecasting short-term, constant price changes in GNP and in just four components of aggregate demand (consumption, non-farm residential constriction, investment in plant and equipment, and non-farm inventory investment) just as accurately with a small system of equations which can be estimated, tested, maintained and used with far less resources than larger models. Whether this is likely to be so depends, as Friend and Taub-man admit, essentially on the extent to which output is determined by demand conditions in the short run so that production functions and demand for labour equations can be dispensed with. Certainly within the terms of the analysis presented in Table 6.3 it would appear that the performance of the Friend–Taubman model compares favourably with that of more complex models. The drawback of this approach lies, however, precisely in its strict limitation to short-term forecasting in constant price terms and in its inability to cope with the kind of analysis required for the design of policy. The removal of these restrictions requires an extension in the scope of the explanation of change offered, both in terms of the existing relationships of the model (in the use of other forecast information in the place of data from surveys of antici-pated consumption and investment, which are only available for the immediate future, and in the addition of policy variables, such as tax rates and thereby the use of disposable income in the consumption function rather than GNP as in the case of Friend and Taubman's model) and in terms of the addition of further relationships in order to replace certain exogenous variables by endo-genous variables and to account for other variables which have a bearing on GNP and which are of interest in themselves in the design of policy, e.g. wage and price levels. These are matters which are considered further in Section 6.5.

The use made of survey information on anticipated behaviour in the con-sumption and investment functions of this model is of special interest in itself. As implied already, this aspect of the study is consistent with its general character and in particular with the simplicity of the structural equations adopted, in which explanatory variables were selected on the grounds of statistical significance as much as theoretical justification, even though the signs of estimated parameters were all in accord with what theory would suggest. The extent to which this kind of information constitutes an accurate forecast depends on the particular variable concerned. Thus anticipated investment is likely to predict actual investment more accurately than anticipated consumption predicts actual consumption because of the relatively close association between a commitment to an investment programme and a series of subsequent expenditures (even though the pace of work may be varied and there may be unforeseeable delays in construction and in the delivery of equipment) in contrast to the more uncertain fulfilment of consumers' declared plans to purchase. The difference suggests the different ways in which the two measures might be appropriately used. Thus until recent advances in the specification of the investment function, anticipated investment often proved a more accurate prediction of actual investment than that which could be obtained by other means.[1] On the other hand, anticipated consumption, even though an unreliable estimate of actual consumption, may be a valuable guide to consumer attitudes and may thus prove to be a useful explanatory variable.

A preliminary study of the utility of anticipatory data in a model of this kind is reported in an earlier study by Friend and Jones (1964). The series looked at included quarterly data for planned expenditures on plant and equipment, business inventory anticipations and consumer intentions to purchase cars, the first two of which refer to anticipations one quarter hence and the third to one year hence. Of these three only the first is reported to have been consistently significant (in the plant and equipment expenditures equation) in all the regressions that were looked at[2] while the other two proved to be, at best, only unreliably significantly associated with inventory investment and consumption. However, housing starts and unfilled orders, which are anticipatory variables if not anticipations, also added to the forecasting accuracy of the model. Much the same results were found for the model used by Friend and Taubman.

[1] As noted already, this source of information has been relied on, for example, for forecasts of new investment in fixed plant and equipment in the Michigan RSQE work although in Friend and Taubman's study these forecasts appear as an explanatory variable in a function for investment in plant and equipment.

[2] The Friend and Jones study looked at the *ex post* forecast performance of this kind of model using quarterly, semi-annual and annual data. It was concluded, that the semi-annual and annual models performed better than the quarterly model, the value of which would in practice be further limited by the lapse of at least one and half months of the period being projected before projections were available. This difference, Friend and Jones ventured, may be the result of averaging out erratic short-term changes in the quarterly data (including observation errors). In view of these results, a semi-annual data model is employed in Friend and Taubman's study although full use is still made of the available quarterly data by means of an overlapping semi-annual observation interval, that is by reckoning the first observation for any year t as

$$\Delta Y_1 = (Y_{t(1)} + Y_{t-1(4)}) - (Y_{t-1(3)} + Y_{t-1(2)})$$

and the next observation as

$$\Delta Y_2 = (Y_{t(2)} + Y_{t(1)}) - (Y_{t-1(4)} + Y_{t-1(3)})$$

and so on. The effect is to enable forecasts for a six-month period to be made at quarterly intervals, at a time when some two months of this six months has passed, which is reported to be six months in advance of the publication of the first estimates of realisations for this period.

Reference has also been made earlier to the use of anticipatory data in the Wharton EFU model, Evans and Klein (1968), in which alternative specifications of two consumer durables functions (for cars and for all other consumer durables) each include an appropriate index of consumer anticipations and in which alternative equations for investment in manufacturing industry, investment in regulated and mining industries and expenditures on non-farm residential construction respectively include investment anticipations of manufacturing firms and of non-manufacturing firms and private non-farm housing starts. Only in the case of the consumption function for durables other than cars were these additional explanatory variables found to be non-significant.[1]

Evans and Klein (1968) have also presented a comparison of the forecasting performance of different econometric models, in this case with reference to *ex ante* annual forecasts of GNP. The records of three econometric models referred to already (the Michigan RSQE, the Wharton EFU and the Friend–Taubman models) are compared with forecasts prepared by the United States Council of Economic Advisors, with forecasts obtained from three naïve models (which include $\Delta GNP_t = \Delta GNP_{t-1}$, setting ΔGNP equal to the average ΔGNP over the sample period to date, and an extrapolation of the change between the first and third quarters of year $t - 1$ through the forecast period t)[2] and with an average of approximately 50 non-econometric contemporaneous forecasts of GNP from various sources, as published by the Federal Reserve Bank (FRB) of Philadelphia.[3] The results obtained can be seen in Table 6.4.

---

[1] In addition, however, a measure of investment anticipations was found to have the wrong sign in the equation for commercial, and other, investment. This was considered to be not too surprising in view of the poorer reliability of anticipations in respect of smaller firms, which account for the bulk of this sector, and some incompatibilities in the coverage of the series used for anticipations and realisations.

[2] According to this procedure predicted GNP for the first quarter of t is $GNP_{t-1(3)}$ plus the change $GNP_{t-1(3)} - GNP_{t-1(1)}$. Similarly $GNP_{t(2)} = GNP_{t-1(3)} + 1 \cdot 5(GNP_{t-1(3)} - GNP_{t-1(1)})$ and so on, where the factors relating to the change $GNP_{t-1(3)} - GNP_{t-1(1)}$ in predicting $GNP_{t(3)}$ and $GNP_{t(4)}$ are 2 and 2·5. The result is

$$GNP_t = GNP_{t-1(3)} + 1 \cdot 75(GNP_{t-1(3)} - GNP_{t-1(1)}).$$

[3] These forecasts represent, broadly speaking, an alternative approach to forecasting in quantitative terms that is based partly on statistical methods and partly on an understanding of past behaviour and an anticipation of future behaviour which is not related to a formal model but which is rather based on personal judgement. A review of the kind of procedures involved in getting short-run forecasts of GNP and its principal components by such means can be seen in the various papers presented in Part Two of Butler and Kavesh's (1966) volume *How Business Economists Forecast*, while a comprehensive analysis of the forecast performance of these methods in respect of GNP and other variables has been presented by Zarnowitz (1967).

Forecasts obtained by these methods, together with those obtained from econometric models, can be contrasted with the more traditional non-quantitative *leading indicator* approach whereby forecasts of changes in the rate of direction or change of certain economic

Again the terms in which the comparison is made can be seen to be somewhat less than ideal: the predictions looked at refer to a rather short time-span for several of the forecast series; not all of the predictions relate to the same variable, since forecasts obtained from the Michigan RSQE model and the Friend–Taubman model are in constant rather than current price terms and have been converted to the latter by means of *actual* price levels over the forecast period; and not all of the forecasts are contemporaneous, since the Friend–Taubman forecasts are not available until towards the end of the first quarter of the forecast year while all the others are made some time towards the end of the previous year or at the start of the forecast year. Furthermore, in contrast to the alternation of boom and recession experienced over the forecast period referred to in Table 6.1, the GNP of the United States rose subject to only relatively minor checks over the period 1961–7. Thus it is that the forecast records of naïve models I and III, and the latter in particular, set a reasonably severe standard which is only bettered conclusively by the Wharton EFU and the Friend–Taubman forecasts.

The possibility that the Wharton EFU forecasts might not have been so much better than those of the Michigan RSQE model if the former had had to cope with recessions has been discussed by Evans (1969*b*). From the first of the Michigan RSQE forecasts in 1953 through to 1967, three recessions are encountered, 1954, 1958 and 1960, for which years the forecast errors of this model are \$0, 3 and −10 billion, i.e. an average absolute error of \$4·3 billion. Since this last figure is considerably better than the average absolute errors of \$8·4 and \$7·8 billion of the model's forecasts for the remaining years of the periods 1953–67 and 1959–67, Evans concludes that the model appears to be more successful in predicting recessions than in predicting upturns and continuing expansions in activity. However, since the error of the FBR average forecast for 1960 is also as low as, if not lower than, the error of this average for any other year in the period 1959–67, Evans (1969*b*) p. 519, further reasons that 'these findings suggest . . . that predicting recessions has not been the major problem of economic forecasters in the postwar period' and, by implication, that the Wharton EFU model should not be at a disadvantage in this respect. Whether this is so or not remains to be demonstrated, of course, and yet one may more readily share his view that the Wharton EFU forecasting record, at least for the five years 1963–7, 'stands as a direct refutation to those who would argue that some combination of sophisticated judgement and simple arithmetic will generate a series of forecasts superior to those from any econometric model'. Moreover, even in the case of the Michigan RSQE

---

variables are based on past observation of how these changes in the growth or contraction of aggregate activity can be fairly accurately based, with different lags, on changes in such variables as orders for machinery and equipment, housing starts and the average number of hours worked per week. Principles involved in these procedures have been reviewed by Moore (1950) and Moore and Shiskin (1967) while the accuracy of the forecasts thereby obtained have been evaluated by, among others, Alexander (1958), Alexander and Stekler (1959) and Evans (1969*b*).

Table 6.4. Comparison of *ex ante* forecasts of U.S. GNP obtained by several different methods. (Billions of current dollars)

| Year | Actual old data[1] | Average FRB compilation[2] | Error | Michigan RSQE[3] | Error | CEA | Error | Wharton EFU | Error | Friend–Taubman[3] | Error | Naive models[4] | | | | | |
												I	Error	II	Error	III	Error
1959	483	470	−13	464	−19							447	−36	464	−19	472	−11
1960	503	507	4	493	−10							521	−18	503	0	502	−1
1961	519	512	−7	521	2							522	3	523	4	511	−8
1962	556	560	4	560	4	570	14					535	−1	539	−17	559	3
1963	584	573	−11	578	−6	578	−6	585	1	588	4	594	10	575	−9	582	−2
1964	623	616	−7	619	−4	619	−4	625	2	628	5	612	−11	606	−17	614	−9
1965	666	656	−10	652	−14	660	−6	662	−4	663	−3	661	−5	646	−20	663	−3
1966	732	725	−7	725	−7	722	−10	728	−4	n.a.		724	−8	708	−24	721	−11
1967	781	785	4	794	13	787	6	784	3	n.a.		791	10	768	−13	788	7
Average absolute error, 1959–67:			7·4		8·8								11·3		13·7		6·1
Average absolute error, 1963–67:			7·8		8·8		6·4		2·8		4·0		8·8		16·6		6·4

Source: Evans and Klein (1968), Table 13, pp. 164–5.

[1] Based on most recent figures available *at the time of prediction.*

[2] Compiled from public statements and releases made in the fourth quarter of the preceding year.

[3] Forecasts are actually made in constant price-terms. Realised price levels were used to convert figures to current price terms.

[4] See text, p. 210.

model's performance it should be noted that although a particular naïve model may have been shown with the benefit of hindsight to have done better, this does not help in anticipating which naïve model can be expected to yield the most appropriate extrapolations of past experience into the future.

Other tests on the forecast performance of the Wharton EFU model reported by Evans and Klein include an examination of forecasts for prediction intervals of one and two quarters ahead as well as an annual forecast made during the fourth quarter of the previous year,[1] all of which are presented for various components of aggregate demand as well as, for a shorter series of forecasts, an implicit GNP deflator, the rate of unemployment, the average annual wage rate in the private sector and the average yield on long-term corporate bonds. While no strictly objective standards of comparison are available in evaluating the relative success of these forecasts, the average absolute forecast error is usually within, and for many series well within, the average absolute change of the variable concerned over the forecast period as well as being usually within the average absolute forecast error of the first of the naïve models specified above, in the case of the quarterly forecasts,[2] or both the first and the third of these models, in the case of the annual forecast. Judged in these terms the most unsatisfactory of the forecasts proved to be inventory investment, owing to some extent to the difficulty in allowing for short-term erratic changes in the level of stocks associated with anticipations of strikes, which may then fail to occur so giving rise to a sudden fall in stocks. One alternative check is available in respect of forecasts of fixed business investment in view of the availability of survey information on anticipations or intentions. The model's predictions are shown to be better, in terms of the average absolute forecast error incurred, than two surveys of this kind, one of annual anticipations and one of quarterly intentions. It may be noted by way of conclusion to this section that it is this kind of evidence which is needed in particular, together with the generally satisfactory performance of the model in other respects, to establish confidence in the value of such a model in the analysis and design of economic policy to which attention is now turned.

6.5 MULTIPLIERS AND DYNAMIC PROPERTIES IN PRACTICE

As noted already in discussing the limitations of the kind of simplified short-term forecasting model proposed by Friend and his co-workers, a macro-economic model which is to be of use in the analysis and design of

---

[1] As the authors point out, this kind of forecast is one which is especially valuable for planning purposes in view of the general leaning towards calendar year planning and one which benefits from there being generally more information about the year ahead during this quarter.
[2] The forecast errors of the model for semi-annual forecasts proved in several instances to be larger than those of naïve model I although GNP forecasts for prediction intervals of one, three and four quarters together with an average of four quarters ahead all improved on the performance of this model.

economic policy must offer adequate expression of the relationships between what may be regarded as the targets and the instruments of economic policy. Given a model which is sufficiently comprehensive in this respect, there is clearly a close connection between what is involved in forecasting and in analysing the implications of different policies. Thus in the case of a linear model in particular, the parameters of the reduced form of the model, which have also been referred to earlier as impact multipliers, are required for both purposes.

For a linear system, like the Michigan RSQE model, the ease with which these multipliers can be calculated and their constancy confers much the same computational facility in tracing the effects of alternative policies as in preparing forecasts. So far as the first of these purposes is concerned, the multipliers may be conveniently set out in the form of either the product $\mathbf{B}^{-1}\boldsymbol{\Gamma}$ or the two arrays $\mathbf{B}^{-1}$ and $\boldsymbol{\Gamma}\mathbf{Z}$, the first of which shows the effects of an autonomous shift in each of the endogenous variables of the model. This interpretation of $\mathbf{B}^{-1}$ can be illustrated with reference to any equation

$$Y_j = \gamma_{0j} + \beta Y_k + \gamma_l Z_l$$

for which the corresponding element in the vector $\boldsymbol{\Gamma}\mathbf{Z}$ is $\gamma_{0j} + \gamma_l Z_l$. In this case, the solution of the model,

$$\mathbf{Y} = \mathbf{B}^{-1}\boldsymbol{\Gamma}\mathbf{Z},$$

shows that an autonomous shift in Y_j by one unit, so that γ_{0j} goes to $(\gamma_{0j} + 1)$, results in a shift in the ith endogenous variable by b_{ij} units if b_{ij} is the i, jth element in $\mathbf{B}^{-1}$. Thus these elements are impact multipliers corresponding to changes in endogenous variables in contrast to the elements of $\mathbf{B}^{-1}\boldsymbol{\Gamma}$ which relate to changes in endogenous variables brought about by changes in predetermined variables.

Suits (1967) has published two rows of the $\mathbf{B}^{-1}$ matrix of the 1965 version of the Michigan RSQE model and these are shown in Table 6.5 together with the unquantified elements of the column vector $\boldsymbol{\Gamma}\mathbf{Z}$.[1] For the sake of convenience of presentation the two $\mathbf{B}^{-1}$ rows are transposed to form the third and fourth columns of Table 6.5 so that a forecast of the level of (private sector) GNP is given by the sum of the products of the corresponding elements of columns three and five. Suits has shown, pp. 262–6, how these results can be used to establish, for example, the GNP and tax revenue effects of reducing the level of unemployment by adding one million to the number employed in government (E_g) and to design a fiscal policy that could be used to hold GNP constant despite this decrease in unemployment.

---

[1] A 17 by 16 segment of a $\mathbf{B}^{-1}$ matrix of impact multipliers has also been published by Fromm and Taubman (1968), p. 26, for the linearised 'real' part (i.e. holding prices, wage rates and interest rates constant) of a condensed version of the Brookings model. However, the concept of the $\mathbf{B}^{-1}$ matrix applies more generally than this to non-linear systems, of course, since the behaviour of the endogenous variables of such a system following an autonomous shift in one of these variables can be traced without having to linearise the model before solving it.

Table 6.5. Two columns from the $(B^{-1})'$ matrix of the 1965 version of the Michigan RSQE model together with the column vector ΓZ

Row number	Endogenous variable(s)	Private sector GNP	Total taxes less transfers	ΓZ
1	ΔA	1·75	0·95	$-\gamma_1 \Delta(X_1 + X_2) + \gamma_2 \Delta L_{-1} - \gamma_3 t \Delta L_{-1}$ $- \gamma_4 (NR - SC)_{-1} + \gamma_{01}$
2	$\Delta F_n + \Delta OD$	1·70	0·92	$-\gamma_5 \Delta P_{fn} + \gamma_6 \Delta P_{od} - \gamma_{02}$
3	$\Delta FB + \Delta CS$	1·48	0·84	$-\gamma_7 \Delta P_{fb} - \gamma_{03}$
4	ΔGA	1·66	1·00	γ_{04}
5	ΔOND	1·68	0·92	γ_{05}
6	$\Delta HSR + \Delta OS$	1·22	0·68	$\gamma_8 \Delta OS_{-1} - \gamma_9 \Delta P_{os} + \gamma_{06}$
7	ΔPE	1,71	0·85	γ_{07}
8	ΔHS	0·11	0·60	$\gamma_{10} \Delta HF - \gamma_{11}(HS - HF)_{-1}$ $+ \gamma_{12}\hat{J} - \gamma_{08}$
9	ΔH	1·40	0·75	$\gamma_{13} \Delta HS_{-1} + \gamma_{09}$
10	ΔFI	1·22	0·66	$-\gamma_{14} FI_{-1} + \gamma_{0,10}$
11	$\Delta(IND - FI)$	1·22	0·66	$-\gamma_{15}(IND - FI)_{-1}$
12	ΔID	1·35	0·71	$\gamma_{16}(D_g)_{-1} - \gamma_{17} ID_{-1}$
13	ΔR	−1·23	−0·62	$-\gamma_{18} \Delta P_{uf} - \gamma_{19} \Delta P_{fb} + \Delta R_{sr}$ $+ \Delta R_{sug} + \Delta R_{mtt} - \gamma_{0,13}$
14	ΔG^*	1·22	0·66	$\Delta(S_g + NS_g) + \Delta(F - R)$
15	ΔG^{**}	0·00	0·00	$-\Delta S_g$
16	ΔVA^d	0·23	0·35	$\gamma_{20} \Delta(F + D_g) - \gamma_{0,16}$
17	Δh	−0·16	−0·21	$\gamma_{21} h_{-1} + \gamma_{0,17}$
18	$\Delta \pi$	−0·09	−0·04	$-\gamma_{22} C_{-1}^d + \gamma_{0,18}$
19	E_p^d	3·84	1·79	0
20	ΔE_p^{nd}	3·07	1·63	$-\gamma_{0,20}$
21	ΔX_u	0·72	−0·60	$\gamma_{23} U_{-1}^*$
22	ΔE_{cc}	4·80	1·99	$\gamma_{24} \Delta HS_{-1} - \gamma_{0,22}$
23	ΔE_s	3·16	1·65	$\gamma_{25}(\Delta E_s)_{-1} - \gamma_{0,23}$
24	ΔE	−0·16	0·96	$\Delta(E_{np}^m + E_{min} + E_{ag} + E_g + E_{se})$
25	ΔU	0·34	−0·93	ΔLF
26	Δw_f^d	5·05	1·48	$\gamma_{0,26}$
27	Δw_p^{nd}	3·73	0·77	$\gamma_{0,27}$
28	—	−0·46	−0·10	—
29	—	0·00	0·00	—
30	Δw_s	18·75	3·87	$\gamma_{0,30}$
31	ΔW	0·66	0·14	$\Delta(w_{cc} E_{cc}) + \Delta(w_s E_s) + \Delta W_{min}$
32	ΔW_z	0·69	0·10	$-\gamma_{26} \Delta(E_{ag} + E_{se}) + \gamma_{0,32}$
33	ΔPY^d	0·09	0·05	$-\Delta(T_{pp} + T_{os} + SI_r)$
34	ΔCP	−0·70	−0·12	$-\gamma_{27} \Delta PY_f - \gamma_{0,34}$
35	ΔDiv	0·78	0·63	$\gamma_{28} \Delta(CP - T_{fc} - T_{sc})_{-1} + \gamma_{0,35}$
36	ΔY	0·97	0·54	$\Delta W_g + \Delta(X_1 + X_2) + \Delta(ig + X_{gi})$ $- \Delta(T_{eg} + T_{op} + T_{ref})$
37	—	1·09	0·60	—
38	$\Delta(T_{fc} + T_{sc})$	−0·11	0·91	$\gamma_{0,38}$
39	$\Delta(T_{fy} + T_{sy})$	−0·98	0·46	$\gamma_{29} \Delta(W_g + ig) - \gamma_{0,39}$
40	$\Delta(T_{fe} + T_{ss})$	−0·09	0·47	$-\gamma_{0,40}$
41	ΔT_{cd}	−0·09	0·47	$-\gamma_{0,41}$
42	ΔSI_r	−0·09	0·47	$\Delta S_{r_1} + \Delta SI_{r_2} + \Delta SI_{r_3}$
43	ΔSI_e	−0·98	0·46	$\gamma_{30} \hat{W}_{-1} + \gamma_{31} \Delta W_g$ $+ \gamma_{32}(PY - CP)_{-1}$
44	ΔU^*	1·41	−1·19	$-\gamma_{32}(\Delta LF - \Delta LF_{-1})$

Source: Suits (1967) pp. 279–86 and p. 288.

In predicting the effect on GNP of expanding E_g by one unit all that is required is the appropriate reduced form coefficient. So far as Table 6.5 is concerned this means identifying the elements of $\mathbf{\Gamma Z}$ in which E_g appears and summing the product of the parameter of E_g found in each of these elements with the corresponding elements in the GNP column of the $(\mathbf{B}^{-1})'$ array. The result is, from reference to row 24, $- \$ 0{\cdot}16$ billion, which is to be expected if the policy is literally interpreted as taking one million people into the government service, so reducing payments of unemployment benefits, without paying any wages. Suits notes that such an answer serves to emphasise the need to take account of changes in all the exogenous variables associated with a given policy. In this case it is also necessary to add to the total wage bill of government (W_g), say \$5 billion if the average salary paid is, \$5000 per additional employee. The change in private GNP thus effected is (from rows 36, 39 and 43 of Table 6.5)

$$(0{\cdot}97 - 0{\cdot}98\hat{\gamma}_{29} - 0{\cdot}98\hat{\gamma}_{31})5 = 3{\cdot}58$$

where $\hat{\gamma}_{29} = 0{\cdot}20$ and $\hat{\gamma}_{31} = 0{\cdot}06$. To this must be added the $-\$0{\cdot}16$ billion above to find the change in private sector GNP and \$5 billion to find the change in total GNP, that is including GNP originating in the public sector. The result is a multiplier of \$8·4 billion. (It should be evident that these other effects of a policy need only be traced with reference to any exogenous variables that are thereby affected. Thus there is no need to take into account the effects of a reduction of unemployment (U) by one million since this is an endogenous variable, the behaviour of which, in terms of both its determination and its effects, is taken care of by the model.)

The effects of increasing E_g on tax receipts net of transfers can be similarly calculated from elements 24, 36, 39 and 43 of the vector $\mathbf{\Gamma Z}$ and, in this case, the second column from $(\mathbf{B}^{-1})'$ shown in Table 6.5:

$$(0{\cdot}96 \times 1)1 + (0{\cdot}54 \times 1)5 + (0{\cdot}46\hat{\gamma}_{29})5 + (0{\cdot}46\hat{\gamma}_{31})5 = \$4{\cdot}26.$$

(Suits reports from reference to the full $\mathbf{B}^{-1}$ array that roughly half of this amount is in the form of additional tax receipts and the other half is in the form of insurance contributions and reduced payments of unemployment benefits.) Thus some four-fifths of payments to new employees in the public sector is returned in increased tax receipts or reduced net transfer payments.

The information given in Table 6.5 can also be used to design a policy to serve a particular purpose. As indicated earlier, Suits has shown how it could be used, for example, to determine the increase in the level of taxation that would be required to hold GNP constant while still pursuing the policy looked at earlier of increasing the number of employees in the public sector by one million. If the increased taxation were confined to federal (f) and state (s) personal income taxes $(T_{fy} + T_{sy})$ the relevant element in the $(\mathbf{B}^{-1})'$ array is $-0{\cdot}98$, which indicates that an autonomous shift in the income tax schedule of £1 billion reduces GNP by \$0·98 billion so that an increase in this tax of \$8·6 billion produces the required reduction in GNP of \$8·4 billion.

The 39th element in the 'total taxes less transfers' column of $(\mathbf{B}^{-1})'$ shows that the net effect on taxes and transfers of a change in income tax rates which would yield an increase in this tax of $1 billion at *old* income levels would, after having taken account of reductions in production and income, produce an increase in the total tax yield net of transfers of only $0·46 billion, or $3·9 billion for a $8·6 billion shift in the income tax schedules at the old level of income.

The total effect of a policy to reduce unemployment by adding one million employees to the public sector's labour force while raising income tax so that GNP remains at the same level is, therefore, to raise revenues by $4·3 billion (recovered from reducing unemployment by one million) plus $3·9 billion (from increased taxes) which on deducting the increase in $5 billion in the public sector's wage bill produces a budgetary surplus of $3·2 billion.

The effects of other policies, and their design to achieve required goals, may be looked at in the same way. All this is, however, subject to a number of caveats. To begin with whether the effects of different policies can be accurately traced by such means depends on the specification of the model used. As has already been pointed out in the case of the Klein–Goldberger model, a realistic study of fiscal policy requires that a set of tax functions be added to the estimated model in order that tax rates, rather than yields, may be considered as exogenous variables. As in the case of the Michigan RSQE model above, tax yields are thereby made endogenous, changing as the tax base changes, which has the effect of introducing tax leakages into the system. Thus any increase income brought about by an increase in government spending will be less than it would otherwise have been had tax levels remained exogenous since a part of the increase is now removed, as in practice, in increased levels of taxation as incomes, profits, expenditures and imports increase.[1]

Even a large macro-economic model may not, however, include variables which precisely relate to a particular policy option open to government nor may it be sensitive to all the effects that may follow a change in policy. So far as the first of these problems is concerned it may be necessary in practice to relate the effects of proposed changes in a policy variable (P) to changes in the exogenous variables $(\mathbf{X})$ of a model to produce a vector of changes $(\partial \mathbf{X}/\partial P)$ before computing the impact multipliers

$$\partial \mathbf{Y}/\partial P = \mathbf{B}^{-1}\mathbf{\Gamma}(\partial \mathbf{X}/\partial P). \tag{6.80}$$

Thus, for example, in the case of the Dutch forecasting and policy model, which does not explicitly include a production function, de Wolff (1967) notes that in tracing the effects of a reduction in normal working hours information

---

[1] Using linear functions to relate tax yields for wage, corporate, indirect and non-wage, non-farm, non-corporate taxes to their respective bases and comparing the parameters of the reduced form of the endogenous tax version of the model for (i) tax rates which approximate those generally in effect in the U.S. in the post-war years and (ii) rates which are all greater than these by one half, Goldberger (1959), pp. 47 and 48, concludes that the effect of this shift would have been to increase total tax yields by about one third while the impact effect of government expenditures on GNP is lowered by some 4 per cent.

on labour productivity must be used to establish the effect of the change in terms of an additional demand for labour, which can then be introduced into the model as an autonomous shift in the labour demand function of the model. In the case of a non-linear model such a shift can be conveniently allowed for by adding an autonomous variable term, having a unit parameter, to the relevant equation of the model before solving. If the model is solved, as the Dutch model has been, in the same way as a linear model after having replaced any non-linear equations by linear approximations, then the reduced form parameter array $\mathbf{\Pi}_0$ contains an extra column corresponding to that column of the $\mathbf{\Gamma}$ matrix relating to this autonomous shift possibility and which shows the impact of the shift on the endogenous variables of the model, including the shifted variable itself.

Multipliers relating to changes in taxation present a more general need for special caution since these changes must be specific to particular changes in the tax structure. Furthermore, in the case of excise taxes it is not only necessary to consider the sort of goods and services to which the tax change applies but also the extent to which it is expected to be passed on to the consumer in price changes, leaving its remaining effect in the form of an autonomous shift in corporate profits.[1]

Illustration of the need to exercise discretion in taking account of the effects of certain policy changes on *endogenous* variables is also offered in de Wolff's (1967) survey of the value of the Dutch model for the purposes of formulating policy. The case of an increase in the controlled rent of housing is cited. Although within the terms of the specification of the model such an increase produces an increase in consumption prices, its effect, so far as other variables are concerned, is not considered to be the same as a general increase in the price of goods and services for consumption (p_c). Thus although profit margins (K), for example, are related to the price of total output less inventory changes and net invisibles ($p_{v'}$), import prices (p_m), the average wage (l) and the incidence of indirect taxes minus subsidies (T'_K),

$$K = p_{v'} - 0\cdot30p_m - 0\cdot27l - 0\cdot06(T'_K)_{-1/3} \qquad (6.81)$$

and even though $p_{v'}$ and l are explicitly related to p_c, it seems unlikely that profit margins are directly affected by rents so that an amendment of this equation is required in respect of this particular policy, especially since K appears as an explanatory variable in the labour demand and inventory functions of the model.

---

[1] These changes may be reckoned in real terms by means of a price deflator for personal consumption in the case of income taxes and that proportion of excise tax changes that is passed on in price changes. In the case of the other part of the latter the deflator must be chosen somewhat arbitrarily. Some of the resulting increase in corporate profits is immediately paid out in corporate income tax and need not be considered further, some is paid out in dividends which can be deflated by the consumption deflator, and the rest is retained earnings which can be deflated by a deflator for gross output originating in the appropriate sector.

A second complication of a general nature in the computation and interpretation of multipliers concerns the problem of reducing the changes adopted in respect of exogenous variables to a comparable basis. So far as a variable like government expenditure is concerned, a multiplier can be reckoned in the usual way as the effect of a unit change in the level of this expenditure. However, changes in taxation and in monetary variables have to be handed differently. In the case of taxation a similar kind of change can be used to that encountered in dealing with government expenditure if, as was done in the above numerical example with reference to impact multipliers, a tax rate change is considered which corresponds to a unit change in tax yield. In subsequent periods the tax yield may well change, as noted earlier, as a result of changes in the tax base so that the denominator required in the computation of multipliers for these periods has to be changed accordingly. Normalisation of intermediate period dynamic multipliers in this way produces a biased result, however, since if the tax yield is itself subject to change some of the effects of these changes, which are still working their way through the system with varying lags, are overlooked. Hence what is wanted in the denominator in these circumstances is a distributed lag although the bias in failing to meet this requirement is less serious the more rapid the tax adjustment and the smaller the weights on distant periods compared with those on the current period.

In the case of monetary variables the problem is more complicated. Two possible approaches are referred to below. In one of these, adopted by Evans and Klein (1968), the effect of monetary policy on required reserves is used as a basis of comparison with fiscal policy multiplers. An alternative, used by Fromm and Taubman (1968), is to reckon the denominator required in computing a monetary policy multiplier in terms of the expenditure changes directly brought about by the policy as though they were autonomous changes.

A third limitation on the general applicability of the kind of multiplier analysis outlined above with reference to the Michigan RSQE model arises when use is made of non-linear models. As noted earlier, multipliers relating to non-linear systems are not independent of the initial values of variables before any given change is effected. Indeed, one of the main reasons for introducing non-linear functions into a macro-economic model is to give expression to the different behaviour that is to be expected in respect of output, prices and wages in particular depending on the level of capacity utilisation.

Non-linearities also present special computational burdens in overcoming a fourth limitation of the multiplier analysis considered so far, the limitation that it is not enough to know the immediate effects of a policy change. Any realistic model must have a dynamic structure which can be used to examine whether a particular policy is likely to produce any given required result in the future and what other, perhaps undesirable, consequences can be expected. As noted earlier, if the model used is non-linear the computational burden in doing this is usually considerable, while in this case multipliers are more realistically sought by comparing a 'control' extrapolation of the model, representing 'normal' or unchanged policy, with a 'disturbed' extrapolation corresponding to a given policy. The ratios of the shifts thereby induced to the changes by which they were effected gives the required multipliers. (It will be appreciated that non-linearities may mean that these results are a less than precise guide to the effects of policies which involve considerably smaller or larger changes than those for which the multipliers were compiled or which take the form of shifts in a number of variables. The effects of such policies may therefore have to be examined by means of a separate extrapolation.)

The extent to which it is justifiable to use a fitted macro-economic model to stimulate the future depends partly on the specification of the model used. The Dutch forecasting and policy model looked at Chapter 5, Section 5.8 has, for example, only a limited value in this respect since long-term matters are either neglected or inadequately represented. In particular, the absence of a production function means that no account is taken of changes in productivity while the price elasticity of exports of $-2 \cdot 6$ in (5.37) may be considered too low to represent the long-term response to a lasting price change.

However, even where allowances have been made for other than short-term developments it will be necessary to have some assurance that the model can be used to simulate the behaviour of an economy reasonably faithfully over a number of years. The checks on forecast performance reviewed earlier are crucial in this respect but other tests of the dynamic properties of a model may be added. Examples of these tests can be found in I. Adelman and F. L. Adelman's (1959) investigation of whether the Klein–Goldberger model offers an explanation of the business cycle. Thus it is found that the model is stable at least to the extent that if it is assumed that most of the exogenous variables follow linear trends then the behaviour of the endogenous variables is monotonic and essentially linear. The model is also found to be equally stable when government expenditure is subject to a severe shock in the form of an extremely large drop for a single year. In this case the simulation first shows a recession and then a boom but given time most of the endogenous variables return to the same equilibrium growth trends that would have obtained in the absence of this disturbance, while none exhibit a trend that is otherwise unrealistic. Again, therefore, neither oscillatory nor explosive behaviour is observed.

The system is also subjected to two kinds of series of random shocks. The first of these takes the form of the addition of random disturbances to linear trends for exogenous variables of much the same order of magnitude and displaying much the same correlations[1] as found in the observed series for these variables. The effect is to generate cycles of three or four years' duration in the endogenous variables but their average amplitude is small compared with what is observed. In contrast, when random shocks of a 'realistic order of magnitude' are added to the structural form equations of the model and it is then solved as before, the cyclical fluctuations which result are found to be similar

---

[1] It was found that there is a high degree of correlation between long- and short-term interest rates and between the size of the wage bill of government and the number employed by government. It was therefore decided that the shock imparted to one variable of each pair should determine the size of the shock on the other.

to those found in practice for the United States economy in terms of the average duration of the cycle, the mean length of the expansion and contraction phases of the cycle and lead-lag relationships. This is a result which is therefore seen to lend support to the hypothesis that random shocks are the prime cause of business cycles while in more general terms the authors feel that 'it is not unreasonable to suggest that the gross characteristics of the interactions among the real variables described in the Klein–Goldberger equations may represent good approximations to the behavioural relationships in a practical economy', pp. 620.

Other examples of the use of econometric models to simulate the behaviour of macro-economic systems include studies by Duesenberry, Eckstein and Fromm (1960), Liu (1963), Morishima and Saito (1964), and Evans (1966). The first three all involve the construction of *ad hoc* models consisting of a relatively small number[1] of highly aggregated relationships which are used to obtain quantitative answers to questions concerning, for example, the effectiveness of different fiscal and monetary policies in achieving certain goals and the lags involved in the operation of these policies. In the fourth of these studies a much larger, more general, model is developed which is then used to obtain short-run and long-run multipliers for three policy variables: government expenditure, the taxation of personal income and, in combination, the money stock and the discount rate. In the case of the last two variables, the required composite multiplier is calculated with reference to the elasticities for these variables of those expenditure categories which the model shows to be directly affected by the money stock and the discount rate, i.e. purchases of cars, housing, and plant and equipment. The sum of these elasticities can be regarded, albeit inevitably somewhat arbitrarily, as equivalent to an autonomous shift in demand in the private sector, analogous to an autonomous change in, say, exports. The multiplier can therefore be obtained as the product of this marginal shift in demand and the private sector expenditure multiplier.

Evans' study also includes a comparison of his results relating to the government expenditure multiplier for GNP with those reported elsewhere.[2] In particular, the way in which estimates of the various parameters of a model contribute toward the value of this multiplier is discussed with reference to the generalisation

$$\frac{\Delta Y}{\Delta G} = \frac{1}{1 - mpc(\Delta Y_a/\Delta Y) - mpi + mpm} \tag{6.82}$$

which can be obtained from linear functions, or linear approximations where necessary, for aggregate consumption (C), taxation (T), investment (I) and imports (M), all of which can be expressed as functions of either GNP or

---

[1] That is, 14, 21 and 10 equations, respectively.
[2] This analysis has been subsequently extended by Evans (1969*b*), pp. 582–94, to include a discussion of results obtained from the Wharton EFU and Brookings models.

disposable income, e.g. in the case of the simplest static model

$$C = \alpha_1 + \beta_1 Y_d \quad (6.83a) \qquad M = \alpha_4 + \beta_4 Y \qquad\qquad (6.83d)$$

$$T = \alpha_2 + \beta_2 Y \qquad (b) \qquad\quad Y = C + I + G + E - M \qquad (e)$$

$$I = \alpha_3 + \beta_3 Y \qquad (c) \qquad\quad Y_d = Y - T \qquad\qquad\qquad (f)$$

where disposable income, GNP, government expenditure and exports are denoted by Y_d, Y, G and E and *mpc*, *mpi* and *mpm* refer to the marginal propensities to consume, invest and import. The results obtained from the six models looked at by Evans are given in Tables 6.6 and 6.7. The disparities

Table 6.6. Comparison of government expenditure multipliers for GNP

Model	Year					
	1	2	3	4	5	long-run
Klein–Goldberger, Goldberger (1959)	1·23	1·95	2·21	2·27	2·26	2·11
Michigan RSQE, Suits (1962)	1·30	1·62	1·58	1·55	1·34	1·10
Morishima–Saito (1964)	1·86	1·96	2·14	2·09	2·13	2·37[1]
Evans (1966)	2·36	2·71	3·54	3·90	3·92	4·00
Ball (1963)	1·29	1·39	1·53	1·66	1·78	2·45
Verdoorn–Post (1964)	0·54	n.a.	—	—	—	—

Source: Evans (1966), pp. 355 and 359.

[1] Nine-year multipler.

thereby revealed are variously traced to differences in the explanatory variables used, including different measures of the same concept, in the lags and the estimation procedures adopted and in the structures of the economies looked at in these studies.

Thus, for example, the last two factors are, respectively, pertinent in explaining the short-run *mpc* of the Michigan RSQE model and the *mpm* figures for the Ball and the Verdoorn–Post models since the first is estimated by ordinary least squares and such an estimate of the *mpc* is biased upward while the other two parameters relate to the United Kingdom and Dutch economies in which imports have a more important place than in the United States economy which is the subject of the other four models. The short-term *mpm* figure for the Verdoorn–Post model is 1·68 which is this high partly also as a result of the use of GNP plus imports as an explanatory variable in the import function rather than GNP alone. In addition this *mpm* is linked to the high value for *mpi* in the Verdoorn–Post model; the *mpi* for fixed investment is only 0·084 but the combination of GNP and imports is also used in the inventory investment function and of the model's GNP components imports is the most responsive to a change

Table 6.7. Components of impact and long-run government expenditure multipliers for GNP

Model	Impact multipliers					Long-run multipliers				
	mpc	$\frac{\Delta Y_d}{\Delta Y}$	$\frac{\Delta C}{\Delta Y}$	*mpi*	*mpm*	*mpc*	$\frac{\Delta Y_d}{\Delta Y}$	$\frac{\Delta C}{\Delta Y}$	*mpi*	*mpm*
Klein–Goldberger	0·479	0·397	0·190	0	0·005	0·724	0·490	0·355	0·218	0·017
Suits	0·707	0·320	0·226	0·068	0·060	0·476	0·320	0·152	0	0·060
Morishima–Saito	—	—	0·452	0	—[1]	—	—	0·570	0	0·010
Evans	0·612	0·590	0·361	0·216	—	0·888	0·718	0·638	0·112	0
Ball	—	—	0·251	0·313	0·392	—	—	0·677	0·277	0·359
Verdoorn–Post	—	—	0·141	0·924	2·26[2]	n.a.	—	—	—	—

Source: Evans (1966), pp. 355 and 357.

[1] This model has a net foreign balance (*F*) term instead of imports. The marginal shift in *F* with respect to *Y* is 0·01.

[2] This model also treats exports as an endogenous variable and the '*mpm*' parameter here also includes the effect of exports.

in government expenditure. The result is a large change also in inventory investment, the effect of which is itself felt in the import function since GNP is sub-divided in this function into final sales and inventory investment and the second appears as an important influence on imports.

Other examples of the likely effects of different specifications pointed out by Evans include the reduction in the *mpc* of the Klein–Goldberger model because consumption is also made a function of population which, since it shares a similar trend, reduces the increase in consumption associated with income and the high $\Delta C / \Delta Y$ ratio of the Morishima–Saito model because of the absence of lagged consumption in the consumption function and the inadequacy of a capital stock term as an alternative means of introducing the influence of past consumption.[1] In contrast the low $\Delta C / \Delta Y$ ratio of the Ver-doorn–Post model reflects the use in this instance of lagged rather than present

[1] With regard to this last point it can be seen that the *mpc* of the relationship

$$C = \alpha + \beta Y$$

does not distinguish between short- and long-run shifts in income unlike the parameter β in the function, suggested by Brown (1952),

$$C = \alpha + \beta Y + \gamma C_{-1}$$

which is a short-run *mpc*, the long-run equilibrium *mpc* being given by the condition $C = C_{-1} = C_{-2} \ldots$ in which case $\Delta C / \Delta Y = \beta/(1 - \gamma)$.

income. (In the case of the Morishima–Saito, Verdoorn–Post and Ball models GNP is used as a measure of income so that measures of *mpc* and $\Delta Y_d / \Delta Y$ do not apply.) So far as the short-term *mpi* is concerned zeros are recorded for the Klein–Goldberger and Morishima–Saito models because for the former *all* the explanatory variables of the investment function are lagged while for the latter investment is an exogenous variable. Fixed investment in the Michigan RSQE model is also a function of lagged variables alone while the *mpi* for inventory investment is only 0·068 which could be the result of using consumption rather than total sales as an explanatory variable.

Looking at the long-run multipliers of these models it can be seen that the size difference between the Evans model and the others is maintained. However, this model is similar to the Klein–Goldberger and Michigan RSQE models in that all three models have multipliers which register a peak at or near five years in contrast to the slow approach of the Ball model's multiplier to an equilibrium value and to the Morishima–Saito model's multiplier which continues to grow indefinitely because of the continual expansion of the capital stock term in the consumption function. The exceptionally low figure for the Michigan RSQE model is essentially a reflection of the model's unsuitability for long-term projections while the more realistic long-run *mpc* of the Evans model and its more appropriate lag structure are chiefly responsible for the different dynamic multipliers obtained from this model.

The Wharton EFU and the Brookings models have also been used to simulate the behaviour of the United States economy subject to the operation of different economic policies. Following a review of the *ex post* forecast record of the Wharton EFU model,[2] Evans and Klein (1968) present multipliers relating to a number of policy variables including two kinds of government expenditure (defence and non-defence), three rates of taxation (relating to personal income, corporate income and excise taxes), and two instruments of monetary policy (the discount rate and the ratio of free to required reserves). Multipliers for a change in the level of exports, as a result of, for example, a shift in the index of world trade, are also given. So far as the problem of comparability between multipliers relating to fiscal and monetary instruments is concerned, reference is made to shifts in required reserves brought about by the latter as a measure of the change in spendable funds involved.

The results obtained are in the form of projections for the period 1966–75 during which it is assumed that government expenditure and other exogenous variables are adjusted to keep the rate of unemployment at about 4 per cent,

[2] It is interesting to note in passing that published actual values of exogenous variables required in making these forecasts are not accepted unreservedly. Thus the labour force figures are smoothed to remove what is considered to be a 'most unusual' pattern in these figures. The official record of government purchases of goods and services for the same year is also found to exhibit irregular fluctuations which are thought to result from 'some kind of fiscal juggling' so the authors again substitute what they consider to be a more accurate set of figures, subject to the restriction of retaining the same calendar year total as found in the official record.

which results in a 'no change' situation in which the annual growth rates of real GNP and prices are 4 and 2 per cent. So far as the GNP effects of various policies are concerned, it is found that a shift in government spending has a substantially greater influence in the short run than a change in any of the three tax rates looked at as a result of an estimated short-run marginal propensity to consume which is much less than unity. Among the taxation alternatives, a change in the corporate income tax rate has the smallest initial effect since it is found that any change in after-tax profits is distributed to dividends quite slowly and that corporate saving only affects fixed business investment with a substantial lag. With regard to the other two taxation policies considered, it is found that for the excise tax change adopted, which is confined to consumer durables and which is passed on in a 70 per cent reduction in prices, the excise tax multiplier is greater than the personal income tax multiplier in the short term. However, with the exception of the corporate income tax rate, all the changes considered have much the same long-term influence on GNP when normalised by the amount of the change. The reason for the exception in the case of the corporate income tax multiplier is the small marginal propensity to spend out of retained earnings.

Despite a relatively high rate of capacity utilisation at the start of the simulation period, changes in prices are found to take place much more slowly than changes in output for all the multipliers considered. Since this effect applies both to positive changes of price and output and to negative changes, the authors conclude that the fiscal and monetary policy alternatives considered could not be expected to be of immediate help in checking prices, although output and employment would quickly suffer. Unlike long-term changes in GNP, price changes also vary greatly between different policy alternatives even in the long-term. The two monetary policies have the greatest influence on prices, even though their effect on investment and thereby capacity is greater than any of the financial policies, since 'the supply curves for fixed investment are more inelastic than they are for other sectors of the economy, and are also more inelastic in the short run than the long run', p. 68, so that the cost of investment goods changes rapidly thus inducing other price and wage changes. In contrast, the other policies considered influence investment only indirectly and gradually via changes in gross private output. Differences in effects on private investment are also seen to explain the smaller influence of a change in personal income tax on prices than a change in government spending.

Using a condensed, 177-equation, version of the Brookings model, Fromm and Taubman (1968) have similarly tested the *ex post* forecast performance of an econometric model with reference to the results of its non-stochastic simulation,[1] in this case for a period of ten quarters, before going on to compute impact and dynamic multipliers for a number of policy variables. The

[1] The results of a stochastic simulation of this version of the model are reported by A. L. Nagar, pp. 425–56, in a collection of papers on further work on the Brookings model edited by Duesenberry, Fromm, Klein and Kuh (1969).

figures they present relating to the second part of their study show shifts in seventeen endogenous variables corresponding to changes in four categories of government expenditure, in income and excise tax rates (including small and large cuts in excise tax each of which is considered at three rates at which the cut is passed on in the form of reduced prices[1]) and in two monetary variables, namely reserve requirements on demand deposits and the level of unborrowed reserves (as affected by open market operations). Comparability between fiscal policy multipliers and multipliers for the last two variables is sought in this instance by relating changes in the latter to real resource equivalents. The approach adopted has the same point of departure as the method referred to earlier that is used by Evans (1966) to obtain a composite multiplier relating to two monetary variables. Thus attention is directed beyond any change itself and its more immediate effects on the size and distribution of bank liabilities and asset portfolios, to the real expenditure changes which are aimed at. Again a change in monetary policy is taken as equivalent to the sum of the shifts in all those categories of expenditure which are directly influenced by the policy, although in this case the effect of the policy is taken as the simulated shift recorded for the endogenous variable concerned. The approach is therefore different from that adopted by Evans and Klein (1968) who, as noted above, look to a measure of spendable funds as a denominator in tackling this problem. To the extent that direct shifts in expenditure are the result of a change in spendable funds, the Evans–Klein procedure can be seen to reach farther back in the chain of causality which gives effect to a change in monetary policy.[2]

Changes in policy variables, or equivalent inputs, used by Fromm and Taubman relating to fourteen different policies, together with corresponding multipliers for two endogenous variables, are shown in Table 6.8. The multiplier results obtained for GNP are broadly in accord with the results that were reviewed earlier for the Wharton EFU model although there are some minor and some major disparities.[3] The former are to some extent accounted for by

[1] The use of cross-section data to determine the effects of changes in *ad valorem* and specific taxes on prices is discussed in an appendix, Fromm and Taubman (1968), pp. 161–9.

[2] In comparing multipliers obtained from the Wharton EFU and Brookings models, Evans (1969b), pp. 588–92, notes that the required reserves multiplier of the Brookings model for real GNP at the end of ten quarters is increased by a factor in excess of five on using required reserves as a denominator in the placed direct expenditure. This second figure for the Brookings multiplier is manifestly at odds with results obtained from the Wharton EFU model. As noted later, the difference is seen by Evans to reflect inadequacies in the monetary equations of the version of the Brookings model used by Fromm and Taubman.

[3] Fromm and Taubman report that most of the lagged influences found in the Brookings model had had their main effect at the end of ten quarters so that multipliers for this period should be close to equilibrium values.

So far as the results given in Table 6.8 in particular are concerned, it is interesting to note that the excise tax multipliers indicate proportionally larger changes in GNP and consumption follow from larger excise tax changes. The theoretical plausibility of this result is discussed by Fromm and Taubman, pp. 75–7.

the different situations considered in the two studies: since the United States economy was nearer full employment at the start of the period looked at by Evans and Klein, output might be expected to rise less and prices more than in the case of the results obtained from the Brookings model. However, movements in prices and in the consumption of cars indicated by the latter are too different to be explained entirely in this way while substantial differences also occur in the required reserves multipliers. These disparities have been traced by Evans (1969*b*) pp. 587 and 593–4, to defects in equations for prices, the consumption of cars, and the money market adopted in the particular version of the Brookings model used by Fromm and Taubman, thereby further illustrating the link between the specification of a model and its multipliers.

Given a means of achieving some sort of comparability between different policy multipliers, Fromm and Taubman go on to consider ways in which their results can be used to judge the effectiveness of various policies with reference to changes effected in real GNP and aggregate consumption at the end of one, four, seven and ten quarters. They also take account of time preference in computing average quarterly discounted multipliers (AQDM's) for these four alternative time spans,

$$\text{AQDM}_n = \frac{1}{n} \sum_{t=1}^{n} \frac{\text{MULT}_t}{(1 + r)^t} \qquad (6.84)$$

where MULT_t refers to the multiplier in quarter t, r is the social rate of time preference, t is the number of quarters from the start of the simulation and n is the time span, in quarters, to which the result relates.

In exploring the feasibility of evaluating and designing policy subject to more than one criterion of success, reference is made to the possibility of using a utility function to represent subjective trade-offs between various criteria. In particular the properties of a linear function

$$u = \beta_1 x_1 + \beta_2 x_2 + \ldots + \beta_n x_n, \qquad (6.85)$$

a Cobb–Douglas function

$$u = x_1^{\beta_1} x_2^{\beta_2} \ldots x_n^{\beta_n} \qquad (6.86)$$

and a constant elasticity of substitution (CES) function

$$u = [\beta_1 x_1^{\delta} + \beta_2 x_2^{\delta} + \ldots + \beta_n x_n^{\delta}]^{1/\delta} \qquad (6.87)$$

are discussed. As noted in Chapter 3, the marginal rates of substitution between different arguments, x_i, representing target variables, are then respectively measured by

$$-\beta_j/\beta_i$$

$$\frac{-\beta_j}{\beta_i} \frac{x_i}{x_j}$$

and

$$\frac{-\beta_j}{\beta_i} \left[\frac{x_i}{x_j} \right]^{1-\delta}$$

Table 6.8. Actual or equivalent incremental inputs and corresponding multipliers for real GNP and consumption for the U.S. economy

Year and quarter[1] / Number of quarters	1960:3 1	1960:4 2	1961:1 3	1961:2 4	1961:3 5	1961:4 6	1962:1 7	1962:2 8
Government } durables expenditures non-durables expenditures employment[2] construction	3·2	3·2	3·2	3·2	3·2	3·2	3·2	3·2
Income tax cut	3·2	3·3	3·3	3·4	3·5	3·6	3·7	3·7
Income tax plus monetary policy[3]	3·3	3·3	3·3	3·4	3·6	3·8	3·9	4·1
Excise tax cut (small)								
100 per cent pass along	1·5	1·4	1·5	1·5	1·5	1·6	1·6	1·6
80 per cent pass along	1·3	1·3	1·3	1·3	1·4	1·4	1·5	1·5
50 per cent pass along	1·1	1·1	1·1	1·1	1·1	1·2	1·2	1·2
Excise tax cut (large)								
100 per cent pass along	2·5	2·5	2·5	2·5	2·6	2·7	2·7	2·8
80 per cent pass along	2·2	2·2	2·2	2·3	2·3	2·4	2·5	2·5
50 per cent pass along	1·8	1·8	1·8	1·9	1·9	2·0	2·0	2·0
Reserve requirements reduction[4]	−1·1	1·0	1·9	2·8	3·6	7·6	7·1	6·6
Open market operations	−1·1	1·0	1·9	2·9	3·7	7·6	7·1	6·6

Source: Fromm and Taubman (1968), pp. 94 and 96.

[1] Stimulus introduced at the beginning of 1960:3.   [2] Increase in 626,000 employees.

[3] The difference between the expenditure and 'pure' income tax multipliers is not simply an expression of the balanced budget effect. This is because the model shows that the larger direct impact of the tax reductions on personal disposable income gives rise to a greater desire on the part of consumers to hold demand deposits which, given fixed bank reserves, produces higher interest rates and a reduction in investment. In order to remove this effect, an 'accommodating' monetary policy is also tried which keeps interest rates at the same level that they would otherwise have reached without the tax cut by allowing an expansion in bank reserves and the money supply.

[4] Reduction in reserve requirements on demand deposits from 0·149 to 0·139.

Table 6.8 (cont.)

Year and quarter[1] / Number of quarters	1962:3 9	1962:4 10	Multipliers for GNP				Multipliers for consumption			
			1960:3 1	1961:2 4	1962:1 7	1962:4 10	1960:3 1	1961:2 4	1962:1 7	1962:4 10
Government										
Durables expenditures	3·2	3·2	1·6	2·1	2·7	2·7	0·5	0·8	1·0	1·0
non-durables expenditures			1·4	2·4	2·8	2·9	0·4	0·8	1·0	1·1
employment[2]			1·7	2·1	1·9	2·0	0·6	0·9	0·9	0·9
construction			1·6	2·4	2·9	2·9	0·4	0·9	1·1	1·1
Income tax cut	3·7	3·8	0·8	1·1	1·2	1·2	0·7	1·0	1·1	1·1
Income tax plus monetary policy[3]	4·1	4·2	0·7	1·3	1·5	1·7	0·7	1·1	1·4	1·4
Excise tax cut (small)										
100 per cent pass along	1·6	1·7	1·1	1·2	1·6	1·3	1·0	1·0	1·1	1·1
80 per cent pass along	1·5	1·5	1·1	1·2	1·5	1·3	1·0	1·0	1·0	1·0
50 per cent pass along	1·2	1·2	0·9	1·0	1·3	1·1	0·8	0·9	0·9	0·9
Excise tax cut (large)										
100 per cent pass along	2·8	2·8	1·0	1·5	2·2	2·3	1·0	1·2	1·5	1·7
80 per cent pass along	2·5	2·5	0·9	1·4	2·1	2·2	0·8	1·2	1·5	1·7
50 per cent pass along	2·0	2·1	0·9	1·4	2·1	2·3	0·8	1·2	1·5	1·7
Reserves requirements reduction[4]	6·3	6·0	1·3	1·5	1·2	1·5	0·4	0·6	0·6	0·8
Open market operations	6·3	5·9	1·3	1·6	1·2	1·5	0·4	0·7	0·6	0·8

so that the linear and Cobb–Douglas functions can be seen to be special cases of the CES function; for the former $\delta = 1$ and for the latter $\delta = 0$. The elasticity of substitution, σ, of the CES function has also been shown earlier to be $1/(1 - \delta)$; in the case of the other two functions this quantity is therefore ∞ and 1. Utility indices, for which the base is the utility of a particular policy at a point in time, are presented for linear and Cobb–Douglas functions and two versions of the CES function ($\delta = -0.5$, $\sigma = 0.67$ and $\delta = -1$, $\sigma = 0.5$), for either equal or different weights, β_i, applied to a set of six arguments[1] and with and without discounting. An attempt is also made in the multiperiod utility computations to allow for the disutility of larger variances of arguments with reference to the reciprocals of these variances (v_i), which are combined in the same functional form as the arguments in each case, so that for the Cobb–Douglas function

$$u_v = \left(\frac{1}{v_1}\right)^{\beta_1}\left(\frac{1}{v_2}\right)^{\beta_2} \cdots \left(\frac{1}{v_n}\right)^{\beta_n}. \tag{6.88}$$

For the sake of simplicity the same β_i and δ weights are also used and the total utility is reckoned as the unweighted sum

$$u_T = u_0 + u_v$$

where u_0 is the sum of a series of discounted utilities relating to the arguments themselves for the same time span as u_v. Results from these different approaches to the evaluation of the effectiveness of various policies are compared with reference to rankings of the multipliers or utilities thereby obtained.

The opportunity presented by utility functions to use econometric models to design optimal policies is an extremely limited one in practice, of course. Quite apart from the limited range of policy matters which can be handled by this approach, i.e. excluding complications such as equity considerations and problems in quantifying certain costs and benefits, there remains the problem of choosing the functional form, the arguments and the weights to be used to represent the preference function of a policy-maker. The same snag applies to the policy optimisation procedure proposed by Theil (1958), (1964) which assumes that it is possible to express a policy-maker's social welfare function in terms of target variables and policy instruments so that this function can be maximised subject to constraints imposed by an estimated model and the values of lagged endogenous variables and of any other, non-policy, exogenous variables. An alternative approach, first proposed by Tinbergen (1952), (1954), (1956) would be to assume that the policy-maker is able to specify required values for target variables. The solution of an estimated model, expressed in terms of the values of the policy variables that are consistent with these

---

[1] These include personal consumption, private sector domestic investment other than inventory investment, and government expenditure, all of which are in real terms, plus the reciprocal of the rate of unemployment, the government surplus in current price terms and the reciprocal of an implicit price deflator for GNP.

objectives, could then be sought subject to the same restrictions as in the Theil approach. Where the number of targets (m) exceeds the number of policy variables (n) it would be necessary, except in special cases, to bring the two into equality in order to be able to get any solution at all while if the reverse situation obtains arbitrary values can be assigned to ($n - m$) policy variables when the model can be solved for the remaining m policy variables. More serious, however, is the practical problem of deciding what values are to be assigned to target variables. In view of these difficulties, Naylor (1968), (1969) and his associates have proposed an approach which in essence goes no further than using an econometric model to simulate the behaviour of an economy for a number of feasible policies which are of interest before seeking the reaction of those actually responsible for policy to the results obtained to see which policies are preferred or what further experiments with different policies are considered necessary. Thus the need to specify preferences in detail in advance is avoided while the kind of information made available is likely to be more acceptable to policy-makers in practice.

6.6 FURTHER READING

Further details of principles involved in the preparation of forecasts from simultaneous equation models and in the analysis forecast errors can be seen in a recent review of the subject by Klein (1971). Other issues discussed include factors influencing the degree of disaggregation to be adopted in building forecast models and various possibilities of improving forecasts including, in particular, corrections for non-randomness in the residuals of the equations of a model and the development of efficient procedures for dealing with the estimation and error build-up problems that arise in predicting with models having lagged dependent variables.

Should the impression have been gained from this chapter that the adoption of a few simple rules in the preparation of forecasts will guarantee the accuracy of the final product then see Streissler's (1970) cautionary, if somewhat negative, account of all the snares that await the unwary forecaster along the path of data collection, theorising about reality, and model specification, estimation and final use for forecasting. Further details concerning the practicalities of preparing forecasts, with reference to short-term forecasting procedures used by the United Kingdom National Institute of Economic and Social Research, which have already been referred to earlier, can be seen in a paper by Artis (1970).

The analysis of forecast errors is discussed in two substantial studies by Theil (1958), (1966), the first of which also includes an examination of the application of decision theory to economic planning. Both discourses on the evaluation of forecasts are a mixture of theory and application, with the latter illustrated largely with reference to results achieved using models developed by the Netherlands Central Planning Bureau. In view of the wealth of detail and the considerable purely theoretical content of these studies the reader looking for tips on what to do in practice will have to be selective. Further, rather more digestible, analysis of the forecast performance of the Dutch macro-models is presented by Sims (1967). Naïve predictions and the forecast achievements of a smaller model of the Norwegian economy are employed as a basis of comparison. He also examines the benefits of elaborations of the Dutch model over time and the extent to which forecast errors have been attributable to inaccuracies and to random elements in the model's structure as opposed to inaccuracies in forecasting exogenous variables.

Detailed assessments of the accuracy of forecasts obtained from two other models referred to in this chapter have been prepared by Ball and Burns (1968) and Liebenberg, Hirsch and Popkin (1966). Both studies set out predictions and realisations for different variables and for lengthy prediction periods so that the reader may apply some of the tests of forecast accuracy set out in this chapter for himself. Ball and Burns assess their results in terms of a general qualitative appreciation, measures of the fit of regressions of actual levels on forecast levels and a count of large and small over- and under-estimates and of turning point errors. The reader may weigh the value of the second of these procedures against those reviewed in this chapter. The third viewpoint is used by Ball and Burns as a check on Theil's (1958) finding that there is a tendency in econometric forecasting to underestimate change, which the authors suspect may disguise the more serious problem of a propensity not simply to underestimate all changes but rather a bias toward under-estimation in the case of large changes and toward overestimation in the case of small and negative changes. Liebenberg, Hirsch and Popkin examine the breakdown of GNP forecast errors into errors found in forecasting the components of GNP as well as evidence of the non-randomness of errors. Particular attention is given to assessing the accuracy of forecasts for 1965 which lie outside the observation period and which present a special challenge in the form of a number of unusual features which are allowed for by various intercept adjustments. Additional reports on simulation results and the analysis of forecast performance for several macro-models of the United States economy, including the OBE, Wharton EFU and Brookings models, can be seen in a number of the papers presented at a United States NBER/SSRC sponsored conference on econometric models of cyclical behaviour. See Hickman (1972).

Reference has already been made, p. 221, to four studies which use econometric models to examine the effects of various monetary and fiscal policies in different situations. A related objective is to use *ex post* simulations to provide some idea of what might otherwise have happened in the absence of a policy which was actually adopted in order to disentangle the effects of this policy from the effects of other exogenous changes in the economy. Use of the Brookings and Wharton EFU models for this purpose in examining the effects of the United States tax cut of 1964, 'a milestone in the application of modern fiscal theory to an actual policy act', is reported by Klein (1969) pp. 459–72. He considers too what would have happened had this particular tax cut been adopted earlier; Fromm and Taubman (1968) pp. 53–80, also report, in somewhat greater detail, on their use of the Brookings model for the same purpose.

Those unfamiliar with the solution and further analysis of difference equations should consult Baumol's (1959) text on the subject, Chapters 8–13. See also Marshak (1953) pp. 17–24. Theil and Boot (1962) find the final form solution of a linear equation system, using Klein's Model I (1950) as an example, in order to show the effect of a once and for all shock in an exogenous variable on the endogenous variables of the model over successive years. In addition they establish the stability condition with respect to the largest of the latent roots of Φ in (6.70) and generalise this result for (6.73). (See also Baumol (1959) Chapter 16.) Since in practice this root has to be obtained from estimates of the coefficients of an equation system it is subject to sampling error in the same way as these parameter estimates are; Theil and Boot therefore go on to derive the asymptotic standard error of the absolute value of the root in terms of the asymptotic variance–covariance matrix of estimates of reduced form coefficients.

A further example of multiplier analysis can be seen in Evans' (1969*a*) report on his short-term forecasting model of the French economy. An evaluation of the practical value of multipliers obtained from macro-economic models in the design of an optimal multi-year fiscal policy using a decision model has been undertaken by May (1966). Further discussion of the design of policy may be seen in Fox, Sengupta and Thorbecke's (1966) review of the subject.

6.7 REFERENCES

Adelman, I. and Adelman, F. L. (1959), 'The Dynamic Properties of the Klein–Goldberger Model', *Econometrica*, vol. 27, 597–625. Reprinted in Zellner (1968).

Alexander, S. S. (1958), 'Rate of Change Approaches to Forecasting – Diffusion Indexes and First Differences', *Economic Journal*, vol. 67, 288–301.

Alexander, S. S. and Stekler, H. O. (1959), 'Forecasting Industrial Production-Leading Series versus Autoregression', *Journal of Political Economy*, vol. 67, 402–9.

Artis, M. J. (1970), 'Short-term Economic Forecasting at NIESR', in Hilton and Heathfield (1970).

Ball, R. J. (1963), 'The Significance of Simultaneous Methods of Parameter Estimation in Econometric Model', *Applied Statistics*, vol. 12, 14–25.

Ball, R. J. and Burns, T. (1968), 'An Econometric Approach to Short-Run Analysis of the United Kingdom Economy, 1955–1966', *Operational Research Quarterly*, vol. 19, 225–56.

Baumol, W. J. (1959), *Economic Dynamics*, 2nd ed. (New York: Macmillan).

Brown, T. M. (1952), 'Habit Persistence and Lags in Consumer Behaviour', *Econometrica*, vol. 20, 355–71.

Brown, M. and Taubman, P. (1962), 'A Forecasting Model of Federal Purchases of Goods and Services', *Journal of the American Statistical Association*, vol. 57, 633–47.

Butler, W. F. and Kavesh, R. A. (eds) (1966), *How Business Economists Forecast* (Englewood Cliffs, N.J.: Prentice Hall).

de Wolff, P. (1967), 'Macroeconomic Forecasting', in Wold *et al.* (1967).

Duesenberry, J. S., Fromm, G., Klein, L. R. and Kuh, E. (eds) (1969), *The Brookings Model: Some Further Results* (Chicago: Rand McNally).

Duesenberry, J. S., Eckstein, O. and Fromm, G. (1960), 'A Simulation of the United States Economy in Recession', *Econometrica*, vol. 28, 749–810.

Evans, M. K. (1966), 'Multiplier Analysis of a Postwar Quarterly U.S. Model and a Comparison with Several Other Models', *Review of Economic Studies*, vol. 33, 337–60.

Evans, M. K. (1969a), *An Econometric Model of the French Economy* (Paris: OECD).

Evans, M. K. (1969b), *Macroeconomic Activity* (New York: Harper & Row).

Evans, M. K. and Klein, L. R. (1968), *The Wharton Econometric Forecasting Model*, 2nd ed. Philadelphia: Wharton School of Finance and Commerce, University of Pennsylvania).

Friend, I. and Jones, R. (1964), 'Short-Run Forecasting Models Incorporating Anticipatory Data', in *Models of Income Determination*, Studies in Income and Wealth, No. 28 (Princeton, N.J.: Princeton University Press for NBER).

Friend, I. and Taubman, P. (1964), 'A Short-Term Forecasting Model', *Review of Economics and Statistics*, vol. 46, 229–36.

Fromm, G. (1962), 'Inventories, Business Cycles and Economic Stabilisation', in U.S. Congress Joint Economic Committee', *Inventory Fluctuations and Economic Stabilisation*, Part IV, 37–133.

Fromm, G. and Taubman, P. (1968), *Policy Simulations with an Econometric Model* (Washington and Amsterdam: The Brookings Institution and North-Holland).

Fox, K. A., Sengupta, J. K. and Thorbecke, E. (1966), *The Theory of Quantitative Economic Policy* (Chicago and Amsterdam: Rand McNally and North-Holland).

Goldberger, A. S. (1959), *Impact Multipliers and Dynamic Properties of the Klein–Goldberger Model* (Amsterdam: North Holland).

Goldberger, A. S. (1964), *Econometric Theory* (New York: John Wiley).

Goldberger, A. S., Nagar, A. L. and Odeh, H. S. (1961), 'The Covariance Matrices of Reduced Form Coefficients and of Forecasts for a Structural Econometric Model', *Econometrica*, vol. 29, 556–73.

Hart, P. E., Mills, G. and Whitaker, J. K. (eds) (1964), *Econometric Analysis for National Economic Planning* (London: Butterworths).

Hickman, B. G. (ed) (1972), *Econometric Models of Cyclical Behaviour*, Studies in Income and Wealth, No. 36, vols. I and II (New York: Columbia University Press for NBER).

Hilton, K. and Heathfield, D. F. (eds) (1970), *The Econometric Study of the United Kingdom* (London: Macmillan).

Hood, W. C. and Koopmans, T. C. (eds) (1953), *Studies in Econometric Method* (New York: John Wiley).

Hymans, S. H. (1968), 'Simultaneous Confidence Intervals in Econometric Forecasting', *Econometrica*, vol. 36, 18–30.

Johnston, J. (1972), *Econometric Methods*, 2nd ed. (New York: McGraw-Hill).

Klein, L. R. (1950), *Economic Fluctuations in the United States, 1921–1941* (New York: John Wiley).

Klein, L. R. (1964), 'A Postwar Quarterly Model: Description and Application', in *Models of Income Determination*, Studies in Income and Wealth, No. 28 (Princeton: Princeton University Press for NBER).

Klein, L. R. (1969), 'Econometric Analysis of the Tax Cut of 1964', in Deusenberry *et al.* (1969).

Klein, L. R. (1971), *An Essay on the Theory of Economic Prediction* (Chicago: Markham).

Klein, L. R. and Evans, M. K. (1969), *Econometric Gaming* (New York: Macmillan).

Liebenberg, M., Hirsch, A. A. and Popkin, P. (1966), 'A Quarterly Econometric Model of the United States', *Survey of Current Business*, vol. 46, 13–39.

Liu, T. A. (1963), 'An Exploratory Quarterly Econometric Model of Effective Demand in the Postwar U.S. Economy', *Econometrica*, vol. 31, 301–48.

Marschak, J. (1953), 'Economic Measurements for Policy and Prediction', in Hood and Koopmans (1953).

May, S. J. (1966), 'Dynamic Multiplers and their Use for Fiscal Decision-Making, in *Conference on Stabilisation Policies* (Ottawa: The Economic Council of Canada, Queen's Printer).

Moore, G. H. (1950), *Statistical Indicators of Cyclical Revivals and Recessions* (New York: NBER, Occasional Paper 31).

Moore, G. H. and Shiskin, J. (1967), *Indicators of Business Expansions and Contractions* (New York: NBER, Occasional Paper 103).

Morishima, M. and Saito, M. (1964), 'A Dynamic Analysis of the American Economy', *International Economic Review*, vol. 5, 125–64. Reprinted in Zellner (1968).

Nagar, A. L. (1969), 'Stochastic Simulation of the Brookings Econometric Model', in Duesenberry *et al.* (1969).

Naylor, T. H. (1969), 'Policy Simulation Experiments with Macroeconometric Models: The State of the Art', *Journal of the American Agricultural Economics Association*, vol. 52, 263–71.

Naylor, T. H., Wertz, K. and Wonnacott, T. H. (1968), 'Some Methods for Evaluating the Effects of Economic Policies using Simulation Experiments', *Review of the International Statistical Institute*, vol. 36, 184–200.

Sims, C. A. (1967), 'Evaluating Short-Term Macro-economic Forecasts: The Dutch Performance', *Review of Economics and Statistics*, vol. 49, 225–36.

Stekler, H. O. (1966),[1] 'Forecasting with an Econometric Model: A Comment', *American Economic Review*, vol. 56, 1241–8.

Stekler, H. O. (1967a), 'The Federal Budget as a Short-Term Forecasting Tool', *Journal of Business*, vol. 40, 280–5.

Stekler, H. O. (1967b), 'Data Revision and Economic Forecasting', *Journal of the American Statistical Association*, vol. 62, 470–83.

Stekler, H. O. and Burch, S. W. (1968a), 'Selected Economic Data-Accuracy vs Reporting Speed', *Journal of the American Statistical Association*, vol. 63, 436–44.

Stekler, H. O. (1968b), 'Forecasting with Econometric Models: An Evaluation', *Econometrica*, vol. 36, 437–63.

Stekler, H. O. (1969), 'Evaluation of Econometric Inventory Forecasts', *Review of Economics and Statistics*, vol. 51, 77–83.

Streissler, E. W. (1970), *Pitfalls in Econometric Forecasting* (London: The Institute of Economic Affairs).

Suits, D. B. (1962), 'Forecasting and Analysis with an Econometric Model', *American Economic Review*, vol. 52, 104–32. Reprinted in Zellner (1968).

Suits, D. B. (1967), 'Applied Econometric Forecasting and Policy Analysis', in Wold *et al.* (1967).

Surrey, M. J. C. (1971), *The Analysis and Forecasting of the British Economy* (Cambridge: Cambridge University Press for the National Institute of Economic and Social Research, Occasional Paper 25).

Theil, H. (1958), *Economic Forecasts and Policy* (Amsterdam: North-Holland).

Theil, H. (1964), *Optimal Decision Rules for Government and Industry* (Chicago and Amsterdam: Rand McNally and North-Holland).

Theil, H. (1966), *Applied Economic Forecasting* (Amsterdam: North-Holland).

Theil, H. and Boot, J. C. G. (1962), 'The Final Form of Econometric Equation Systems', *Review of the International Statistical Institute*, vol. 30, 136–52. Reprinted in Zellner (1968).

Tinbergen, J. (1952), *On the Theory of Economic Policy* (Amsterdam: North-Holland (second rev. ed., 1955).

Tinbergen, J. (1954), *Centralization and Decentralization in Economic Policy* Amsterdam: North-Holland).

Tinbergen, J. (1956), *Economic Policy: Principles and Design* (Amsterdam: North-Holland).

Verdoorn, P. J. and Post, J. J. (1964), 'Capacity and Short-Term Multipliers', in Hart, Mills and Whitaker (1964).

Wold, H., Orcutt, G. H., Robinson, E. A., Suits, D. B. and de Wolff, P. (1967),

---

[1] All of the six papers by Stekler (i.e. including that co-authored with S. W. Burch) reference here have been reprinted in: Stekler, H. O. (1970), *Economic Forecasting* (London: Longman).

    Forecasting on a Scientific Basis (Lisbon: Proceedings of an International Summer Institute sponsored by the NATO Science Committee and the Gulbenkian Foundation).

Zarnowitz, V. (1967), *An Appraisal of Short-Term Economic Forecasting* (New York: NBER, Occasional Paper 104).

Zellner, A. (ed) (1968), *Readings in Economic Statistics and Econometrics* (Boston: Little, Brown).

Author Index

Subject Index